THE HOUSE THAT HUGH LAURIE BUILT

An Unauthorized Biography and Episode Guide

PAUL CHALLEN

ECW Press

Published by ECW PRESS
2120 Queen Street East, Suite 200, Toronto, Ontario, Canada M4E 1E2

LIBRARY AND ARCHIVES CANADA CATALOGUING IN PUBLICATION

Challen, Paul, 1967–
The House that Hugh Laurie built :
an unauthorized biography and episode guide / Paul Challen.

ISBN 978-1-55022-803-8

1. Laurie, Hugh, b1959–. 2. House (Television program).
3. Actors — Great Britain — Biography. I. Title.

PN2598.L39C43 2007   792.02'8092   C2007-903579-5

Cover Image: CP/AP/Reed Saxon
Back Cover Image: Everett Collection/The Canadian Press
Cover and Text Design: Tania Craan
Typesetting: Mary Bowness
Production: Rachel Brooks
Printing: Victor Graphics

The publication of *The House that Hugh Laurie Built* has been generously
supported by the Government of Ontario through the Ontario Book
Publishing Tax Credit, and the Government of Canada through the Book
Publishing Industry Development Program (BPIDP).

Canada

This book is set in Sabon.

DISTRIBUTION
CANADA: Jaguar Book Group, 100 Armstrong Avenue,
Georgetown, ON, L7G 5S4
UNITED STATES: Independent Publishers Group, 814 North Franklin Street,
Chicago, IL 60610

PRINTED AND BOUND IN THE UNITED STATES

ECW PRESS
ecwpress.com

TABLE OF CONTENTS

HOUSE BUILDER

EPISODE GUIDES

"Humanity is overrated."

— Dr. Gregory House, MD

CHAPTER ONE

WHAT WE TALK ABOUT WHEN WE TALK ABOUT HUGH LAURIE

So, how is it, exactly, that an American TV series about an abrasive, limping, pill-popping doctor with the bedside manner of Attila the Hun — played by a depressive, Cambridge-educated, English actor, doing a fake New Jersey accent — has emerged as one of the most popular primetime dramas in recent years, among fans and critics alike?

And why do so many people love Fox's *House, MD* — the casual fans watching at home and the more rabid ones who build websites devoted to the show, the newspaper and magazine writers, and the folks who vote on the Golden Globe and Emmy awards? And, despite having been on the air only three seasons, why are many people already talking about *House* as a classic, a series that, despite its relative youth, is mentioned in the same breath as other great dramas like *ER* and *Law & Order?*

Certainly, the quirky juxtaposition of a lead character who works in a profession devoted to helping people but who delights in insulting patients, residents, and humanity in general is part of the reason. Television — or, more broadly, drama — has always loved the idea of characters whose jobs or positions in society are just the opposite of their true personalities (such as the bumbling cop who always manages to catch the crook, the hooker with a heart of gold, etc.).

But let's face it: That kind of contrast in a lead role isn't enough. Ted Danson tried the grouchy doctor shtick in *Becker*, the CBS offering that ran from 1998 to 2004 ("His bedside manner is no manners at all," ran the show's tagline) and although the show did have a pretty good run, with 128 primetime episodes in total, with all due respect to Danson, *Becker* was . . . well, *Becker* — a show with lots of easy laughs and convenient plots, but not much depth.

And there have surely been a sufficient number of grouchy MDs on shows like *Ben Casey, ER, St. Elsewhere* and even *General Hospital* to take enough shine off this type of role, such that the mere presence of a "sure I help people but I'm a jerk" character alone cannot explain the huge success of *House*.

Taking the dramatic analysis one step further, could it be that the strength of the show comes from its brilliant writing and directing? Certainly, the lines delivered by the lead and supporting characters in *House* are among the snappiest — and at times, funniest — heard on the small screen in decades. And it's true that the show's Canadian creator and lead writer, David Shore, has invented characters who talk in ways that are unique on primetime, delivering pronouncements on complicated medical cases in specialized scientific lingo one minute, then engaging in witty banter about their personal lives or their complicated relationships with one another the next.

And the several directors who have been brought in to work their magic on the show — including veterans like Paris Barclay, Deran Sarafian, Bryan Singer, and Daniel Sackheim — have all managed to give this medical drama just exactly the right pacing and its clever, behind-the-scenes look and feel, including the show's popular close-up plunges inside the human anatomy as *House*'s doctors discuss and cure the myriad of medical problems that come their way.

But great writing and directing alone can't be the answer — or at least not *all* of the answer — to the success of *House*. There have been — and indeed, are currently — lots of shows that thrive on zippy, smart dialogue (*The West Wing, Seinfeld*, and *The Sopranos* all come to mind as fairly recent examples). And for those cool techno-effects that feature the "camera" zipping through a human heart or stomach, well, nobody does that little trick as well as *CSI*. Certainly, good writing and directing play a big part in the overall impact of *House* — but they don't explain it all.

Instead, you have to look to the man behind the show's main character — that Englishman doing the phony American accent — to truly understand the foundations upon which this *House* has been built. That's Hugh Laurie, former member of the Footlights comedy troupe at Cambridge, veteran of the British stage, television, and movie scene, motorcycle and boxing enthusiast, depressive, novelist, crack musician, husband, father of three, and former world-class rower, who really provides the show with the legs it has needed to become one of primetime's best.

In fact, it's exactly that varied, multifaceted background that has allowed Laurie to excel as much as he has in *House*. In an age where specialization is king, and when many actors seem to get their start as kids and then do little else of note their entire lives (adopting weird religions or African orphans, just for the great publicity it brings, doesn't really count), it's heartening that someone with a list of accomplishments and talents as long and diverse as Laurie's can bring the kind of energy, maturity and poise that a smart, serious drama like *House* — and the title character that drives it — really need. If *House*-watchers — professional critics, bloggers, and casual fans alike — note one thing about the pull that Laurie exerts in the show's lead role, it's that he brings "depth" to the character; there seems to be a lot more behind the three-days-stubble mask than simply a vacuous, polished actor with a pretty face, mailing in a weekly performance for a steady paycheck.

But at the same time, as Laurie has managed to convey a great deal of his personality to the public since becoming a hit on *House*, we've learned that his off-screen life is far from a self-satisfied, smug existence. For all of his accomplishments, both off the stage and on it, Laurie remains, if not exactly a tortured soul, at least a person who, as one U.K. reviewer put it, "is a big hit at everything but being happy."

Or, as Laurie himself has said about his career, "I've been lucky and I've always found stuff to do, but there have been times when I've thought, Am I really cut out for this? Is this what I really want to do? Should I go off and become a teacher? . . . Or should I try to write *Ulysses?* . . . But that's been done."

Certainly, those closest to the working Laurie — fellow actors, directors, producers — have all pointed out that while Hugh seems to have every element needed for a happy life, he just can't seem to shake off a basic sense of inner gloom. Katie Jacobs, one of the show's executive producers, told an interviewer about a typical day for Laurie on the Los Angeles set of *House:* "Every day at about four or five o'clock, Hugh's sitting on the curb, completely despondent. He's miserable no matter what he does. Never thinks he's good enough — never thinks he's got it right."

And of course, that sense of isolation and general confusion about the world has been a perfect match for Laurie's character on *House.* One reviewer, writing in the *Times* of London, summed up that Laurie's character "at times seems a more suitable subject for treatment than his patients."

In the pages that follow, we'll look at how all of these aspects of Hugh Laurie — as dramatic and comic actor, athlete, writer, musician, moody fellow who has struggled with depression, and family man — came to be, and how he's brought all those aspects of his character into the role of Dr. Gregory House, the role that so many fans and critics have praised and enjoyed.

(Dave Pickhorn/BBC Photo Library)

I went there to row . . . and anthropology was
the most convenient subject to read while spending
eight hours a day on the river.

— Hugh Laurie, on why he attended Cambridge University

CHAPTER TWO

BACK IN THE DAY

To begin at the very beginning: Hugh Laurie — born James Hugh Calum Laurie (although he has never used the first name James) — came into the world in Oxford, England, on June 11, 1959, the youngest of four children. His father, William George Ranald Mundell Laurie — he went simply by Ranald — was a medical doctor, a Cambridge-educated general practitioner. His mother, Patricia, was a stay-at-home mom, busy with Hugh and his older brother and two older sisters.

From his many comments in interviews, it's clear that Laurie's early upbringing was governed by a relationship with his mother — who died when Hugh was 29 — that was very different than the one he had with his father.

In June 2005, Laurie did an interview with the U.K.'s *Mail on Sunday* — just before *House* premiered on British TV — in which he discussed candidly these widely differing parental relationships.

"I did have problems with my mother and she with me," he said. "I was an awkward and frustrating child. She had very high expectations of me, which I constantly disappointed. She had moments of not liking me. When I say moments I use the word broadly to cover months."

Laurie described how, while his mother had moments of kindness and good humor, she was for the most part, "contemptuous of the goal of happiness, of contentment, ease and comfort. She even disliked those words. When she was in a good mood, she was a joy, funny and bright. Then she could just switch off, spending days, weeks, months, nursing some grievance."

On the other hand, Hugh's relationship with his dad seems to be one marked by respect and, if anything, a profound sense of having let his father down a little. Indeed, Hugh did attend the Dragon School, a famous preparatory school in Oxford, and then Eton College, one of England's most prestigious public — or, in North American terms, private — schools, before going on to Cambridge University.

But Laurie has noted that his dad, who in fact became an MD only after entering med school when he was 40, having served in the Second World War, did have medical aspirations for his son, but following in Ranald's footsteps was simply not something Hugh was interested in when he attended Eton.

"My father had high hopes for me following him into medicine," Laurie told the *Mail on Sunday*. "I wanted to, and was going to choose the right subjects at school but in the end I copped out. Medicine is awfully hard work and you have to be rather clever to pass the exams. Seriously, this is a source of real guilt for me."

Of course, the coincidence of a young man who grows up with a father who wanted him to enter the medical profession, never makes it as a doctor, and then many years later goes on to play one on a popular TV show, has not gone unnoticed — and certainly not by Hugh.

"One of the things that makes me feel guilty about playing this role is that my dad was such a good doctor and believed passionately in the Hippocratic oath. He was a very gentle soul," Laurie says. "If every son in some way is trying to live up to his father it is irksome — but here I am prancing around with three days of stubble because the part calls for it and faking being a doctor, when my father was the real thing and a very good one at that. I'm probably being paid more to be a fake version of my own father."

By his own admission, Hugh's work in his early years of schooling was marked not necessarily by a lack of intelligence — but instead by a seeming non-existence of anything resembling drive. In a witty article he wrote for the (U.K.) *Daily Telegraph* in 1999, Laurie summed up his younger years, and his performance in school during them, like this:

> *I was, in truth, a horrible child. Not much given to things of a bookey nature, I spent a large part of my youth smoking Number Six and cheating in French vocabulary tests. I wore platform boots with a brass skull and crossbones over the ankle, my hair was disgraceful, and I somehow contrived to pull off the gruesome trick of being both fat and thin at the same time. If you had passed me in the street during those pimply years, I am confident that you would, at the very least, have quickened your pace. . . . You think I exaggerate? I do not. Glancing over my school reports from the year 1972, I observe that the words "ghastly" and "desperate" feature strongly, while "no," "not," "never," and "again" also crop up more often than one would expect in a random sample. My history teacher's report actually took the form of a postcard from Vancouver.*

Although the lack of ambition that Laurie cites as the factor that prevented him from ever going to medical school seems to characterize his early years, that same dearth of drive, however, did not plunge him into complete slackerdom. Instead, Hugh was saved from a total couch-potato existence by a pastime that was to define a large part of his early life, and indeed, was to develop in him the kind of discipline and character he would need to draw upon in his later career as a successful actor: the sport of rowing.

Now, many foreign-born celebrities, upon making it big in North America, find that the years they spent before coming to the New World become subject to a kind of quasi-historical scrutiny into both their personal and their professional lives. In much the same way that the North American media — and the adoring public — seemed stunned at times to discover that such stars as Penelope Cruz, Mel Gibson, or Antonio Banderas had actually managed to build certain reputations in their home countries before appearing in Hollywood, many North American magazines and TV reporters spilled gallons of ink and hours of airtime on the fact that Hugh had enjoyed a successful career on stage and on the big and small screen before he struck it rich on *House*.

But as amazed as North Americans were about that, they seemed equally enthusiastic about another fact of Laurie's life before coming to the U.S. — namely, that at one point, he had been one of the best young rowers in Britain, and, indeed, one of the top junior oarsmen in the world.

If you want to know much about what Hugh Laurie was up to in his youth, the sport of rowing provides most of the answers. It defined his teen years, dictated many of his educational choices, and helped him develop many of the character traits that would lead to his future success as an actor.

Certainly, achievement in sport prior to screen success is nothing new for actors, as proven by such diverse stars as Bruce Dern (running), Kris Kristoffersen and Burt Reynolds (football), or Geena Davis, one of Laurie's co-stars in the *Stuart Little* films (archery). And many a journalist has commented on the fact that several of the same skills needed for success in acting — willingness to put in long hours of practice, self-confidence, the ability to suffer defeat as well as embrace success — are similar to the ones you need to be good at sports.

But for Laurie, who plays a scruffy, half-lame, drug-dependent curmudgeon in primetime, the idea of international success in a sport as demanding as rowing just didn't seem to fit. (Although on the occasions in *House* when the good doctor reveals a forearm during a complex operation it's easy to see — if you look closely — some very well developed muscles.)

But it is indeed true — in his younger days, and especially during his time at Cambridge, Laurie was a world-beater on the water. As a student at Eton, he had progressed in the sport to the point that he and his partner J.S. Palmer, had been junior national champion in the coxed pairs event, and came fourth in the world junior championships in Finland, in 1977.

In fact, his whole choice of university — and the course of study he followed while at Cambridge — was based on rowing. "I went there to row. I'll be blunt with it," he has said. "That's really what I went for, and anthropology was the most convenient subject to read while spending eight hours a day on the river."

Laurie started at Cambridge in 1978, and rowed there for his college, Selwyn, as well as for the university, although a bout of glandular fever in early 1979 interrupted things a bit. In 1980 though, he returned to qualify as a Blue, or varsity team member, in that year's Oxford-Cambridge boat race, a race imbued by a rivalry that in England is similar to the one that underlies Red Sox–Yankees baseball games or the Harvard-Yale football contests in the U.S.

In the 1980 Oxford-Cambridge race, he was in the Cambridge boat that waged a spectacular come-from-behind effort that nevertheless ended up in a narrow defeat at the hands of the hated Oxonians. In an entirely House-ian move, to this day, Laurie still points to this loss — and not some win — as his strongest memory as a rower.

"I was [rowing in the] number-four [seat] in this particular encounter," Laurie says, "and the result was a loss by Cambridge by a distance of five feet, which is something which I will carry to my grave. In fact, I really shouldn't say this, because I still to this day wouldn't want to give any pleasure or satisfaction to the opposing crew. But yes, it's true — it was a very bitter defeat."

Still, a few months after the disheartening loss to Oxford, the Laurie and Palmer duo competed in the coxless pairs event at the legendary Henley Royal Regatta, becoming the only British crew to make it to a Henley elite final, and finishing second to an American duo.

The hard-to-believe contrast between Laurie's decidedly un-athletic character on *House* and his real-life athletic success might be easier to understand in light of a very strange story involving both the sport of rowing and his family life. In fact, Hugh had enjoyed considerable success as a young rower before he discovered something important about his father: namely that Ranald had actually been an Olympic gold medalist in the sport, having been, at the age of 33, one half of the coxless pair that was victorious at the 1948 Games in London. In fact, Laurie really did "discover" his father's hidden sporting life, only coming across the medal, stuffed inside an old sock and a cardboard box while poking around in the attic one day. (Indeed, it was a historic Olympic gold medal to have around the house, since it was another 40 years before a British pair would win another one.)

"My father was very modest," Laurie told the (U.K.) *Mail on Sunday*. "He never told me he had won an Olympic gold. It was tin with gold leaf as it happens, because of the war. There were no frames, no glass cases, in fact hardly any rowing memorabilia was on show in the house. It was astounding humility of a sort that people would barely comprehend nowadays."

Today, a framed photograph of the elder Laurie and his rowing partner and Cambridge alumnus Jack Wilson receiving their medals adorns Laurie's desk in his home in England. "Jack is loose-limbed and dashing, my father ramrod straight to attention," says Hugh, describing the photo. "These were two really remarkable men. Tough, modest, generous and, I like to think, without the slightest thought of personal gain throughout their entire lives. A vanished breed, I honestly believe."

With all that in mind, is it really so surprising that this formerly great athlete hides his one-time prowess behind the role of a self-destructive, un-athletic doctor, the same profession followed by his father who was too modest to tell his own son that he's once won the Olympics in that son's favourite sport? "Humility," says Laurie, "was a cult in my family."

Despite Laurie's claim that rowing was the only reason he went to Cambridge, he did manage to get enough studying done to graduate with a third-class undergraduate degree in anthropology and archaeology, in 1981. As well, the esteemed English educational institution was the place where — to the everlasting gratitude of *House* and Hugh Laurie fans everywhere — the lanky oarsman also discovered acting.

At Cambridge during a spell in which he was too ill to train for rowing seriously, Laurie found his way into the Cambridge University Footlights Dramatic Club, a venerable theatrical troupe, founded in 1883. Anyone who follows British acting will know about the Footlights, as their alumni list reads like an all-star list of U.K. theater, TV, and movies. Famous Footlights alumni include *Hitchhiker's Guide to the Galaxy* author Douglas Adams; Sasha Baron Cohen of *Ali G* and *Borat* fame; playwright Alan Bennett; Graham Chapman, John Cleese and Eric Idle from *Monty Python*; TV interview legend David Frost; author Germaine Greer; writer and critic Clive James; and stage and screen star Emma Thompson.

But while starring as a varsity rower and joining a theatrical club as an undergrad seems like a pretty straightforward thing to do, Hugh himself has suggested that at least the theatrical part was anything but a mainstream move at Cambridge in the early 1980s. "I was an annoying kid who talked back and made a fool of myself in class," he remembered in a 2002 interview with the *Chicago Sun-Times*. "Acting is not an 'English' thing to do. It's not a thing that schoolteachers ever advise kids to look into or take seriously. In fact, generally speaking, they probably frown on it. 'Sure, you want to play around with it, but grow up and get a proper job.' Which is something I plan to do very soon."

Certainly, this perception that acting is a trivial pastime, or at least not something worthy of a well-educated, "serious" Englishman, is something that has always bothered Laurie — especially in light of his father's achievements as both a man of medicine and an athlete. But, paradoxically, acting has also proven to be the one thing that Laurie has consistently been able to do very well — despite his protests that "the world doesn't need any more actors . . . one more twit like me joining the back of the queue seems completely unnecessary."

And despite those protests, acting has also provided financial gain well beyond what most of his more "serious" Cambridge classmates could ever dream of. Consider, for example, the fact that in the summer of 2006, *Entertainment Weekly* pegged Laurie's salary at about $300,000 per episode of *House* . . . that's about $7 million for a season. "Serious" money indeed!

Hugh eventually ended up as president of the Footlights in 1980–81, and during his time in this position, he was joined by Emma Thompson as vice president — a fact that illustrates two important things about his early acting days in college. First, the Cambridge theatrical group's comedy revues and skits provided Laurie's early introduction to the stage and to the various dramatic building blocks upon which he would construct his career. But it would be a mistake to think that Cambridge provided Laurie with any kind of classical acting background. "People assume that I'm very highly trained, that I studied and did years and years of Shakespeare," he has said. "I have no training whatsoever and I've only done one Shakespeare play at university. If people want to believe that, I'm happy to go along with it."

Instead, those Footlights years are also significant in that they represent a very important step for Laurie's long-term prospects as an actor. His time at Cambridge brought Hugh into contact with a group of young actors — including Thompson, whom he dated for a while (Thompson has described him as a "lugubrious, well-hung eel" and "the funniest person I've met") and who would soon go on to become some of the leading lights of British theater, films, and TV. And it was an annual Footlights tradition that allowed Hugh to develop a friendship with a fellow actor which was likely the most significant personal contact he was to make in the first two decades of his acting career.

The tradition holds that at the end of the year the Footlights players hit the road for a tour, and while on one of these tours, Thompson introduced Laurie to a budding playwright and actor named Stephen Fry. (Fry had written a 1980 play called *Latin!* that Laurie liked so much he asked Thompson to introduce the two men.) Today a well-known actor in Britain, Fry's main fame in North America lies mostly among American and Canadian devotees of British comedy shows, although true theater fans also know, thanks to a classic 2006 article in the *New Yorker* by veteran critic John Lahr, that Fry contracted, in 1995, what might well be the worst case of stage fright in a big-name actor.

Appearing in a London play called *Cell Mates*, Fry suddenly, and seemingly unexplainably, became so terrified of performing that he not only left the theater — he left England, taking off for Denmark in an attempt to overcome what he called a "sort of clammy horror — just a feeling of impossibility." (Since what he calls his "debacle" Fry has written several books, appeared in several films, and made several documentaries — but he has never gone back on stage.)

But, back in the early 1980s, Fry and Laurie were still just a pair of spirited youngsters looking to have some fun while developing their acting chops. They worked together to develop a sketch called *The Cellar Tapes*, which they entered, in 1981, in a competition in the Edinburgh Festival Fringe — an event that bills itself "the largest arts festival in the world." Sure enough, the sketch was awarded the "Perrier Pick of the Fringe" award, which led to a tour of England, a three-month stint in Australia, and ultimately a London West End production and an offer from Granada TV for Hugh, Fry, and Thompson to appear in two sketch comedy series.

It was the trip to Australia that seemed to cement the Fry-Laurie duo. "By the time we came back," Thompson has joked, "they were married." And certainly, these early '80s years marked the start of a great friendship and a great collaboration — both of mutual respect and a high degree of acting skill. In fact, in 1982, Laurie, Fry, and other Footlights members collaborated on a TV movie called *The Cambridge Footlights Revue*, which shows the group in a number of sketches and skits.

"He's absolutely brilliant but also painfully self-critical," Fry told the *Los Angeles Times* about his friend. "[But] I don't think I have ever heard him say that he's pleased with anything he's done, except things that really matter to him, like friendships, parenthood, or love. He's just a remarkable man to have as a friend; the wisest I have ever known."

Almost 30 years later, the friendship endures — and although the two have not collaborated seriously since the mid-1990s, they do occasionally cross paths, as happened in Los Angeles in early 2007.

"He was over here recently doing a couple episodes of *Bones*," Laurie told *Men's Vogue* magazine, referring to Fry's appearances in the Fox mystery-thriller series based loosely on the Kathy Reichs novels. "After 26 years of knowing each other, we end up 8,000 miles from where we started, on adjacent stages, working on American TV shows? Very weird."

I still had much to learn. How to smoke plain
cigarettes, how to drive a 1927 Aston Martin, how to
mix a Martini with five parts water and one part water
(for filming purposes only), how to attach a pair of
spats in less than a day and a half, and so on.

— Hugh Laurie, on preparing for his role in
Jeeves and Wooster

CHAPTER THREE

BREAKING THROUGH

We've seen how his early days in the Footlights formed the backbone of Laurie's acting career — and, just as importantly, how his early work with the Cambridge group brought him into contact with people like Emma Thompson and Stephen Fry, both of whom he would continue to work with for many years to come. In fact, it was those early connections that would carry Laurie along through the next crucial stretch of his acting life — a period that was characterized by success on British television, and a number of other projects that began to establish him as a well-known figure in the U.K.

Springing from the success of *The Cellar Tapes*, and following the airing of a 1982 Footlights made-for-TV film, Hugh continued by teaming up with Fry, Thompson, Ben Elton — a University of Manchester grad who would go on to become one of the U.K.'s most popular standup comedians and the writer/star of *Saturday Night*, another comedy show on which Laurie appeared as he was making his name on British TV — and another Cambridge alumnus, Paul Shearer, for a season of a new comedy ensemble show. The group, assembled by the

Granada production company, who had scouted the Footlights members at the Edinburgh Festival, put together three sketch episodes of a show called *There's Nothing to Worry About!* that aired in the northeast of England in 1982.

The following year, the show was renamed *Alfresco*, with Shearer dropping out of the cast and Scottish actor/comedian Robbie Coltrane — who North American TV viewers know best as the star of the import detective series, *Cracker*, and as the enormous half-giant Rubeus Hagrid in the *Harry Potter* movies — moving in. The show featured Elton as its lead writer, with other cast members contributing material as well. It lasted for 13 half-hour episodes (1983–84) on British TV, and made a little bit of U.K. television history: as its name suggests, it was not shot in a studio but rather in the "open air" in which the production crew used, for the first time on a comedy show, ENG — or Electronic News Gathering — equipment usually used for news footage.

Following *Alfresco*, Hugh had another chance to appear in the big-time of British TV comedy, on the show (or, more properly, *shows* — more on that in a minute) *Blackadder*. For the millions of fans in the U.K. (and, in smaller numbers, North American fans of British comedy) who love it, *Blackadder* — the general name for no less than four series and several stand-alone episodes of a wacky historical comedy — needs no introduction.

Non-addicts, however, need a little explanation on how the series actually worked. If nothing else, *Blackadder* would be famous as the show that helped boost the career of Rowan *(Mr. Bean)* Atkinson in the title role of Edmund Blackadder — a part that actually represents four generations of the Blackadder family, each supported by a general, all-around servant named Baldrick (all played by Tony Robinson). This bizarre tradition also holds that in each incarnation the Blackadder/Baldrick duo is joined in comic mayhem by a useless aristocrat — which is where Laurie comes in: in the third and fourth series, he took on the roles of the bumbling Prince George and the equally bumbling Lieutenant George, respectively.

In the former, called *Blackadder the Third*, Hugh plays a late 18th/early 19th century English Prince Regent, a character that the official BBC history of the show describes as "a man of severely limited intellect and foppish habits." Blackadder (assisted by Baldrick) is charged with the responsibility of being the Prince's butler. Although the Atkinson character has "a stinging wit and a cowardly cunning," according to the BBC history, "his demeaning position, in service to a man with a 'brain the size of a peanut,' only strengthens his resolve to move up in the world."

And in the latter *Blackadder* — called *Blackadder Goes Forth* (and subtitled *Goodbyeee*), Hugh took on the role of the excellently named Lieutenant the Honourable George Colhurst St. Barleigh, an upper-class British military man who gets shot, along with the rest of his troops, trying to charge a German battalion. Hugh also appeared in a one-off *Blackadder* episode called *Blackadder's Christmas Carol* (1988), and in an uncredited bit in 1988's *Blackadder: The Cavalier Years.*

Following *Blackadder*, Hugh had yet another chance to strive for laughs in tandem with Fry in a two-man series called, logically enough, *A Bit of Fry and Laurie*. The show featured a 35-minute pilot, which aired in 1987, and grew into a 26-episode series, which ran on the BBC from 1989 to 1995. It followed the sketch-show format that the Laurie-Fry duo had been working with for more than a decade, and contained lots of clever, wordplay-based humor and more than a touch of vulgarity and innuendo.

Fans also enjoyed the show's many instances of both Laurie and Fry breaking out of characters and into their "real" personalities in the middle of a skit, and the rather large amount of musical numbers in the show, with Laurie often on piano and many other instruments. In fact, Laurie has trotted out some of these songs in appearances on the American shows *Inside the Actor's Studio* and *Saturday Night Live*. On *A Bit of Fry and Laurie* — available since 2006 on DVD — *House* fans can see (and hear) the early strains of Hugh's excellent American accent.

Just to give the reader some idea of the kind of musical and comedic fare on offer on the show, here's a description of one of the musical numbers, from a summary on a fan web site devoted to the show:

> America: *a parody of Bruce Springsteen. Laurie dresses in what was, at the time, the "standard" American uniform — flannel, white T-shirt, jeans, sneakers, and a bandana headband in the style of Springsteen and Jimi Hendrix. Laurie dramatically sings the song, the lyrics of which consist of ". . . America, America, America . . ." and ". . . the States, the States, the States . . ." until Fry comes on stage quite annoyed, and punches him.*

While 1989 was a banner year in Laurie's career because of the launch of the series *A Bit of Fry and Laurie*, that professional accomplishment must have paled in comparison to a much more significant personal milestone: getting married, on June 16, to a theater administrator named Jo Green. Although rocky unions and fast divorces aren't uncommon in the TV and movie world, the couple's marriage has endured almost 20 years at the time of writing — although, predictably, the tabloids and gossip magazines have speculated, since the time Hugh started filming *House* episodes on the other side of the Atlantic, that the long-distance relationship might at some point feel the strain. But Hugh has always been reluctant to commit to moving the family — which includes three kids — Charlie (born 1988), Bill (born 1991, and who once auditioned, unsuccessfully, for a role in one of the *Harry Potter* movies), and Rebecca (born 1992, and who played a very small role in the 2001 Emma Thompson film *Wit*) — to Los Angeles.

What's more, Laurie is not all that sure that his kids would like it there. "My oldest son [Charlie] is very English," Hugh told the *Mail on Sunday* in the summer of 2005. "He loves cricket and rugby and probably wouldn't want to leave London. But my daughter would love to go to an American high school. I must say I rather like the energy and vivacity Americans have, but I admit L.A. does look rather like a giant petrol station." Hugh has also speculated that even if his family did relocate to the States, his filming schedule on *House* is so demanding that they would be able to see their dad for only about an hour a day when the show is in production.

Hard on the heels of the success of *A Bit of Fry and Laurie,* the pair was back on British series TV in the title roles of a show called *Jeeves and Wooster* that ran, in 23 original episodes as part of the legendary *Masterpiece Theater*, from 1990 to '95.

Laurie's appearance as the bumbling English upper-crust gent Bertie Wooster — opposite Fry as Jeeves, his much smarter manservant — actually had deep significance for him. Certainly it gave Hugh a chance to sink his teeth into a starring role in a popular primetime series in Britain, an undoubted plus in the career-advancement department. But it also put him in a role created by P.G. Wodehouse, one of his favorite writers — if not his all-time favorite writer, period. In fact, Laurie has referred, very often and very publicly, to the effect that Wodehouse's writings have had on him, once going so far, in an only half-kidding essay written for *The Daily Telegraph* in 1999, to say that "Wodehouse saved my life."

Now, Laurie is by no means the first modern-day Englishman to make his love of the work of Pelham Grenville Wodehouse

(1881–1975) clear in print. The *New Yorker*'s much-loved, English-born-and-raised film critic, Anthony Lane, opined in a long 2005 article that:

> *Logic tells me that there must be people on the planet who do not know who Catsmeat Potter-Pirbright is, or the meaning of the heliotrope pajamas with the old gold stripe, or what Lady Sprockett-Sprockett drank in the drawing room when Mordred Mulliner was hiding on a high-backed sofa . . . but logic and I have nothing to say to one another. The thought of not reading Wodehouse strikes me as no less indecent, and in some ways no less impractical, than walking down Madison Avenue wearing only a pair of loafers.*

But in his *Telegraph* essay, Laurie went even further than Lane, proclaiming just how important Wodehouse had been — for his life and career as an actor. We've already seen that Hugh's early years were characterized by a lack of ambition, and it's clear that rowing was the main thing that saved him from a life of sloth and underachieving. But according to Laurie, reading Wodehouse — who he calls "the funniest writer ever to put words on paper" — also went a long way toward lighting a life-long spark in him.

"In about my 13th year, it so happened that a copy of *Galahad at Blandings* by P.G. Wodehouse entered my squalid universe, and things quickly began to change," Laurie wrote:

> *From the very first sentence of my very first Wodehouse story, life appeared to grow somehow larger. There had always been height, depth, width and time, and in these prosaic dimensions I had hitherto snarled, cursed, and not washed my hair. But now, suddenly, there was Wodehouse, and the discovery seemed to make me gentler every day. By the middle of the fifth chapter I was able to use a knife and fork, and I like to think that I have made reasonable strides since.*

So, you would think, based on this kind of tremendous admiration for Wodehouse, combined with Laurie's opinion that the Jeeves and Wooster stories are the finest examples of the author's craft — what Hugh calls "the best of the best" — that an offer to take on the role of Bertie Wooster in a 23-part TV series would be something that Laurie would jump at immediately.

Not so. When a TV producer approached Laurie and Fry, the reaction was, recalls Laurie, one of disdain. "Wodehouse on television? It's lunacy. A disaster in kit form," Laurie recalls he and Fry telling the producer, noting that for a true Wodehousian, even one who has just been given a chance to take on a plumb role based on the Master's work, the possibility of transferring the sacred texts to the small screen seemed fraught with danger.

"[T]he thing that really worried us . . . was this business of The Words," Laurie thought. "Wodehouse on the page can be taken in the reader's own time; on the screen, the beautiful sentence often seems to whip by, like an attractive member of the opposite sex glimpsed from the back of a cab. You, as the viewer, try desperately to fix the image in your mind — but it is too late, because suddenly you're into a commercial break and someone is telling you how your home may be at risk if you eat the wrong breakfast cereal."

Of course, when the producer, faced with the two actors' seeming dismissal of the roles, decided to move off in search of another comedic pair who would not be so literary-minded and fussy, Laurie and Fry thought the better of it and — to the eventual delight of *Jeeves and Wooster* fans on both sides of the Atlantic — accepted. "And so it was that, a few months later, I found myself slipping into a double-breasted suit in a Prince of Wales check while my colleague made himself at home inside an enormous bowler hat," wrote Laurie, "and the two of us embarked on our separate disciplines. Him for the noiseless opening of decanters, me for the twirling of the whangee."

Of course, Laurie and Fry had not been completely wrong in anticipating that their Wodehousian roles would be tough to play. "I soon learnt that I still had much to learn," recalled Laurie of his work as Bertie Wooster. "How to smoke plain cigarettes, how to drive a 1927 Aston Martin, how to mix a Martini with five parts water and one part water (for filming purposes only), how to attach a pair of spats in less than a day and a half, and so on."

Similarly, Fry had to learn the tricks of the trade to get into his role as Jeeves — but at least the duo had already developed the timing and familiarity with one another they needed to make the show work.

The entire effect was to produce a show that fans and critics loved. But in typically pessimistic fashion, Laurie was not convinced that the book-to-TV transition of Wodehouse was entirely successful as he and Fry enacted it. "Naturally, one hopes there were compensations in watching Wodehouse on the screen — pleasant scenery, amusing clothes, a particular actor's eyebrows — but it can never replicate the experience of reading him," he says. "If I may go slightly culinary for a moment: a dish of foie gras nestling on a bed of truffles, with a side-order of lobster and caviar may provide you with a wonderful sensation; but no matter how wonderful, you simply don't want to be spoon-fed the stuff by a perfect stranger. You need to hold the spoon, and decide for yourself when to wolf and when to nibble."

In fact, all that concern over the ability of Wodehouse to move successfully from the page to the small screen was largely unfounded. That's because the adapting duties were handled so well by veteran writer Clive Exton, who came up with a good formula of writing scripts by linking together three short stories, or about one-half of a novel, into the one-hour episodic format. As Michael Brooke, writing on the British Screen Institute's website described it, Exton seemed to get the balance just right. "Although much sublime comic material still had to be sacrificed, and *Jeeves and Wooster* is ultimately no substitute for Wodehouse on the page," wrote Brooke, "Exton's adaptations come surprisingly close to capturing the flavour of the originals — and, as one critic pointed out at the time, a production that regularly managed to slip words like 'opprobrious' into a peak-time TV slot is something to cherish."

The mid '90s saw Hugh go, as the Brits like to say, "from strength to strength." On top of his roles on *Blackadder, Jeeves and Wooster*, and *A Bit of Fry and Laurie*, Hugh added work — as both actor and director — on the miniseries *Look at the Shape We're In!*, a show that starred Hugh's fellow Cambridge alum John Cleese. And he appeared in an excellent, Brit-flavored example of the then-burgeoning art of the music video: in full Blackadder Regency-period Prince George garb in Annie Lennox's *Walking on Broken Glass* (1992), which complemented his earlier video appearance, as a scientist in Kate Bush's *Experiment IV*, from 1986.

While Laurie was developing a name for himself as a mainstay on British comedy television, he was also busy expanding his career in another important direction — the movies. Although the glamour of the big-screen seems like a good, logical next step for an actor who has been developing his craft on shorter-form TV series, Hugh explained in a 2002 interview with Luaine Lee of the *Chicago Sun-Times*, that this is not exactly the case in Britain — at least not for an actor with his background.

"There is among the British acting fraternity — which it isn't, by the way, it's a backstabbing snake pit. But let's pretend it's a fraternity," said

Hugh, "[a] snobbery about the movies; that they're kind of commercial and then particularly American movies are more so."

Regardless of that attitude — or maybe simply to fight against it — Laurie began working increasingly in films in the early 1990s. In 1992, he played a character called Roger Charleston in the ensemble comedy *Peter's Friends*, a movie about a group of former university chums getting together for a New Year's Eve party/10-year reunion at one of their number's massive countryside manor to talk about the good old days. Directed by Kenneth Branagh and co-written by Rita Rudner, who both appear in starring roles, the cast also includes Laurie, Fry, and Thompson. For the glimpse it provides into the early work of these successful British actors, the film still stands as a minor classic among those fans who also flocked to U.K. group-of-friends movies like *Four Weddings and a Funeral* (1994) and Laurie's supporting role still holds up well today.

Throughout the 1990s, Hugh appeared in several other films, including *A Pin for the Butterfly* (1994) and *The Borrowers* (1997), and did voice work on a few others, like *The Snow Queen's Revenge* (1996) and *The Ugly Duckling* (1997) — none of them headlining parts, but in all of them, you can see Laurie in small-to-medium sized chunks of screen time, building his actor's résumé, step by step in preparation for bigger things to come.

Of course, since his success on *House*, Laurie's 1990s oeuvre has come under serious scrutiny by fans eager to see how their beloved Hugh's career looked before he became a New Jersey doctor on the small screen, in much the same way that *X-Files* fans started obsessing over old episodes of *The Red Shoe Diaries* for glimpses of David Duchovny, or devotees of George Clooney developed a fondness for *Facts of Life* reruns.

One of the early Laurie film efforts that's often talked about as his best among fans and critics alike is 1995's *Sense and Sensibility* — and for good reason. For one thing, the film itself — directed by Ang Lee and adapted by Laurie's longtime collaborator and ex-short-term-girlfriend Emma Thompson — is an excellent adaptation of the Jane Austen novel.

Classic books don't always make such great screen fare — remember Hugh's concerns about adapting P.G. Wodehouse — but Thompson produced a pretty faithful version of Austen's 1811 book for the screen. And for another, the cast, which includes Thompson, Kate Winslet, Hugh Grant, Alan Rickman, and Tom Wilkinson — along with Laurie — provides some all-star acting to go along with the superb period costumes and setting. Critics and fans both loved the film, as evidenced by the fact that, in 1996, Thompson captured an Oscar and a Golden Globe for the script, won the award for best film at the Berlin Film Festival and was nominated for an Oscar in the best picture category as well.

Sense and Sensibility gave Laurie a chance to shine in a substantial role — as the bedraggled husband Mr. Palmer — in a film that got wide exposure outside of Hugh's regular fan base in the U.K., and into North America as well. British TV fans of *Blackadder*, *Jeeves & Wooster*, and other series had known for a few years about Laurie's comedic chops, and now, for the first time, movie buffs in the New World were able to see him in action as well. That's not to say that Laurie was anything like the "star" of *Sense and Sensibility*, but his turn as Palmer certainly took him to another, higher-visibility level of his acting career.

As Thompson wrote in the diary excerpts that accompany the published version of the screenplay, "There is no one on the planet who could capture Mr. Palmer's disenchantment and redemption so perfectly, and could make it so funny."

Critics also praised Hugh's small but significant role. In Britain, *Film Review* gave Hugh "special mention" in a film it called "a celebration of exemplary acting"; the *Independent on Sunday* described Hugh as "laconically hilarious"; the *Sunday Express* said that "Hugh Laurie's cameo as Mr. Palmer threaten[ed] to steal the film"; and Adrian Sington, writing in the *Tatler* called Hugh's role "a classically understated piece of acting," adding that "his looks and bearing are made for the period."

With those very positive reviews — and several others — it looked as though Hugh Laurie was poised to break into the big-time of the British screen world. And with *Sense and Sensibility* garnering praise and awards outside of the U.K., most notably in the United States, it looked there was every chance that the up-and-coming former oarsman from Cambridge was poised to break through into the next level of acting and comedic success, with higher-profile roles in bigger-budget productions on both sides of the Atlantic. As we'll see, the future might not have been quite that rosy for Hugh, but good things — and a few bad ones — were certainly right around the corner.

(CP/© Columbia/Courtesy: Everett Collection)

I figured that I might as well give someone 100 bucks
an hour to hear my woes. At least someone can make
a living listening to my tedious problems.

— Hugh Laurie

CHAPTER FOUR

TO THE BRINK

Of course, in Hollywood — the fictional one, not the real one — a supporting role in *Sense and Sensibility* would almost immediately lead to Hugh's being "discovered" by a big-bucks producer and signed to an immediate, three-film deal that would establish him firmly as an "exciting new import" actor. But since Laurie's acting career developed in the real world, it's necessary to report that his next major appearance in front of North American audiences was in the role of Jasper, the hapless henchman of the notorious Cruella DeVil, played by Glenn Close in the 1996 remake of the classic animated film *101 Dalmatians*.

The expression "remake of the classic animated film" should immediately throw up a few red flags for anyone who's never seen *101 Dalmatians*. At least for Laurie fans the film was not a total disaster. The role of Jasper, the tall, skinny bumbler who is paired with a shorter, squatter bumbler named Horace (played in the film by British funny guy Mark Williams) are in the story solely to provide slapstick comedic moments as they try to carry out the sinister plans — including the kidnapping of those 101 spotted canines — of the nefarious Cruella. Laurie and Williams aren't exactly doing high comedy in this one, but they do provide the intended yucks in a movie that sadly had all too few of them.

This period in Laurie's life also saw the continuation of a couple of interests he'd had since his teen years — namely, motorcycles and music. Ranald had bought Hugh his first bike when he was 16, and they'd been a passion of his ever since. Indeed, when fans of *House* saw their leading man appear at Princeton-Plainsboro Teaching Hospital on a snazzy new bike in season two — the good doctor in fact borrows the money to buy the bike from Robert Sean Leonard's character, Dr. Wilson, he says, as a "test of friendship" — many knew that the fictional character was actually bringing a real-life interest of Laurie's to the screen. In fact, to celebrate getting the role of House in 2004, Hugh bought himself a 1960s-replica model Triumph Bonneville.

"[It's my] dream bike," Laurie told *Men's Vogue* in a 2007 interview, when asked about the Triumph. "It's just so odd that it's a dream bike — you could buy three of them for the price of an average Harley — but we all have to decide in life: are we going to remain faithful to a single example, or are we going to become collectors? I'm quite anti-collecting. One must commit."

And on the musical side Hugh continued a longtime interest in music — what he told the BBC radio program *Desert Island Discs* as a "trifle with piano, guitar, and a few other things" by playing keyboards with a pickup soul and R&B band called Poor White Trash. U.K. audiences had seen his musical abilities on *Jeeves and Wooster* and *A Bit of Fry and Laurie*, and London club-goers in the mid '90s could also see him jamming with the band, which included Sophie Elton, the wife of Ben Elton, his former cast-mate in *Alfresco*.

A burgeoning acting career, combined with a marriage and kids, plus a growing passion for music and motorcycles would seem to represent a pretty full life for anyone, but it all wasn't quite enough for Hugh Laurie in the mid-1990s. That's because, starting in 1996, you could add "published author" to his list of accomplishments. That year, Penguin U.K. released Laurie's novel *The Gun Seller* in Britain. At the time of writing, Laurie's second novel, *The Paper Soldier*, was due out in the fall of 2007, much later than he or Penguin had anticipated — due in part to Hugh's busy acting schedule, and in part to his nervousness about writing a follow-up book as good as *The Gun Seller*. "I wrote the first one strictly for me," Laurie told *Men's Vogue* magazine, "and when I submitted it to a publisher, I did it under another name. I can't fool myself the second time around. I've just got to bite the bullet and be me, but that's the difficulty of life, being me — I mean, being oneself."

Hugh had originally submitted *The Gun Seller* under an assumed name, because, as he says, "I wanted to get a sort of fair reaction that had nothing to do with my name, such as it is." Of course, reality soon intruded on that little scheme, when, as Hugh remembers, his publisher asked him, "Do you know how hard it is to sell any book anywhere without you mincing around behind a veil of secrecy?"

The book is a spoof/tribute to the spy novel genre — a Laurie favorite bed-time type of book — and most notably, to his favorite author, John le Carré. "There are few things quite as beautiful as a well-constructed thriller," Hugh told *O Magazine*, adding about le Carré's writing that "it has the mathematical precision of a piece of Bach."

The Gun Seller was a best-seller in Britain and got good critical notices there and in North America as well. Typical of the praise it received was a review in the prestigious *Times Literary Supplement* which called the book's humor "sharp, knowing and contemporary." The *Express* said Laurie had used "all the right ingredients to write a really good thriller," and had "constructed a web of international intrigue worthy of an embryonic Forsyth," while the *Sunday Telegraph* reviewer called it "A terrific debut . . . a Boys' Own thriller so good that I was putting it down all the time to make it last longer," adding, "I thoroughly recommend it."

After *The Gun Seller*'s U.K. publication, there was some speculation as to the possibility of an American edition of the book — with Hugh himself going on record as saying he was in doubt that it would find sufficient readership on this side of the Atlantic because of its unflattering portrayal of Americans. But *The Gun Seller* was in fact released in the U.S., in April 1997.

As it turns out, Laurie need not have feared a parochial reaction on the part of American readers and reviewers. Christopher Buckley, writing in the *New York Times Book Review*, called it nothing less than "the most engaging literary *mélange des genres* since George Macdonald Fraser's *Flashman* arrived on the scene" adding that "[a]s a writer, Mr. Laurie is smart, charming, warm, cool (if need be) and high-spirited. He has Ian Fleming's dash, flash, slam-bam plotting and technical knowledge of hardware — especially with exotic weaponry — as well as P.G. Wodehouse's wit and sense of detachment."

Another prestigious U.S. paper, the *Washington Post*, also had these encouraging words in a summer review: "If you can allow yourself only one more 'light' book, just one, before the encroaching darkness of fall guilts you into re-reading *Being and Nothingness*, this has to be it," wrote Jay Fernandez in the paper's Book World section. "*The Gun Seller* is fast, topical, wry, suspenseful, hilarious, witty, surprising, ridiculous and pretty wonderful. And you don't need a permit to buy it."

Of course, given the subject matter and Laurie's comic twists to the plot, it was only logical that *The Gun Seller* would be considered for a movie adaptation. Indeed, not long after publication, Laurie sold its film rights to MGM/United Artists, who had John Malkovich lined up as one of the producers, and Hugh slated to do the adaptation, and perhaps even to star as the title character, a man named Thomas Lang. In the end though, the terrorism that is such a big part of the plot meant that the movie deal had to be scrapped — at least temporarily. "It's at the bottom of the pile now," Hugh told Amy Jory of *The Evening Standard* (London) in 2002. "I was working on it for about two years, which is a shame, but people lost a lot more than I did, so it's one of those things."

Hugh had always been a big fan of *reading* books, so it made sense that actually *writing* one would follow. "[T]here are the books that shine in my memory, milestones along the horizontal course in my life," he wrote in an introduction to a list of his favorite books in *O Magazine*. "I remember not just the books themselves but the chair I sat in, the shoes I wore, the woman I loved, what song was on the charts at the time."

But in addition to this romanticized view of books, Hugh had a much more practical reason for enjoying writing: "I much prefer it to acting because you can do it lounging on a pillow rather than running upstairs 14 times. But I'm a very shallow person and I'm simply attracted to the idea of sitting there in some Bloomsbury way."

With "successful novelist" to add to his growing c.v. of television and film credits as the 1990s moved past the midway point and into the 21st century, Hugh Laurie was seemingly making a climb to the top of the artistic world. In the latter part of the decade, he added roles as Baron Hector Hulot in 1998's *Cousin Bette*, an adaptation of the 1846 book by Balzac, and, much more significantly for North American audiences, appeared in two excellent supporting roles, as Mr. Frederick Little, the father of the lead character in *Stuart Little* (1999) and *Stuart Little 2* (2002); and as Vincente Minelli, the husband of Judy Garland (and father of Liza Minelli), in the critically acclaimed 2001 TV movie *Life with Judy Garland: Me and My Shadows.*

In the *Stuart Little* movies, Hugh plays the human dad of a cute, ambitious little mouse. In both the films and the original *Stuart Little* story from 1945 (written by E.B. White, who many know as both a long-time *New Yorker* contributor and the co-author of the legendary writing manual *The Elements of Style*), no real mention is ever made of the fact that it is more than a little strange that a family with human parents and another human kid happens to have one child who is a mouse — there's never any discussion that Stuart is adopted, or had been found one day scurrying around the floorboards or anything like that. He dresses in human clothes, sleeps in a human bed, and does all the things the other Littles do, just on a smaller scale.

So while it may seem weird that a role as the human father to a tiny rodent would mark a significant stage in any acting career, that assumption would miss the significance of *Stuart Little*, both to Hugh's progress as an actor, and to audiences in North America.

For one thing, Laurie was part of a great cast in both of these films. The adorable little rodent was voiced by Michael J. Fox; his mother was played by Geena Davis; and other voices were supplied by well-known actors like Nathan Lane (Stuart's friend and ally, Snowbell the cat), James Woods (the evil falcon who tries to capture Stuart), Melanie Griffith (as Margalo, a bird who is sweet on Stuart), and Chazz Palminteri and Steve Zahn (two thuggish cats who make life tough on Stuart). Certainly, these two high-budget films, which drew on the popularity of White's book that has been standard bed-time reading for kids ever since its release in 1945, put Hugh's face in front of his largest North American audience yet.

The role as Frederick Little gave Hugh a chance to trot out his well-crafted Yankee accent, supplying advice to the Little family like the all-American dad his character is. An important step between the Britcom version of Laurie and the very American Gregory House, MD, role he would soon fill, the *Stuart Little* movies proved he could "do American" as well as any import — although it's true that it is not possible to imagine any greater contrast between the optimistic and always-cheery Mr. Little in his brightly colored almost cartoonish suits, and the rumpled abrasive Dr. House.

As well as his role as Stuart's dad in the live version of the *Stuart Little* film, Hugh supplied voice work on the 2003 animated version of the *Stuart Little* TV cartoon. This was actually a culmination of another important aspect of Hugh's career, namely, supplying voices to commercials and animated shows in Britain. This work included voices on such shows as *Preston Pig*, *The Adventures of Mole*, and *Santa's Last Christmas*, as well as ads for companies like British Telecom, Daewoo, and Fisher Price, to name just a few from a long list of commercials.

Laurie's role in the TV biopic *Life with Judy Garland* was also a huge one for the profile it gave him among North American audiences. The enduring fame — and controversial life — of singer/actor Garland (1922–69), played in this one by Judy Davis, meant that the film had wide viewership in North America when it was released by ABC in February of 2001. The TV movie, written and produced by Garland's real-life daughter Lorna Luft, was nominated for five Emmy awards, with Davis winning one for best actress. And as Garland's second (of five) husband and father of future star Liza Minelli, Hugh joined a cast that included Victor Garber (a native of London, Ontario — the same hometown as *House* creator David Shore), Sonja Smits, and Marsha Mason that also helped the two-part film garner a Golden Globe nomination for best made-for-TV movie.

The late 1990s/early 2000s period also saw Hugh active in other TV projects, in the U.S. and in Britain. In 1998, he appeared in a small guest role on the mega-hit series *Friends*, and in 2002, also guest-starred in two episodes of the British spy series *Spooks*, which also aired in North America on the A&E network as *MI-5*. As a long-time fan of spy novels, Laurie welcomed the chance to guest star in this series, developed in consultation with real British anti-terrorist experts, that won a lot of critical acclaim because of its realistic portrayal of espionage.

"They're subtle about it," said Laurie of the real-life spies he was portraying on screen. "But they are unfettered. John le Carré said that the operations of agencies such as MI5 and MI6 reveal the true nature of a nation's politics. Because they're free to do so much, what they choose to do and not do reveals a lot about their national character."

And in 2003, he played a doctor (a GP, like his father, no less) in the British three-part comedy-drama miniseries *Fortysomething*, adapted from a novel by Nigel Williams and directed by Hugh himself. In this one, Laurie's character, named Paul Slippery, is a midlife crisis–facing guy with a wife and kids. Reviewers noted that Hugh was, in real life, about the same age as his character, and wondered if getting a little older was something he feared off-camera as well. "It took time for it to sink in," he told the Coventry (U.K.) *Evening Telegraph*. "I still had that teenage feeling that there was lots of time to do the things I wanted to do. And then suddenly I found myself grunting as I got out of a low chair, and you think, hold on, I'm not 17 anymore, I've got to get on with stuff."

Of course, as both lead actor and director, Hugh could have been expected to put quite a lot of emotion into both his role and the production as well. But in fact, he was his usual philosophical self when analyzing the subject of his getting older. "Sometimes I worry a lot about this, about whether myself at 40 is a betrayal of what I hoped I would be when I was 20," he said. "When I was 20 I certainly thought I'd have opened the batting for England by now, and I'd have climbed Everest and written a great cello concerto. I've done none of those things and therefore I've let the side down. . . . [But] I suppose I'm more bemused rather than panicked. I'm not as neurotic as Paul. Friends of mine might disagree but I think of myself as vaguely puzzled by life rather than neurotic."

So, as the 20th century gave way to the 21st, Hugh Laurie had been able to put together a résumé that would have satisfied most actors in their early forties. "Not that life is unbearable in Britain," he told an interviewer at this point in his acting life. "In fact the really nice thing about my career is that the only people who *do* recognize me are those who actually like me. Which is a good thing."

What Laurie couldn't have known, however, was that in his professional life, things were only going to get better — a lot better, in fact. But — and remember the now-familiar theme that there's a difference between the plots you find in movies and the ones you find in real life — there was one factor in his life that would remind him, and those close to him, that life was far from perfect.

That's because in the first few years of the 21st century, Hugh finally started to come to grips with a long-standing problem. He had always been characterized — by himself and by others — as "moody," and his professional life as an actor specializing in funny, and often downright wacky, roles had always stood out in stark contrast to his real-life persona as a guy who, quite frankly, could be something of a downer for long stretches at a time.

Finally, in 2002, Hugh made a decision to confront what he determined was fairly serious depression — and he has been up-front about his battles with the condition ever since, an admission which has caused more than one reviewer to note that this real-life personal battle with a documented medical problem may be a source that Laurie is able to draw on when he explores his character House's struggle with his substance addiction on TV.

At any rate, Hugh has been candid about the very occasion on which he decided to confront his demons. "I was in the middle of a stock car race for charity, with cars exploding and turning over . . . when it suddenly hit me: I was bored," he recalled in a 2005 interview with the *Mail on Sunday*. "'I thought, this can't be right. I should either be hating it with every fiber of my being or loving it, because this is an extreme experience. I realized this was the state of mind of a depressed person."

After this self-diagnosis, Laurie realized that his depression was not something he could ignore any longer. "It affected everything — my family and friends," he recalls. "I was a pain in the arse to have around. I was miserable and self-absorbed. It went on for long periods of time and had all the other symptoms, like lethargy and not wanting to get out of bed in the morning. I was amazed that people put up with it. I would cling to unhappiness because it was a known, familiar state." He added, in a comment that sounds not unlike his character on *House*, "It's actually selfish to be depressed and not try to do anything about it."

Hugh decided that the solution was to look for help from a psychotherapist. As he put it in a interview with the *Mirror* (London), again sounding not unlike Dr. House himself, "People are more open about seeking help these days. They recognize the fact that the alternative to having a shrink is that you bore your friends stupid. So I figured that I might as well give someone 100 bucks an hour to hear my woes. At least someone can make a living listening to my tedious problems."

Despite all that House-ian cynicism, Hugh has said that he believes therapy is helpful — both to him and to others suffering from depression — not only because it can help alleviate problems on a personal scale, but can ease the burden on friends and family as well. "I know a lot of people think that therapy is about sitting around staring at your own navel," he said. "But it's staring at your own navel with a goal. And the goal is to one day see the world in a better way and treat your loved ones with more kindness and have more to give."

Having more to give — as a husband, father, friend, and, of course, an actor and an artist — was going to be very important to Hugh Laurie by 2004. That's because, every aspect of his life was going to change enormously, bringing everything he had done to that point to hone his craft to a fine edge.

Now *this* is the sort of strong American actor
I'm looking for!

— *House* executive producer Bryan Singer, upon

seeing Hugh Laurie's audition tape

CHAPTER FIVE

BUILDING THE HOUSE

When those legions of hardcore TV buffs who like to bore friends silly reciting small-screen trivia over beer and popcorn — or populate online forums with details about obscure sitcoms or actors — look back on significant moments of television history, they may well remember an anecdote about an actor who played a small role as an oil company executive named Ian (we never do find out his full name) in the 2004 movie thriller *Flight of the Phoenix*.

It's not as though *Flight* — a remake of the 1965 James Stewart film of the same name — was a particularly successful venture, either in terms of critical review or the box office. And it isn't as though the actor in question — Laurie — played a role in this tale of a plane crash and its survivors that was a particularly huge or memorable one. It was, rather, a little bit of after-hours, looking-ahead-to-the-next-project work, done during the filming of *Flight of the Phoenix* in the southern African nation of Namibia that took Hugh's career from good to great.

After a long day of shooting, Laurie decided to audition for an American TV pilot, for which he had been faxed a few script excerpts from the States. He took the audition without any major expectations about what the role might bring. "At the time I was thinking, 'It's a pilot, that's all. Maybe 10 or 12 days' work," Hugh told *Men's Vogue* magazine. "I didn't assume it would go any further than that. Most times they don't."

Perhaps calling the whole event an "audition" is to invest it with a little more glamour than it really had. In fact, Hugh, with his fellow *Flight of the Phoenix* actors Jacob Vargas and Scott Michael Campbell holding the camera, actually read his lines off those faxed sheets in a Namibian men's room. "The only place that had enough light was the shaving mirror in that bathroom," Hugh recalls. "But you could tell straightaway that it was different. Even from the few pages that I saw, I thought, 'Now this is good stuff.'" What's more, Hugh decided not to change out of the dirty, dusty clothes he'd been wearing during the day's filming, including the beat-up leather jacket that was part of his *Flight of the Phoenix* costume. As well, he let a few days' growth of beard remain.

It might have been part of a grand strategy, hoping that the stubble and the disheveled-looking clothing would give him an advantage over all the other inevitably well-turned-out actors vying for the part. But then again, doing the audition tape in his *Flight of the Phoenix* get-up might simply have been a case of being too tired to shower and change — and indeed, Laurie does apologize for his appearance on the audition footage.

Whatever the case, Hugh determined to do as good a job as possible in pitching his talents at the pilot show's producers. "I didn't want to fail again at an audition I knew I could have done well," Laurie told the *Sunday Times* in 2005. "So I worked at it, and I did get it right." Bringing his top-notch American accent — honed on such parts as the *Stuart Little* films and bits in his various sketch comedy shows — Hugh took what little he knew about the role and gave the audition the old champion-rower effort, both in its preparation and its execution.

Of course, it helped that even in the early drafts, the role of Gregory House, MD, was a complex and challenging one. "He was all there in those pages they faxed me," Hugh recalled in an interview with *Entertainment Weekly* just before *House* started its third season in the fall of 2006. "I could hear him in my head — the rhythm of his speech. What he was hiding behind the meanness and sarcasm. I could see him very clearly in my head from the start."

Somehow, all those years of work on student productions, TV shows, films, and all the rest came together that day in the Namibian bathroom.

Laurie's audition for the part of a quirky American doctor — complete with New Jersey accent — ended up being a winner.

In fact, *House* legend has it that when executive producer Bryan Singer saw Laurie's audition footage, he enthused, "Now *this* is the sort of strong American actor I'm looking for!" In fact, Singer — and the other members of the executive production team, including lead writer David Shore, Paul Attanasio, and Katie Jacobs — had already cast half of the other actors on the show *before* they saw Hugh's audition tape. Originally, Denis Leary, Rob Morrow, and Patrick Dempsey were considered for the role, and even Shore, who was familiar with Hugh's past work, didn't initially think he was a good fit. "I was a fan of his comedy," Shore told *Entertainment Weekly*. "But I honest-to-God never thought he'd be right for this role."

It is worth mentioning here that what Laurie didn't know — at least not initially — was that the role he was reading for in Namibia was in fact the *lead* role in the pilot. Thinking that he was trying out for a secondary role was a logical enough assumption, since angry, irascible doctors don't usually carry the action on high-budget primetime series. "I couldn't believe House was the main character," he recalls. "The tradition on American TV is that the hero is always morally good — which also means he's good-looking, since good looks and moral rectitude go together in Hollywood. The character wasn't any of those things. I couldn't believe that anyone would put him in the middle of a one-hour drama."

And although Hugh argues that he lacks leading-man looks — a contention that his legion of fans might dispute — it's nevertheless true that he has established a certain trademark appearance on *House*. That disheveled, *Flight of the Phoenix* look in Hugh's audition not only went a long way in securing the role of Gregory House, MD, for Laurie — it also established for once and for all, the well-known scruffy "House look" — the few days of beard, the jeans, scruffy suit or leather jacket, the running shoes — that would remain part of the show's aesthetic appeal from the very first episode.

Of course, the perfect match between Hugh's talents and the character the executive producers of *House* were aiming to develop was a career-making convergence of factors for Hugh Laurie. But for the *House* creative team, that match was no less gratifying.

"Hugh walked in the room and I said, 'Okay, *that* is what I wrote,'" Shore recalled in the summer of 2006, addressing a master class on TV writing at the Banff Centre for the Arts in his native Canada, adding that as a writer, working with Laurie's versatility means that it's possible to combine comedy, drama, and the medical-procedural elements of the show through one strong lead actor. "He frees you up to write almost anything," Shore told the audience in Banff. "You can have the most dramatic, heavy, emotional scene, and you can throw a one-liner in the middle of it, and he'll pull it off. People will laugh, and yet you'll still have all that emotion, which is really unbelievable."

According to Shore though, falling in love with Laurie on his audition tape and getting the Fox network to fall in love with a lead who was, after all, 45 years old the year he was cast as House, was a bit of a challenge. (Remember, too, that in 2003's British show *Fortysomething*, Hugh had already started to play middle-aged dads, which of course he was in real life.) In the increasingly youthful world of primetime show casting in the U.S., Shore and his team realized that they would have to sell Fox on Hugh's depth and complexity as an actor — and the fact that those very traits were perfect for the main character in their new show.

Though it was quite a challenge to get Fox to agree to a 40-something lead actor, "the script really didn't change that much after he came on board," recalls Shore. "What he did was he made it work. It's very easy to sit in a room and write 'the character is tall yet short, crusty yet lovable.' [But you] want characters who are complex and tricky and who have characteristics that are self-contradicting. But it's much easier to write that, than to act that."

Shore gave a lot of the credit for getting the show off the ground, as well as allowing Hugh and his fellow cast-mates to develop their roles, early on, to his co-executive producer (and director of the pilot episode) Bryan Singer. Although as a director Singer might not be a household name to the extent that blockbuster helmers like Spielberg, Cameron, or Lucas are, he's certainly gained a following for his work on action flicks like the *X-Men* trilogy and *Superman Returns*.

"It was such a pleasure as a writer, having a director who you'd hear talking to the actors about what was going on in this scene, and what the character is all about," recalls Shore. "And he'd identify stuff in my own work that I didn't know was there. I'd say, 'yeah, that's good, that works really nicely.' He really, really got the material."

That "material" originated in an idea from Paul Attanasio, another one of the series' executive producers, who thought up the basic concept of a medical procedural series after reading an article about obscure diseases in the *New York Times*. Attanasio and Shore combined forces, because, as Shore told Dylan Callaghan of the *Writer's Guild* magazine, "We knew the network was looking for procedurals, and Paul came up with this medical idea that was like a cop procedural. The suspects were the germs. But I quickly began to realize that we needed that character element. I mean, germs don't have motives."

Of course, to be a show that any major network would want to pick up — and invest millions in to put on primetime — the medical-procedural idea would need to be fleshed out in a considerably more sophisticated way. "On a more philosophical level, it asks the question: What's more important, kindness or truth?" explains Shore, who has also written episodes for such series as *NYPD Blue*, *The Practice*, *EZ Streets*, *Due South*, and *The Outer Limits*. "We're looking to create the same thing that most shows are: drama and an opportunity for people to examine various ethical issues."

And since *House* was going to deal with life-and-death medical cases in pursuit of answers to this complicated philosophical question, it would need to represent both the science of the cases, and the correct — or in the case of Laurie's House character, pointedly incorrect — hospital procedures involved in curing them. So Shore and his team called in an expert, in the form of an MD who, as "executive story editor," helped give the early episodes the medically accurate detail they would need to convince viewers that House and his staff were real doctors working in a real hospital.

"There's a doctor named David Foster who works with us on the show," Shore explained, adding that part of the writing exercise in the early episodes — a practice that has essentially continued throughout the life of the show — involved putting a certain disease or condition at the heart of the 45-minute story line. "To some extent we work backwards," Shore explained. "We start with the disease and then work back through the character of Dr. House."

But it would be a mistake to give too much importance to the disease angle when assessing whether or not the creators of *House* have come up with a winning formula for a primetime show. After all, as Singer told *Entertainment Weekly*, "There's a procedural element to it, sure, but if all House did was cure a disease every week, he'd get boring pretty fast."

And, simply put, the responsibility for avoiding that boredom fell squarely on the shoulders of Hugh Laurie. If the show's production team were to have any chance of making the show work — any chance of the pilot being turned into a true series, and then avoiding the fate of a huge percentage of new shows, the fate of getting a network start and then being canned after a few episodes — Laurie was going to have to take on the role of his life, and keep that role going through weeks and weeks of grueling filming as season one of *House* was produced.

It may, however, be a mistake to put the whole responsibility for *House*'s success or failure in those early days on Laurie's shoulders. After all, as Shore has mentioned, the show could count on solid directing and the promise of some top-notch acting from the other members of *House*'s main cast — Omar Epps, Lisa Edelstein, Robert Sean Leonard, Jesse Spencer, and Jennifer Morrison — to boost it into a life beyond the pilot stage.

When Fox first put *House* on the air on Tuesdays at 9 p.m. in the fall of 2004, early ratings were solid, but not spectacular. A core of fans began to coalesce around the show's fairly standard plot lines in season one: a patient presents with a strange but serious illness; the diagnostic team assesses, with Dr. House's "differential diagnosis" technique, what is wrong with the patient; whatever prescribed treatment the doctors come up with works at first and then goes wrong; House himself comes up with the true diagnosis, seemingly at random and based on an offhand comment or obscure factoid the patient's friend or relative happens to slip in to a conversation; House and team cure the patient, often with a simple procedure and all is well; House wraps up the episode by deflecting all compliments and, more often than not, insulting the now-well patient for whatever bad habits caused his or her sickness in the first place.

Even as the action unfolded along these fairly predictable lines, critics loved Hugh's portrayal of the grouchy doctor in season one. Many noted (correctly) that the show was more like a detective or crime-solving procedural with a quirky lead character than a standard "medical" show — and more than a few TV writers compared House and his cane to Peter Falk's detective on *Columbo* and his raincoat. Others appreciated the depth — a product of Shore's great writing and Hugh's great acting — of the show's lead role.

"Gregory House is a sort of superman, but way more Nietzsche than Clark Kent," wrote Mary McNamara in the *Los Angeles Times* in an excellent analysis of why the character worked so well on the small screen. "Still, in the end, he always comes through; he just uses his wits and eye for detail rather than using the Batmobile or an Uzi. Which makes him a much better fit for the contemporary feminist-ish working gal but tough on the writers — if serialized, the man of mystery must reveal something to keep from being static, but not too much or he will become banal." As well, McNamara noted that, self-deprecating remarks about his looks aside, Hugh was able to provide a certain kind of subtle eye-candy appeal that was not lost on the average viewer, but had at the same time to be kept in check. "The sexiness has been suitably acknowledged by various plot developments (none of which involve so much as a kiss — the kiss must be saved for 'a very special *House*,' possibly a holiday episode)," McNamara wrote, "but it can't become the staple of the show or the seductive power of the non-romantic romantic lead will be lost."

The cleverness of the writing and sexiness of the lead character was not lost on the folks who hand out TV awards either. In September 2005 — just as season two was kicking off, with almost 16 million viewers watching the opening episode — *House* won an Emmy award for best dramatic writing. And although he was nominated for best actor — an award many, including, not surprisingly, the *House* production team, thought he had a great chance to capture — Hugh did not win. (That honor went to James Spader, for his role in *Boston Legal*.)

"I think the show would not be on the air if we did not have Hugh Laurie in this role," Shore told the *Chicago Tribune*. "It's a tough character to play and play well. To have turned that character into one of the sexiest characters on TV, that is not something I foresaw when I was writing this."

Clearly, in season one, Laurie and *House* were off to a great start. With solid ratings, an Emmy award and a cast and storylines that were getting good reviews from both fans and critics, it was a show that was certainly worth keeping on the air. But in contemplating season two, Fox executives made a masterful scheduling decision regarding *House's* placement in primetime that would go a very, very long way toward boosting the show into TV mega-success, and would establish Hugh Laurie as one of the biggest stars in the TV universe.

That scheduling decision, as it turns out, involved putting *House* on the air just after the enormously popular *American Idol*. For those who are unfamiliar with the scheduling practices of major U.S. networks, this placement of *House* on the TV grid might seem insignificant. But in fact, putting a show on after another, more popular program — often called "giving it a lead-in" — can have a huge effect on viewership, for the very simple reason that people who love one show will often stay on the couch and watch whatever else comes on just after it. For Fox, and for

House, this pairing with *American Idol* had the effect of turning a whole new group of watchers into fans of the show — and fans of Hugh Laurie. "We had a core of fans who discovered us on our own before *Idol* moved," executive producer Jacobs told *Entertainment Weekly*. "But we never imagined we would have this huge an audience."

Certainly the partnership with *American Idol* was huge for *House*. But that explanation for the show's success in the early going only tells part of the story. The other part is best told by Laurie's fellow cast-mates, and it has everything to do with the hard work, dedication, and, of course, weird obsessions of their leading man.

Listening to the comments of his fellow actors, it becomes clear that Laurie considers himself to be, at the very least, something close to an assistant director on the series. "Hugh co-directs every show we do," Robert Sean Leonard, who plays Dr. James Wilson, an oncologist and seemingly House's only true friend in the world, told *Men's Vogue*. "It's not an exaggeration. He really does say, 'Are you cutting from that shot to this shot? Because if so, that would be awkward.' Are you kidding me? I'm thinking about what I'm having for lunch."

For his part, Hugh — who, after all, does have experience on both sides of the camera — doesn't try to deny that he likes to get involved, as more than just an actor, on the set of *House*. "I have tried to exert an influence," he admits, "and as the show grows in its success an increasing burden is placed on — no, that sounds sort of pompous. I meddle."

That meddling was made all the more difficult because it had to be done on a shooting schedule that was very different from the one typically followed in Britain, where six episodes in a TV series season are the norm, as opposed to 22 per season in North America. As well, because he is in a vast majority of the scenes of *House*, Laurie found himself in front of the camera almost constantly. "I show up every week and do eight scenes," says Leonard. "Hugh does, like, 40. I would shoot myself in the mouth if I were him. There are a lot of adjectives for [the character] House, like 'cantankerous' and 'curmudgeonly.' That's all great, but it's very tiring unless the person's enjoying it."

Co-star Jennifer Morrison, who plays Dr. Cameron, a physician who is as moral and caring as House is corner-cutting and cynical, adds to Leonard's assessment of just how difficult it is to play Hugh's role. "You know, for Hugh, it's not just showing up and saying a few lines," she says. "He's saying medical terms constantly. . . . And then, along with the accent, he's got the limp and then figuring out how to handle all the props because he's only got the use of one hand. He's constantly juggling — and that's a lot to think about when you're just trying to act."

For his part, Laurie often jokes that he "forgot to read the contract" in signing up for such a tough role — and that his work on *House* cannot really be all that hard — after all, it's just acting. But when you examine his career and his life, with all of their ups and downs, it becomes clear that hard work on the set of *House* is really in the end one of the things that makes Laurie happy — or at least as happy as he is ever going to be.

"Probably, I fear happiness because I don't know what follows," he said in the 2007 interview with *Men's Vogue.* "To say 'I've accomplished something,' or 'I look around and I see that my life pleases me,' that would feel like a kind of death. If things ever were good enough, I wouldn't know what to do afterwards. I wish I could silence that part of my brain. Or remove it."

Co-executive producer Jacobs confirms that this kind of existentialist dilemma of "not knowing what to do afterwards" is not something that is merely all in Hugh's head — but rather a drama that the cast and crew of *House* get to see played out on a regular basis.

With season one of *House* in the books, the cast and crew now had to face the familiar "sophomore challenge" of giving the critics and fans more of what they had come to expect from the show — and, in fact, to exceed those expectations and make the series even better and more packed with both drama and comedy. As we have already seen, Fox's efforts in teaming the show up with *American Idol* would certainly go a long way toward beating the second-year, what-can-you-give-us-for-an-encore jinx.

But for Hugh Laurie to really take off as a bona fide American TV star, he'd have to reach down even deeper into his actor's bag of tricks for season two and beyond.

(CP/AP Photo/Kevork Djansezian)

I swank around during the week thinking I'm the big cheese. But you don't feel like that when you are in the ring with a chap who knows what he is doing.

— Hugh Laurie, on the challenges of boxing

CHAPTER SIX

IN THE RING

On *House*, Hugh Laurie's character deals with pain and stress by popping Vicodin pills. But in real life, Hugh seems to be able to cope with the pressure of an insane schedule in less self-destructive ways. Despite the crazy, all-out schedule that came with the territory of starring on a big-time American series — or, more likely, because of it — Laurie began following a few other, non-acting pursuits as he acclimatized to life in Hollywood. Of course, with rowing so strongly in his background, it was already clear that he was not a one-dimensional actor concerned only with life in the theater and on screen. And indeed, an education at Eton and Oxford, no matter how slackly pursued, has been known to lead people to develop multiple interests and pastimes, along the lines of the "sound mind in a sound body" philosophy.

So, in 2005, Laurie went back to the athletic side of his personality — that same side that helped him end up a champion rower, decades earlier — by taking up boxing. But while rowing was a life-changing activity for Hugh, his time spent pursuing the sweet science is fueled by more modest ambitions. And although he's tasted success at the highest levels in rowing, he's realistic about his abilities as a pugilist. "I swank around during the week thinking I'm the big cheese," he says. "But you don't feel like that when you are in the ring with a chap who knows what he is doing."

A 2007 profile of Hugh (and *House* in general) in *Men's Vogue* magazine, noted that Laurie's main attraction to boxing seems to be the fact that he loves it "precisely because it's the hardest thing he's ever tried — and probably because it hurts." Throwing a good punch, said Hugh, "is as hard as hitting a good forehand or a good golf shot. But those guys hitting good forehands and golf shots don't have someone hitting them in the face while they're doing it, which, I can tell you, throws you off your game a bit."

In addition to getting involved in the sporty side of things, Hugh pursued his love of music, as *House*'s popularity grew. We've seen earlier how he became involved with his friends in the pickup band Poor White Trash, and in Los Angeles, he helped put together another loose assembly of television actor/musicians, called, logically enough, Band From TV.

Hugh plays keyboards in the band, with James Denton (from *Desperate Housewives*) on guitar and Greg Grunberg (from NBC's *Heroes*) playing drums; *The Bachelor*'s Bob Guiney and Lisa Somerville from *Kitchen Confidential* supply vocals. The band does cover tunes, and raises money for charity. The idea for it came about when Grunberg — whose son has epilepsy — realized that a musical group made up of TV stars would be a great way to raise cash for good causes.

For his part, Hugh joined Band From TV after Grunberg made an appearance on *House*, and has taken on the unofficial role of the act's funny man. In an interview during a rehearsal in the summer of 2006, he told *USA Today* that being unsure of exactly which songs the band would play, he simply "went to iTunes and downloaded all songs in C major." And when asked whether he found playing music more enjoyable than doing *House*, he joked, "I'm a miserable person — the sort of person who finds whatever he's not doing more fun. The grass is always greener," but added, in all seriousness, that he was intending to donate the money he earned from Band From TV shows — all members split the money evenly, and *USA Today* reported that they have been able to receive corporate donations of up to $200,000 for concerts — to the Save the Children fund.

But while Hugh's musical talents might have been a way for him to escape from the tough rehearsal and filming schedule needed to put

House together, those same talents also ended up making an appearance in the show. Once the *House* production team got an earful of Laurie's keyboard skills, it was only logical that they would want his character to show them off on screen. "The character initially didn't play the piano," recalls executive producer Katie Jacobs. "But Hugh's piano playing is so exquisite that it was written in."

Hugh's own analysis of his musical skills, and how they might progress was, typically, equal parts serious and self-deprecating. "I am going to form a jazz trio along the lines of a Ramsey Lewis or Herbie Hancock kind of thing," he said in the *Men's Vogue* profile. "I'm gonna find some regular gigs, and we'll play a very groovy set. If girls in tight-fitting cocktail dresses want to drape themselves over the piano, that's fine, but the music's the thing. That's one of the few things I'm sure about — I know, I just know, that will make me immensely happy."

In season two, Hugh had a chance to take a very good character in Gregory House, MD, and transform him into one of the great all-time small-screen roles. It was, in fact, a chance he grabbed with both hands — a fact that did not go unnoticed by critics, fans, and, perhaps most significantly for the future annals of TV history, the awards judges.

About halfway through *House*'s second season, Hugh captured a Golden Globe award for best actor in a drama series. At the awards' evening in Los Angeles, Hugh got huge laughs with his acceptance speech, telling the audience that, since there were so many people to thank — he had compiled a list of 172 of them — he had decided to write each name down on a separate piece of paper, put all of them in his pants' pocket, and simply pick out three at random. ("And everyone else," said Hugh, "can just lump it.")

After recognizing *House*'s script supervisor and hair stylist, Hugh thanked his agent, Christian Hodell, before exclaiming "That's not my handwriting. . . . Oh, he's good," to much laughter. In all seriousness, Hugh went on to thank Paul Attanasio ("whose original concept the show *House* was"); Bryan Singer ("whose rampant hypochondria has informed the entire thing"); Katie Jacobs ("whose wit and taste has stamped itself in every frame of every show"); and "the incomparable David Shore who is one of the — yes, who is one of the finest writers it has been my privilege to say the lines of," adding, to much more laughter, "I could have done with him in the middle of that sentence."

Hugh wrapped things up by thanking the other cast members of *House*, the show's crew, and its other writers, as well as Stephen Fry, who was sitting in the audience, and wife Jo, who was also there. Finally, Laurie thanked his three children. "They're sitting at home," he explained, "in which case I say to them now, go to bed."

Despite being recognized for his acting excellence with a 2006 Golden Globe, Hugh failed, in an occurance that allegedly drew the ire of the folks at Fox, once again to win an Emmy that year — and in fact he was not even nominated.

Although failing to garner a primetime Emmy nomination in 2006, the televised awards show did provide an opportunity for Hugh to shine. On the event broadcast on August 27, Hugh joined host Conan O'Brien in a pre-taped, scripted introduction, doing a funny bit in a spoof of his *House* character with Conan, who pretends he is looking for assistance in getting to the Emmys on time. Later on in the evening, Hugh presented fellow Brit Helen Mirren with an award for best actress in a miniseries, for her role in *Elizabeth I*, showing the audience his ability to speak French in the process.

But although not getting a 2006 Emmy nomination must have been a little grating for a foreigner trying to make it big in North America, it was another honor, announced in December in Laurie's home country, that represented one of the biggest recognitions of his talents. That was the OBE, or Officer of the British Empire, which Hugh accepted, a few months later, in May 2007, from Queen Elizabeth (the real one, not the one played by Helen Mirren), at a ceremony at Buckingham Palace.

For those not familiar with this legendary British honor, it is in fact an order — or rank — of chivalry, with five classes, the top two of which allow the recipient to use "Sir" and "Dame" before his or her name. (As an OBE, Hugh cannot be called "Sir Hugh Laurie" — that honor is available only to those who have earned the titles of Knight [or Dame] Grand Cross or Knight [or Dame] Commander.) These honors were developed in 1917 by George V, as a way of recognizing outstanding achievements by citizens of Britain and the Commonwealth.

In Hugh's case, as reported by the BBC, the OBE was given to him "for his services to drama, in recognition of his more than 20 years in show business." Explaining Laurie's North American success to its British audience, the BBC explained how his "role on *House* has introduced Laurie to a whole new audience, and he surprised fans with his convincing American accent," reminding Brits that, "previous to this, Laurie was known for playing quintessentially British characters, albeit usually extremely quirky ones."

In keeping with Bryan Singer's contention that *House* really deserves to be seen as more of a detective show, TV fans started drawing comparisons between Hugh's character and the legendary Arthur Conan Doyle creation, Sherlock Holmes, as the show's popularity grew. Beyond the obvious similarities in their names, fans started going online to post their observations on such things as the two lead characters' dependence on drugs (Holmes on cocaine, House on Vicodin); their sidekicks with similar names, whom they always refer to by surnames (Watson and Wilson); their extreme arrogance; and, most interestingly, their similar street addresses. As every Sherlock Holmes fan knows, the English crime-solver lived at 221B Baker Street, and, as astute *House* buffs pointed out online, a close look at an episode in season two reveals that the front of House's house shows the number 221B.

And perhaps the final word in House/Holmes comparisons comes in the many quotes posted on-line by fans of the show eager to demonstrate how descriptions of the Victorian detective in the Doyle series of books actually mesh with modern ways of describing Hugh's character on TV. For example, here's one from the second Holmes story, *The Sign of Four*, which sounds an awful like House's "differential diagnosis" approach: "Eliminate all other factors and the one which remains must be the truth."

While fans were busy noting the similarities between Holmes and House, Hugh was also busy rehearsing and filming their beloved show — on a schedule so packed it prevented him from taking part in a feature-length movie about another iconic hero, the comic book idol Superman. He was cast as Perry White, the editor of *The Daily Planet* newspaper and the daytime boss of the Man of Steel's alter ego, Clark Kent, in the 2006 film *Superman Returns*. But, sadly for *House* fans who would have loved to see more of Laurie on the big screen, he had to give up work on that one (the role was originally filled by veteran Frank Langella) because of his busy schedule on the medical show. In fact, working on *Superman Returns* would have been a bit of a homecoming for Hugh, since the film was directed by Singer.

Now, anyone who's the least bit familiar with North American media knows one thing about fame on that side of the Atlantic — and that is that no matter how famous you become, you've never really arrived until you have hosted the classic show *Saturday Night Live*. And, sure enough, in the fall of 2006, just a couple of days before Halloween, Hugh appeared on the legendary NBC comedy series as host.

The highlight of Laurie's appearance on *SNL* is generally regarded by his fans as his role in a short skit — and in a short skirt — about a man who goes to see a dubious doctor about a broken leg. The man, played by funny guy Kenan Thompson, visits the doctor, and accuses the medic of cheating him, in the company of his wife — a giant, six-foot-plus woman, played, of course, by Laurie. As several fans pointed out on the Internet, Hugh, as a veteran of U.K. sketch comedy, was no stranger to the very British tradition of funny gags that involve men in drag. As well as being welcomed by an enormous amount of cheering and applause when he first hit the set, and delivering the traditional guest monologue, Hugh appeared in several other skits and even performed his song from the *A Bit of Fry and Laurie* days, "All We Gotta Do."

Among the stage and screen crowd, another pretty good indication of having "made it" is an invitation to appear on the show *Inside the Actor's Studio*. Just a few months before going on *SNL*, Hugh also appeared on this interview-based series, which features host James Lipton having in-depth chats with some of the acting world's legends. During his visit to the show, which was taped at New York's Pace University, Hugh chatted with Lipton about his development as an actor and his struggles with depression, as well as performed another one of his songs, "Mystery," on the piano.

In season three, Hugh continued his strong work on *House*. Before the season started, various published estimates held that the show was drawing between 18 and 20 million viewers per episode, and reports out of Hollywood said that the show's producers had extended Laurie's contract for another year, meaning that a fourth season (in 2007–08) of the show would be produced. Those same sources also reported that Laurie's contract had been bumped to something like $300,000 per episode — which would earn Hugh somewhere between $6 million and $7 million a year — making him one of the highest paid actors on the small screen. (TV networks and studios are typically close-mouthed about actor salaries, although it is also conventional wisdom that if the right people want information to get out into the press about these statistics, they can usually find a way to make that happen.)

Likely the most reliable of the accounts of Laurie's big raise came in a July 2006 article in the *Hollywood Reporter* by Nellie Andreeva, who reported that the salary bump came following a two-month long negotiation, and that the $300K per-episode fee represented a "dramatic increase from Laurie's starting pay on the Fox series, which is said to have been in the mid-five figures."

The Hollywood Reporter also confirmed that Fox and *House*'s production company, NBC Universal TV Studio, were committing to the extra year of production, adding that "it is understood that Fox has helped NBC Uni TV foot the bill for Laurie's new deal," and that "Laurie is also said to have received a small stake in the backend of *House*," meaning that Hugh would make a small profit from the advertising and other revenues (like DVD) sales realized by the show.

In early 2007, as *House* hit the midway part of its third season, the awards kept on rolling in for Laurie. He captured his second Golden Globe for best actor in a drama series in January of that year, and, just a couple of weeks later, won the award for best actor in a television drama from the Screen Actors Guild. Following up on the 2006 Golden Globe acceptance speech, Hugh again elicited big laughs with his remarks after winning the 2007 GGs.

This time, instead of the names-in-my-pocket routine, Hugh tried a different tactic. "I am speechless. I'm literally without a speech," he confessed. "It seems odd to me that in the weeks leading up to this event, when people are falling over themselves to send you free shoes and free cufflinks and free colonic irrigations for two, nobody offers you a free acceptance speech. It just seems to me to be a gap in the market. I would love to be able to pull out a speech by Dolce & Gabbana."

Despite all the kidding around, Hugh was able to get serious about what he believed was his tremendous good fortune in being able to play the lead role in *House*, a big-time American series, after all those years honing his craft in lower-budget British comedies. Indeed, in his acceptance speech at the 2007 Screen Actors Guild, he put that gratitude into words — although Laurie being Laurie, he was not able to stay serious and somber for very long.

> *It seems . . . that this business, for actors anyway, is not so much about whether or not you do good work, it's about whether or not you get the chance to do good work. . . . Every day I am extremely grateful for the chance I've been given to play what is to me such a fascinating character, to do it here in America. I'm British, by the way. Which accounts for why I'm so smooth. And what's more, to do it at a time when American television drama, it seems to me, is absolutely at its zenith. It's a phenomenal honor and a great chance, and I am — I know it will pass very quickly . . . it might even have passed while I've been standing here. But it's still amazing.*

Adding that "my therapist made me promise that I wouldn't thank anybody — something to do with ownership, I didn't really understand it," Hugh went on to acknowledge what he called "the people who gave me the chance": *House*'s executive producers. He concluded on a metaphysical note: "[A]nd to chance, thank you. Thank you very much."

Even though Laurie had, since the start of the filming of *House*, insisted that he was too busy to engage in any other large-scale acting jobs, he has, at the time of writing, thrown his lot in with an upcoming 2008 movie, produced by Fox Searchlight Pictures, called *Night Watch*. The film is being directed by David Ayer, writer of the Oscar winning *Training Day*, who has adapted the movie from a book by crime-writing legend James Ellroy. Laurie will play a supporting role in *Night Watch*, and will join Oscar winner Forest Whitaker, veteran Keanu Reeves, and Chris Evans, best known for his role as the Human Torch in the *Fantastic Four* movies.

According to *Variety*, Laurie and Evans will reportedly team up as internal-affairs investigators for the Los Angeles Police Department, in *Night Watch* (which at one time had been called *The Night Watchman*) in a plot that will feature Reeves as a LAPD officer who starts to soul-search over some dubious tactics he's used during his career, while being confronted by a veteran cop (Whitaker) over the death of another officer. The film had reportedly started production in April 2007.

Early 2007 was also a time that Hugh ramped up his charity work — most notably for the American Red Cross. In March, he attended a gala "red tie affair" — wearing red socks, just to be thematic — to commemorate 90 years of service by the Santa Monica chapter of the ARC. At the event, he autographed a replica of the motorcycle he rides on *House*, for an American Red Cross online auction.

With one of the highest per-episode salaries of any TV actor in the world, plus a growing array of honors, a legion of followers, raving critics, and an upcoming foray into the world of big-time American movies with *Night Watch*, Laurie's career has certainly come a long way from the Cambridge days, and his time on British sketch comedy shows. He's become a published author, a successful dabbler in music, and a budding boxer as a recap of his earlier career as a world-class rower. As a husband and parent, Laurie is also a family man, trying to juggle work on one side of the Atlantic with his home on the other. And in the end, it has all be made possible by an acting talent that, for whatever reason, has seen him go from a wacky prankster on British TV to a flawlessly accented American grouch of a doctor — all in a primetime TV market-place that usually relegates this type of misanthrope to secondary roles.

When asked by the British publication *Time Out*, between seasons two and three of *House* to sum it all up, Hugh put it succinctly, "I have played stupid people. I don't know if it's something about my face. I appear to be well suited to play stupid people and it is a difference in style between British TV and American TV." He explained:

> *American writers tend to write about clever people. That's just what they do. . . . [but] it has been a terrific challenge to try and do the [House] character justice and the whole issue of chronic pain and drug dependency. . . . If my life was hanging by a thread, I would go to the good doctor rather than the kind doctor, definitely. Kindness is lovely, but if lives are at stake, then you want the best. . . . Maybe TV is the best place for this guy. In real life, he'd be in jail or someone would have punched his lights out. But there's an exhilaration in seeing someone say the un-sayable.*

I'm sort of reasonably good at a lot of things but not great at anything yet.

— Hugh Laurie, on his diverse career

CHAPTER SEVEN

ALL-ROUNDER

Probably the most significant thing about the career of Hugh Laurie, when you try to sum it up and figure out his overall place in the entertainment world, how he matches up with all the other actors who are busy in TV and movies today — and, by extension, how he rates within the pantheon of stars who have come before — is that his professional and personal lives have been marked by five main themes.

These relate to various aspects of Laurie's personality, his interests on stage and off it, and the fact that he's managed to fashion a great acting career on both sides of the Atlantic. And they derive in large part from the public personality that Hugh has put "out there" — the way he has talked about himself in interviews, shaping what his millions of fans know about him.

So, in no particular order, these organizing themes in the life of Hugh Laurie go like this:

1) Hugh Laurie as the depressed, I'm-no-good-at-anything actor guy: Clearly, Laurie has struggled with depression for a long time, and he has been very public about that, and his attempts to overcome it through therapy. But he has also gone out of his way to be self-deprecating and self-critical when asked about his special talents — always, of course in a humorous way, with typical British modesty mixed in with that sketch-comedy-inspired ethos that makes it funny to expose oneself to ridicule by dressing in an outrageous woman's costume or taking a pie in the face.

The amateur-psychological approach would be to say that Hugh never quite made it past wanting to please his successful-but-humble dad, but that would be a little too easy. Whatever the reason, when Laurie says things like he did when he told *Extra* magazine, after discovering he was nominated for an Emmy award in 2005 — "It feels absolutely terrific . . . partly because I've never been entirely sure that I should be an actor" — it is hard not to appreciate that down-to-earth modesty. Especially in light of the fact that it is coming from one of TV's reportedly highest paid actors.

2) Hugh Laurie as the nice guy who just happens to play a jerk on TV: This trait goes hand in hand with the first. A huge part of the appeal of *House* lies, of course, in the fact that the show's lead character is a misanthropic curmudgeon who, somehow, enjoys great success in a profession that is supposed to be all about helping people — not about insulting them. And it doesn't hurt that, even though you might think Dr. House acts meanly to his patients and colleagues most of the time, he does so in a way that is consistently amusing.

But this contrast between the supposed "good" intentions of the job and the "bad" intentions of the real person doing the job goes even further when you consider the public persona of Hugh Laurie, because people also love the idea that one of TV history's grouchiest lead characters is, in real life, and by all indications, a nice, friendly guy with a wife and three kids.

It's almost a relief to see Hugh cracking wise, in his very non–New Jersey accent on some awards show or *Saturday Night Live*, because it reinforces the fact that for all the realism on *House*, playing that character is just an act for Laurie. As Hugh himself says, his ability to play a convincing American is the product of "a misspent youth [watching] too much TV and too many movies."

3) Hugh as the Brit-com funny guy who thinks it's just one big lark to be in America: Because Laurie has a comic turn of mind, and because a big part of comedy in general comes from pointing out differences in things and magnifying those differences in ways that are funny, Hugh has never shied away from accentuating the fish-out-of-water aspects of his being an Englishman who has come to the former colonies and, almost despite himself, made it to the big-time. As he told an online chat group sponsored by *USA Today*, "I tried to get some time [doing research] in American hospitals but the whole thing happened so fast that I ended up just having to fake it. That's what actors do, after all!"

Those Brit critics, recalling Laurie's days of the slightly undignified, do-what-you-have-to-to-get-ahead routine of a young British actor on the way up are past him, like to imply that his new life — what some of them have called his "reinvention" — as an American star has only come about because of his days in the Brit-com boot camp of the 1980s and '90s.

4) Hugh as an athlete, or at least an ex-jock: It is entirely possible to overestimate Hugh's sporting legacy, and talk about his success as an athlete and his rise as an actor as a cause-and-effect relationship. But if we are being honest, it is very difficult to argue that those two very different accomplishments are not the result of some singular characteristic — a drive and determination that, in the end analysis, has led to high-performance results in both fields. Although it is hard to imagine Hugh saying much positive about himself in any context, he does allow that his success at rowing ("I was pretty good at that") and being in front of the camera ("I'm not easy on the eye or the ear or anything else so I have to come up with something which one could loosely describe as acting") could be the result of the same driven, dedicated personality.

And finally, **5) Hugh as the artistic Renaissance man:** People who like to talk about success — and how we achieve it — love to debate whether the correct path in life is choosing just one thing to try to be good at, and working your entire life at achieving success at that one pursuit. Certainly, history is full of these single-minded geniuses, and the accompanying stories about how other aspects in their lives (Einstein's mismatched socks, Bobby Fischer's crazy political views, etc.) tend to suffer from neglect.

But the opposing school of thought holds that the best way to go through life is to try to be good at a wide range of things, focusing on balance and not necessarily specializing. Of course, Hugh has pursued the athletic side of his life — at one point, following it to the highest levels of international competition. This alone would qualify him as Renaissance man by most standards, but it's also true that within the narrower field of the arts, Hugh has achieved success in a number of areas. Nobody would argue that he hasn't reached much higher heights in acting than he has in writing, directing, and music, but it is still impressive that Laurie is, in addition to being an actor at the top of the profession, a published novelist and accomplished musician.

Of course, cynics could contend that he's been able to be successful in those other fields exactly because of his success in acting (remember his publisher's argument about how hard it is to sell books with a visible author, never mind an invisible one), but reading Hugh's work and listening to him perform — both on *House* and with Band From TV — it would take a truly jaded mind to argue that there is not a huge helping of talent packed into that particular brain and body.

As we have seen is so often the case in his exploits, Hugh is able to sum up the truth about his multi-faceted career better than anyone else ever could. In a 2002 interview with the *Chicago Sun-Times*, he explained himself as a kind of jack-of-all trades.

"I'm sort of reasonably good at a lot of things but not great at anything yet," he said. "I'm a reasonably good writer. I don't write like Martin Amis, but I wish I did. But I can probably act better than Martin Amis. But I can't act as well as Kenneth Branagh, but I can probably play the piano better than Kenneth Branagh. But I can't play the piano as well as Dr. John. I may be able to cook better than Dr. John."

It is too early to know just how Laurie will be judged, years from now, when casual fans and the people who dole out those "lifetime achievement" awards or produce hour-long documentaries about celebrities get around to assessing his life and career. Of course, a lot of that depends on how *House* holds up in its remaining seasons, and how well Hugh manages to avoid becoming too typecast in grouchy-doctor roles.

Two things are for sure though. One is the fact that Laurie has managed to crack a North American TV market that has not traditionally been an automatic "win" for U.K. actors — and has done it by giving life to a main character who is really unlike any other in small-screen history.

And the other is that he's managed to pull it all off with a sense of humor — most of the time self-effacing — that's won legions of fans for providing a refreshing alternative to all those stars who just seem to take themselves way too seriously, all of the time.

As always, it's best to leave the final word on the subject to Hugh Laurie. When asked to sum up his approach to his life and career, he answered:

> *I still amble along and I don't have answers. I never have had. In fact, that would be my epitaph:* I just don't know. *Because, let's face it, who does? Either that or:* Here lies Hugh Laurie. He always cleaned up after himself.

(CP/Patrick Rideaux/Rex Features)

"Trying to minimize the amount of cruelty you participate in, I think, is healthy for anybody to do."

— Lisa Edelstein, on her experiences with being a
vegan

LISA EDELSTEIN

Any actor who is even *thinking* about playing a role that involves supervising the work of a character widely regarded as one of the most obnoxious employees in the history of television had better be prepared to bring an equal combination of experience and determination to the set every day. And for the character of Dr. Lisa Cuddy, Dean of Medicine at Princeton-Plainsboro Teaching Hospital on *House*, the show's producers have definitely found that actor in Lisa Edelstein.

But then again, David Shore and crew did enlist the services of an experienced stage, film, and TV performer who'd tackled such unusual on-screen tasks as Rob Lowe's prostitute/ law student girlfriend on *The West Wing*, James LeGros's transsexual boyfriend on *Ally McBeal*, David Conrad's lesbian sister on *Relativity*, an Orthodox Jewish woman in a custody battle on *Family Law*, and the object of James Spader's romantic attentions on *The Practice*.

Edelstein, who was born on May 21, 1967, in Boston, and grew up in New Jersey, developed the chops for these varied roles by studying theater at New York University's Tisch School of the Arts. But academic pursuits did not take up all of Edelstein's time in the Big Apple. She got involved in the "club kid" scene in NYC, where she took on the nickname "Lisa E" and became so well-known in after-hours clubs that writer James St. James (author of such pop classics as *Disco Bloodbath* and *Freakshow*) appointed her "Queen of the Night" in his book *Party Monster* (2003). As well, *Newsweek* noted her prominent position in the clubs by calling her a "celebutante."

As an established actor turning the corner toward 40 as *House* was becoming successful, you might expect Edelstein to be a little ashamed of all that late-night partying during her younger days. But that's not the case, as she revealed in a 2006 interview with the Bullz-Eye entertainment site online. "It was great! I was a kid! I had a great time," says Edelstein. "I met amazing people, it was really exciting and fun. It was a growing experience, for sure! It was everything I wanted at the time; I couldn't have been happier."

Of course, some people are able to make a lie of Andy Warhol's claim about 15 minutes of fame by turning that brief celebrity into something a lot longer-lasting — and that is exactly what Edelstein did with the club-kid notoriety she'd developed. Proving that she was a lot more than just a partygoer, she began by writing, composing, and starring in a musical she called *Positive Me*, which ran at the La Mama experimental theater in Manhattan — and which many people in the New York theater scene still recognize as one of the first stage efforts to confront AIDS and its spread in the 1990s.

"I had a built-in audience," she says today about the currency of her subject. "People were wondering what I did, since I was being famous for no reason! But, thankfully, I did something. And it was something of value . . . something of social value."

Given the momentum that MTV was developing at the time, it's also not surprising that the producers of the cable network's *Awake on the Wild Side* were eager to gain her talents, casting her as a VJ on that experimental show which — in retrospect, somewhat bizarrely — represented MTV's attempts to secure a foothold among young viewers in the early morning hours. For her part, Lisa does not see her time on *Awake* in 1990 as a supremely productive period. "It was, I like to say, four hours of national humiliation every day," she told Bullz-Eye. "It was a really stupid show."

Despite the fact that Edelstein's MTV stint was a "stupid" one, at least her humiliation was *national* humiliation. That exposure soon led to appearances on mainstream TV, with small guest parts on popular shows such as *Mad About You* (1992) and *The Larry Sanders Show* (1994) and a tiny role in the 1991 Oliver Stone film *The Doors*. But those were just the beginning of some serious TV exposure, as Lisa also played a memorable role as George Costanza's girlfriend Karen on the mega hit *Seinfeld* in two episodes in 1993, followed by those other notable spots on *Relativity* (1996), *The West Wing* (1999–2000), *Ally McBeal* (2000–01), *Family Law* (2001), *Felicity* (2001–02), *The Practice* (2003), and *Leap of Faith* (2002). As well, Edelstein did guest stints on *ER* (1997), *Frasier* (1998), and *Sports Night* (1999), a critically acclaimed but short-lived offering from Aaron Sorkin, creator of *The West Wing*.

On the big screen, Edelstein also built up her c.v. with appearances in *As Good As It Gets* (1997), *What Women Want* and *Keeping the Faith* (both 2000), and *Daddy Day Care* (2003). And, since the working life of any actor must seemingly nowadays include animated productions, Lisa has done character voices on TV shows that include *Superman: The Animated Series* (1996–97), *Justice League* (2003–05), the video game adaptation of *Blade Runner* (1997), and, most recently, *American Dad* (2007).

But all that movie, TV, and animation work was just a prelude to Edelstein hitting the big time on *House* in the role of Dr. Cuddy. Her audition, as she explained in a panel discussion at the William S. Paley Television festival in early 2006, was helped by the fact that *House* producer Bryan Singer had seen — and liked — her as the prostitute on one of his favorite shows, *The West Wing*.

"I'm a hot hooker — that's my thing," joked Edelstein, adding that her transvestite role in *Ally McBeal* might have helped as well. To that, Singer said that in hiring Edelstein, "the biggest challenge was getting Fox to see her as a woman" — to which Lisa shot back, "that's why you never see Cuddy wearing pants!"

In all seriousness, Edelstein — who has appeared in every episode of *House* — declares that on a professional level, she was very attracted from the outset to the lines her character delivers on *House*. "I think the writing is so smart, and I love the snappy dialogue that my character has with House," she says. "And I look forward to them writing even more of that. I like their relationship a lot."

The combination of Edelstein's acting experience and the snappy dialogue she prizes on *House* have certainly paid off — both in terms of fan support and critical acclaim. In 2005, she won a Satellite Award for outstanding actress in a supporting role, and she is the subject of numerous fan sites on the Internet.

And although her role on *House* represents the peak of her acting career so far, Edelstein is not about to get carried away with her success. "I'm just enjoying it," she told Bullz-Eye. "[P]eople ask me, 'Is it surprising, the success of *House*? . . . [But] I think anything in our business is surprising. You really just can't tell what's going to happen with a show, and it's very nice to have this experience."

That level-headed approach to her career is supported by Edelstein's non-acting pursuits. Perhaps surprisingly to those who recall her "Lisa E" party days in New York City, Edelstein now lives quietly in an old house in Los Angeles with a cat and three dogs named Sandwich, Wolf-E, and Bumpa. In fact, one of her main non-acting interests is volunteering for the Best Friends Animal Society, an organization that runs the U.S.'s largest sanctuary for abandoned and abused animals.

As part of her interest in animals, Edelstein is also a vegetarian — though not, as she points out, a vegan. "Politically, I agree with veganism. I mean, nobody dies making milk, but the dairy industry has some very cruel practices," she said. "Trying to minimize the amount of cruelty you participate in, I think, is healthy for anybody to do. And it doesn't mean you have to be perfect. But I think making the effort makes a difference. Making different choices, even a couple of days a week, makes a difference." Despite several reports to the contrary on online pages about Lisa and her career, she says she is not currently a vegan. "The hardest part about being vegan is shoes," she confessed. "I mean really that's the only difficult part — finding shoes that don't have leather on them."

Another pastime that keeps Edelstein grounded is her practice of Ashtanga yoga, a vigorous form of yoga that, according to the official site of the Ashtanga Yoga Research Institute in India, "involves synchronizing the breath with a progressive series of postures — a process producing intense internal heat and a profuse, purifying sweat that detoxifies muscles and organs. The result is improved circulation, a light and strong body, and a calm mind."

As Edelstein explained to TV host Rachel Ray on her online magazine, the yoga is part of a regular morning routine. "When I wake up, I always drink tons of Guayakí organic yerba maté tea," she said. "After tea, I do Mysore-style Ashtanga yoga. I can't eat anything beforehand or I'm really, really uncomfortable."

It's certainly a long way from the night-owl party life of the New York club kid scene to a tea-drinking, yoga-doing primetime TV star. But thanks to her role on *House*, Edelstein has been able to make that switch, and has entered her forties on top of the acting profession after a couple of decades struggling to make it big.

"In my business . . . one thing really *does* lead to another," she says. "If you're good to work with and you enjoy people, then I think it makes a difference. There are so many good roles for women out there, I don't understand it when people say the role choices are fewer as you get older. I find the opposite to be true: there are less good roles out there for the hot 20-year-olds because the normal girl parts just aren't interesting."

House fans the world over are grateful for Edelstein's "interesting" role on the show — and for the poise and experience she brings to it every week as Dr. Cuddy.

(CP/Carlos Diaz/INFGoff.com)

"All I really want to do is [act in] plays, play with my dog, have kids."

— Robert Sean Leonard on his aspirations in life

ROBERT SEAN LEONARD

If you're one of the producers of a hit primetime series and you're faced with the challenge of developing a character who's going to play a role that involves being the only true friend of one of the least amicable characters in the history of television, what kind of actor do you choose?

That was the challenge facing *House*'s creative team when they looked to fill the role of Dr. James Wilson, the head of the oncology department within the complicated world of the Princeton-Plainsboro Teaching Hospital, and the grumpy Dr. House's only confidant.

That kind of role demands an actor with great comedic timing of the straight-man variety, plus an on-screen presence that's unassuming while at the same time bold enough to confront the leading man. Because Wilson has, relative to the other characters, little screen time, *House*'s creative team knew that the actor chosen to play him would also need to be one whose ego will not demand star turns every two or three minutes. And above all, the role of Dr. Wilson requires the sort of normal-guy bearing and demeanor against which the quirky, risk-taking and rule-breaking persona of Dr. House can stand out in contrast.

In short, the role of Dr. Wilson demands an actor with the kind of solid, classical training and discipline to succeed as one of TV history's top friend-of-the-leading-man roles, someone to take his place in the small screen hall of fame alongside such great characters as Don Knotts' Barney Fife on *The Andy Griffith Show*, Ron Howard's Richie Cunningham on *Happy Days*, and Hervé Villechaize's Tattoo on *Fantasy Island*. (Okay, maybe Tattoo is pushing it a bit, but you get the idea.)

The diverse bag of tricks any actor would need to bring to a successful portrayal of Dr. Wilson suggests a firm grounding in the fundamentals of the acting craft — and that's certainly true of Robert Sean Leonard, the man picked to play Wilson.

Indeed, prior to joining the cast of *House*, the native of Westwood, New Jersey (born February 28, 1969), honed his skills primarily as a stage actor. Leonard made his debut on stage in 1981, playing the Artful Dodger in *Oliver!* at the New Players Summerstock Theater in New Jersey and continuing, over the next two decades, to appear on Broadway in such plays as *The Music Man, The Iceman Cometh, Arcadia, Candida, The Speed of Darkness, Breaking the Code, Brighton Beach Memoirs,* and *The Violet Hour,* as well as the West End production of *Our Town*. In recognition of his stage talents, Leonard got a 1993 Tony nomination for his role in the revival production of George Bernard Shaw's *Candida*, in which he played the role of Eugene Marchbanks.

In 2001, Leonard — a graduate of New York's Fordham University and Columbia University's School of General Studies and Continuing Education — went one better than his nomination in the Tony department, winning the award for best actor for *The Invention of Love*, a play by Tom Stoppard about the life of A.E. Houseman, in which Leonard took on the lead role.

Leonard was also nominated in 2003 for a best-actor Tony for his role in Arthur Miller's *Long Day's Journey into Night*, which also starred Brian Dennehy, Philip Seymour Hoffman, and Vanessa Redgrave. But although his run on *Long Day's Journey* was very successful, Leonard describes the actual production of the play as "hell." As he related in a 2003 interview, "The play's too long, the cast was weird, I hated going to work. Every evening at six, when the church bells rang near my house, I'd think 'Here we go again; four hours of screaming and crying.' I understand and embrace the success it was artistically and financially, and wouldn't trade it for anything. But I wouldn't say it was fun."

Although best known for his stage successes before *House*, Leonard did have considerable experience in film as well. In fact, many viewers of the primetime series of a certain age recalled, upon seeing Leonard as Dr. Wilson, that he had appeared, at age 19, in the very popular 1989 movie *Dead Poets Society*, alongside Robin Williams and Ethan Hawke (a close friend of Leonard's), playing one of Williams' students who eventually kills himself. He followed that up with a part as Joanne Woodward and Paul Newman's son in the Merchant-Ivory film *Mr. and Mrs. Bridge* (1990), and major roles in three 1993 flicks: *Swing Kids, Married to It*, and *Much Ado About Nothing*.

Following that big year in the movies though, Leonard returned increasingly to theater work, including those aforementioned Tony-nominated and Tony-winning roles. (One notable foray into the film world during that time was *Tape* with Uma Thurman and his friend and fellow *Dead Poets Society* cast-mate Ethan Hawke, a 2001 movie about a reunion of three friends who relive some of their glory — and not-so-glorious — days from high school.) In fact, even though he has established Wilson as a central character on *House*, Leonard admits that theater is his one true passion — and that he's not even that familiar with the intricacies of television, and almost never watches the show on TV.

"I watched in the first year," he told Maureen Ryan of the *Chicago Tribune*, midway through the show's second season, explaining that he and his fiancée, Gabriella Salik, a classics scholar whom he met while at Columbia, had relocated briefly from their home in New York to California. "But then she left, she had to come back to New York, and what are you going to do? The idea of me watching myself on TV, alone in Santa Monica, was just about . . . just short of, like, a bottle of Maker's Mark and a shotgun away from shooting myself. . . . So I haven't watched it all season. But when I have watched it, I've been mildly confused and Hugh is appropriately grumpy."

But the pull of the theater remains strong. "I don't want an Emmy," he told Ryan. "I've never been happier than where my career is now. And I don't want it to change necessarily. Money's good, and I'm glad I'm getting that, and I'm putting it away for later in life when I do more Tom Stoppard plays at Lincoln Center and make no money. But really, I'm great. I don't mind working two days a week." (The "two days a week" quote is a reference to the fact that, unlike Drs. Cameron,

Foreman, Chase, and, of course, House, Leonard's Dr. Wilson is in relatively few scenes — meaning that Leonard does not need to put in the 16-hour shooting and rehearsing days that his cast-mates do.)

Way back in 1997, when *House* was not even a gleam in David Shore's eye, Robert did an interview in *Play by Play* magazine, in which he described why he enjoys theater so much, in contrast to the movies he had been working on at the time. "I have had great experiences in both, and I have had terrible experiences in both," he said. "Theater has, for me, a better work structure. I like going to rehearsal at ten in the morning and sitting with the script and tearing it to pieces and finding new things and working till 6:00, then going home and making dinner, watching a Knicks game and then going to sleep. Movies are a little more frenetic and ever changing. . . . You are usually working 16 hours a day and your life tends to get put on hold when you are in a movie."

So what is the allure of doing *House*, especially if it is only a two-day-a-week commitment that involves little time on screen? Part of the payoff, Leonard admits, is that the chemistry between his Dr. Wilson character and Hugh Laurie's Dr. House continues to keep the show interesting for many fans — and for him as an actor. "The only way I've found to define it, and it's so pretentious that it makes me want to jump out a window, is like King Lear's fool," he told Maureen Ryan. "I'm like the only one who tells him the truth. And [Wilson] has nothing to lose. I don't work for [Dr. House] and he doesn't work for me. I'm the only character who chooses to be with him as opposed to being there because of a job. And because of that I have the freedom to tell him what I think."

When asked about the appeal of *House* for him as essentially a theater actor trying to determine if he really wanted to do a weekly TV series at the 2006 William S. Paley Festival in Los Angeles, Leonard was direct. "It's going to be a boring answer," he warned. "It was a great script, great writing," he said adding that in playing Wilson, he had relished the chance to duplicate with Hugh Laurie one of the great on-screen relationships of TV shows past — *The Odd Couple*. "I like being the guy who isn't the guy but that the guy counts on," he said. "Plus I've wanted to be Tony Randall all my life."

In the end, Leonard says that with all the success *House* has enjoyed, he'd still be happy to continue doing plays instead of TV. "I've achieved everything I ever wanted to do. I've done 14 Broadway shows and got a Tony award, and now I'm making money and no one even really knows," he told Ryan. "I'm getting away with murder. If I come back to

New York in two years and nothing's changed, I'll be thrilled. All I really want to do is [act in] plays, play with my dog, have kids. My desires are pretty simple. I don't really want to do movies anymore. I'm pretty tired of camera acting."

(CP/Jane West/INFphoto.com)

"You only live once. I'm the type of person who just wants to fulfill my potential — no matter what it might be."

— Omar Epps, on his acting career

FROM BROOKLYN TO FOREMAN

OMAR EPPS

Since the series first made it to the airwaves in the fall of 2004, fans of *House* have been fond of pointing out that when push comes to shove, there is really only one character on the show who can stand up to the curmudgeonly lead character on a consistent basis — and that's Dr. Eric Foreman, the neurologist played by actor Omar Epps.

And while it is always a stretch to say that life imitates art when it comes to actors taking on roles that match their real-life personalities, it's not pushing things too far to say that in Epps' case, playing a no-nonsense, won't-get-pushed-around character is not all that much of a stretch. That's because Epps, who was born in Brooklyn, New York, on July 23, 1973, has, since taking up acting at a young age, specialized in tough, gritty roles that match his determined, hard-driving personality. This is, after all, an actor who started writing screenplays and poetry before he turned 10 and claimed, well before his success on *House*, that he was "going to be the first black president of the United States," adding that, "if Reagan can do it, I know I can."

Epps — whose full name is Omar Hashim Epps — attended Fiorello H. LaGuardia High School of Music & Art and Performing Arts in New York, and credits his mother with inspiring and motivating him. "My mother, who was a teacher, then vice principal and superintendent, is one of my inspirations," Epps told *TV Guide* in an interview held just after the *House* season three finale in May 2007. "She was the first person to believe in me and my talent."

That talent is multi-faceted. In addition to acting, he formed a rap group, called Wolfpak, with his brother in 1991, has appeared as a backup dancer for pop star Queen Latifah, and has recently written a romantic comedy — one that, he told *TV Guide*, he was planning on starring in alongside Tracee Ellis Ross, actress and daughter of singer mom, Diana.

As well, Epps has taken a few turns behind the camera, including directing videos by musicians Heather B. and Special Ed. "You only live once," Epps told *TV Guide* when asked how one person can manage to pack all those abilities into one body. "I'm the type of person who just wants to fulfill my potential — no matter what it might be. . . . My template, actually, is Will Smith. He's won Grammys, been nominated for two Academy Awards, and is a film producer. It *can* be done."

Epps' first big screen role came in the 1992 movie *Juice*, a film directed by Ernest Dickerson and starring the late rapper Tupac Shakur, about the lives of four young men growing up on the mean streets of Harlem. He followed that one up with a role as a college football player in 1993's *The Program*, and in 1994 appeared in another sports movie, this time as a baseball player in *Major League II*. The sports roles continued with a much harder edge, with Epps starring in the 1995 John Singleton-directed *Higher Learning*. Epps plays a track superstar who wins an athletic scholarship, only to find that the powers that be in U.S. college sports are often more concerned with performance in sports than they are in the classroom.

Certainly, those film roles had built a solid base of credentials for Epps as he entered his late twenties. He had developed a reputation as a young actor who specialized in playing African-American parts in movies with messages about inequality and people struggling to overcome tough odds and tough backgrounds. Certainly, this was one young actor who directors and producers had come to value for his ability to take on difficult roles in challenging films that would mean more to audiences than simply an excuse to chew popcorn. But even with his fine work on movies like *The Program* and *Higher Learning*, Epps was still one step shy of breaking into Hollywood's top echelon.

Of course, in the acting profession, that "one big step" almost always takes several years, and in fact several smaller steps, to happen — if it ever actually happens at all. And in Epps' case, there was a medium-size break before the actual big break of getting onto *House* occurred. That transitional TV step came in the form of a recurring part on one of the all-time great primetime series, *ER*. Given the similar settings of the two shows, it was likely a role that added a lot of credibility to Omar's résumé when it came time to audition for *House*.

In 1996–97, Epps played a surgical intern named Dr. Dennis Gant on *ER*. He appeared in 10 episodes, before his character died in a mysterious accident with a train — within the *ER* plotline, some of the other doctors question whether it might have been a suicide — in the episode entitled "Night Shift" that aired on January 16, 1997.

Even though his run on *ER* was relatively short, the wide exposure changed Epps' perception of what it meant to be a "big time" actor. "Before *ER* a lot of people knew my name and some people knew my face," he recalls. "I saw a big difference after *ER*, like, wow, I didn't know television was that powerful."

Still, Epps would have to wait a few more years before he could feel the truly "powerful" impact of TV through his role on *House*. He followed up his work on *ER* with appearances in the films *First Time Felon* (1997), *Scream 2* (1997), and the updated movie version of the classic TV show from the late-1960s, *The Mod Squad* (1999). (To this day, Epps still jokes about the tight pants he had to wear in this one.)

And while *The Mod Squad* wasn't exactly a home run among critics or at the box office, 1999 also saw Omar appearing in a much more somber and critically acclaimed role in *The Wood*, a film from writer/director Rick Fumuyima that traces the lives of a group of African-American kids from a middle-class neighborhood. In 1999, Epps also appeared in the cop-thriller *In Too Deep*, and alongside Jada Pinkett Smith and James Earl Jones in the murder mystery/1950s period piece *When Willows Touch*. The following year, he returned to the sports genre as a hoopster with dreams of playing in the NBA in *Love & Basketball*, as well as the comedy *Big Trouble*, and the made-for-TV movie, *Conviction*.

For *Love & Basketball*, Epps received two Teen Choice Awards nominations, a Black Reel Award nomination, and nominations for an NAACP Image Award and an MTV Movie Award. And for *Conviction*, the story of a man named Carl Upchurch who spends most of his life in jail, Epps also received an Image Award in the TV-movie category.

In 2004, Omar starred in yet another sports film, *Against the Ropes.* In that one, Epps' most mature role prior to appearing on *House*, he played a former drug dealer called Luther Shaw, who, with the help of advice and training from real-life boxing promoter Jackie Kallen — played in the movie by Meg Ryan — turns into a successful pro fighter. 2004 also saw him in *Alfie*, a remake of the 1966 Michael Caine classic that starred Jude Law.

But all of this work was just a lead up to Epps' trip to the truly big time on *House*. He secured the role of Dr. Foreman with a little bit of an advantage over his fellow eventual cast-mates, as he explained at a panel discussion held in conjunction with a screening of a *House* episode in early 2006 at the Director's Guild Festival in Los Angeles, alongside *House* producer Bryan Singer, creator David Shore, and other members of the production team and his fellow cast member.

As reported in *Blogcritics Magazine* online, Epps revealed that he was the only one of the actors eventually chosen for lead roles on the show to have read the entire script of the pilot. (Laurie claims to have read three pages, while Jesse Spencer said he only got six.) But surprisingly, Omar revealed that when it came time for his audition, he and Singer "talked about life and everything but the script."

The show's producers though, were looking for a supporting cast for star Hugh Laurie that would serve as more than just foils for the lead character's quirky genius and odd brand of humor. They wanted Epps and his fellow *House* actors to be able to carry the show in their own right, and, in the case of Dr. Foreman, needed a character who could oppose his mentor and even rise above and outrank him on occasion, like in season two when House is temporarily suspended and Foreman becomes his boss.

And, as *House* buffs who watched the show through the end of season three can attest, Epps' Dr. Foreman was even strong enough to quit House's team in the final episode. When *TV Guide* asked Epps, who's been nominated for two more NAACP Image Awards for his work on *House,* to explain why his character had taken such a dramatic step — being tough and not backing down is one thing; quitting is altogether another — he responded bluntly.

"The short answer is he doesn't want to become House," Epps said. "House is judgmental — he's callous toward humanity. Foreman is an optimist [but] he sees the dark side that House always talks about. It's getting to be a bit much. . . . The show has good ratings, but it's been three years of the same formula, and we should push it a bit."

Epps, who has two small children and is married to singer Keisha Spivey, says that Dr. Foreman will certainly be back on the series in season four — but if he knows in exactly what form, he's not saying. One thing he is sure of is his ability to continue with his own unique, multi-talented approach to the entertainment world.

"The only limitations that I can have," he says, "are the ones that I set on myself."

(CP/Carlos Diaz/INFphoto.com)

"She exudes a lightness and she has a beautiful soul. . . . Whenever she laughs, everyone laughs."

— Omar Epps, on his fellow *House* cast member Jennifer Morrison

JENNIFER MORRISON

They say that early success in acting is sometimes the best path to a short screen career. And certainly, for many young TV and movie stars, securing high-profile roles before you're old enough to secure a driver's license has led to nothing but heartbreak and ruin — not to mention decades spent trying to convince producers and directors that, if only given the chance, you could easily reclaim past glories.

Happily for Jennifer Morrison, who plays the morally upstanding and ethically solid Dr. Allison Cameron on *House* — a character convinced of the basic goodness of humanity, and the need to practice medicine by conventional rules, in distinct contrast to Hugh Laurie's lead character, who believes that people are basically corrupt and that all shortcuts are worth taking — a background as a teen star has led, not to a place in the Has-Been Hall of Shame, but to a major role on one of the top series of the decade.

Morrison, who was born in Chicago in 1979, and raised in the affluent Arlington Heights suburb of the Windy City, actually started appearing in print ads at the tender age of 10. Morrison herself is a little reluctant to invest that very early work with too much glamour, but it did mark an important first step. "I was a kid, so I wouldn't consider that real modeling," she said in a 2003 interview with *Playboy* magazine. "But every Sunday you could open the paper and see me in ads for Kohl's, JC Penney, Montgomery Ward, and stuff like that. The big scandal was when I was in seventh grade and I modeled a bathing suit. Everybody freaked out!"

As well, Morrison took the newspaper-ad modeling a step further when, at age 11, she appeared on the cover of *Sports Illustrated for Kids* with none other than the legendary (and, at the time, fellow Chicagoan) Michael Jordan. As well, Morrison practiced dancing seriously as a kid. She attended Prospect High School, where her father David was a teacher and band leader. (In 2003, David was named the 2003 Illinois Teacher of the Year.) A strong student, Morrison played the clarinet in both the school's marching band and orchestra, played soccer, and was a cheerleader. But she now admits that it wasn't always easy having a dad teaching at the same school she attended. When asked by *Playboy* if having her dad so close nearby put a crimp in her social life, she replied, "I think 'crimp' is a real understatement. It was not good. I love my dad so much, and he's an amazing teacher, so I really wouldn't trade that for the world. But it didn't make me too popular."

Her popularity must have got quite a boost in 1994 though, when, as a 15-year-old, Morrison appeared in the drama *Intersection*, playing the young daughter of Richard Gere and Sharon Stone. She followed that part up with small roles in the 1994 re-make of *Miracle on 34th Street*, and the 1999 Kevin Bacon thriller *Stir of Echoes*.

Having a dad teaching at the same school she was attending might have been a bit of a hassle on the social scene, but did not hurt Morrison's academic performance. She was admitted to prestigious Loyola University in Chicago, where she graduated in only three years, with a B.A. in theater and an English minor in 2000. Fueled by that educational background and a stint studying with Chicago's legendary Steppenwolf Theater Company, Morrison decided to move to Los Angeles to try her luck at breaking into movies and TV.

The move paid off, as Morrison began to string together a solid c.v. of film and television roles. In 2000, she appeared in the movie *Urban Legends: Final Cut*, and backed that up with appearances on series *Touched by an Angel* and *The Chronicle*. Then, in 2001–02, she got her first big mini-break, appearing in two episodes of the very popular series

Dawson's Creek. In that one, Jennifer played a character called Melanie Shea Thompson, whose main claim to fame was that she was the sometimes girlfriend of heartthrob Joshua Jackson's character, Pacey Whitter.

Then, in 2003, Morrison increased her profile yet again, appearing in a popular road-trip comedy about skateboarders called *Grind,* the film that secured her the aforementioned interview in *Playboy.* Morrison's background in dance and soccer came in handy for that one, as the part included some fairly difficult skateboarding stunts.

"We had two days to learn everything. They gave me *Tony Hawk's Trick Tips* videos," she recalled. "I'd be in my pj's at night with my board trying to learn how to Ollie on my carpet or skate up and down my alley at 2 a.m. I almost got evicted from my apartment complex. We spent the entire time on set on our boards, so we constantly got more comfortable and got better and better."

Clearly, Morrison was getting "better and better" as an actor as well, a fact that shows up in the 2004 film *Surviving Christmas* in which she appears opposite Ben Affleck. The wholesome-good-looks persona she had perfected in these latter two films made a perfect fit for the character *House*'s production team was looking to establish with Dr. Cameron — someone tough enough to stand up to House and the other members of the staff, but someone also attractive enough to bring in a heavy dose of sex appeal and to make the interest shown in Dr. Cameron by both Dr. House and Jesse Spencer's character, Dr. Robert Chase, seem altogether convincing.

But actually getting the part of Dr. Cameron on *House* is the subject of a funny story that Morrison shared with the audience at a panel discussion in Los Angeles in June 2006 that also featured her cast-mates, creator David Shore, and executive producer Bryan Singer. It seems as though Jennifer had concluded that her audition for the show went absolutely terribly, and was quite possibly the worst she had ever done. To make matters worse, she had run into Singer in the hotel lobby before going to bed and had come across, in her words, as a "sopping mess."

But, as Singer confessed, his skill as a director does not always necessarily mean he is great at remembering faces. He recalled that the Fox network had sent him a bunch of footage of the various candidates for the Dr. Cameron role, and that he had then pared the choices down to two finalists — one blonde and the other a brunette. Luckily for Morrison, they were both her — as a blonde in her *Dawson's Creek* episodes, and the other "in something else" as Singer remembers it.

"And you picked both of them," Morrison recalled, laughing. "I ended up being my own worst competition."

Of course, when you've only got yourself as a competitor, it's not that hard to win, and Morrison got the role — one that would win accolades from fans and critics, right from the show's opening episode in the fall of 2004.

Season three of *House* was a particularly good one for Morrison, especially as the calendar flipped into 2007. That year, the actor was given the lofty — and uniquely 21st-century — accolade of appearing, as a character called Kirce James, in a video game, *Command and Conquer 3: Tiberium Wars*. As well, 2007 saw Morrison get a nod as one of TV's "top 10 sexiest stars." Talking to *Entertainment Tonight*, Morrison's fellow *House* cast member Omar Epps revealed that for him and the other actors on the show, Jennifer's beauty was much more than skin deep. "She exudes a lightness and has a beautiful soul," Epps said. "Whenever she laughs, everyone laughs."

But aside from the media accolades, Morrison had a much more personal reason to be happy in 2006–07 — a reason that emphasized Epps' point about how much the other members of the *House* cast think of her.

That's because, after several months of speculation about just how serious their dating had become, Jennifer revealed that cast-mate Jesse Spencer had proposed to her during a trip to Paris during the Christmas holidays.

"It was so romantic!" Morrison told *People* magazine. "We were at the Eiffel Tower and the ring was not in a ring box but in a little old pill case with a butterfly on top. Jesse gave it to me and said it was my Christmas present."

The proposal though, took a little while to sink in. "I was in so much shock when he proposed that it took me two days before I cried! My brain couldn't catch up to everything," Morrison admits. "Jesse laughed at me for a couple of days because I wandered around not really able to grasp everything. But then I realized that all these things that I was hoping for in my life — all these things you don't dare to hope for too much just in case that's not your path — all of a sudden it was at the forefront and possible. I realized, 'I will have a home and a family with him!' That's when it finally hit me and I cried — but it was a happy cry!"

All tears of joy aside, Morrison was not about to let marriage — or plans of marriage, at any rate — slow her down. In 2007, she filmed the comedy *Big Stan* (with Rob Schneider) and a TV film called *The Murder of Princess Diana* based on the Noel Botham book. As well, in 2006, Morrison had extended her talents into the field of producing, taking on that role for a film called *Flourish* — in which she also co-starred with Jesse Spencer — and it's a good bet she'll be trying her hand at the producing game again in the near future. Unfortunately for fans of the on- and off-screen couple, Morrison and Spencer called off their nuptials in August 2007, issuing a joint statement assuring *House* viewers, they "are still very close, and . . . look forward to continuing to work together."

However Morrison chooses to move forward in her career, it's clear that she's one kid star who didn't get hung up on those youthful roles, but has instead parlayed that experience into a major part on a hugely successful series. It's a pretty good bet too that as well as Morrison does with Dr. Cameron on *House*, there's lots more career in store for this talented young actor.

(CP/Jane West/INFphoto.com)

It's tough in this industry — it doesn't matter whether one is auditioning for an advertisement or for a role in theater or television — you just learn to take the hundreds of knockbacks!

— Jesse Spencer, on the acting business

JESSE SPENCER

Australian actor Jesse Spencer finds himself in a slightly unusual position within the *House* cast when it comes to researching the medical science he needs to know about for his role as Dr. Robert Chase. That's because any time he wants some information about one of the specialized terms or factoids that populate the show's dialogue so densely, he can simply make a call or send an e-mail to his father, Rodney, or his two brothers, Tarney and Luke — all three of them doctors back home. (Although Hugh Laurie's late dad, and Lisa Edelstein's still-alive father are also MDs, three in the same immediate family is certainly a *House* record.) In fact, as Spencer revealed at the William S. Paley Television Festival in early 2006, he gets free medical advice from his three close relatives without even asking for it. "My brother e-mails me when he thinks he's seen something wrong," reported Spencer, "and he writes 'ha ha' at the end."

In addition to having spawned two real life doctors and one who plays one on TV, Jesse's parents, Rodney and Robyn, are well known in Australia for a very different reason — their political

activism. They are the founders of the controversial conservative political party, Australians Against Further Immigration, a group the elder
Spencers started in 1989 and registered for official party status in 1990.
As a self-described "eco-nationalist" party, AAFI opposes immigration to
Australia on the grounds that increasing the population through the
arrival of people from other countries is harmful to the Australia's environment and the people who already live there. The AAFI has often run
candidates in federal and state elections, but has never won a seat.

For Spencer, who was born on February 12, 1979, in Melbourne, the
role as Chase almost didn't happen — as a result of the actor's pro-
nounced Aussie accent, or, perhaps more accurately, because of his
attempts to hide it. It seems as though *House*'s creators had initially
intended Chase to be a 35-year-old American radiologist, but when
meeting the much-younger Spencer, they decided to ask him to read for
the part a little differently. "At one point we were going to make him
English," he recalls. "I'll never forget Hugh's face at the read-through."
Finally, Spencer says, after mangling the part as both an American and
a Brit, the producers were convinced that the best approach was simply
to let him do it in his normal Aussie voice.

But although he's now a star on a hugely successful American TV
show, it's no accident that Spencer's Australian-ness comes through so
strongly on *House*, since his roots — family, artistic, and even political
— are so firmly planted in Oz. Just before he turned eight, Jesse, who
had already begun honing his musical skills on the violin, joined the
Australian Boys Choir, remaining with it until his voice changed. On his
official website, Spencer says his years spent in the choir "provided great
training and discipline" for his future artistic pursuits, but he has also
been quoted as saying that, "Mum decided that I could sing a bit, so she
put me in a choir, which I hated and it was just a nightmare. I was a
rebellious sort of choirboy."

It was also during the choir years that Spencer met a man named Bill
Shanks, whom he credits with being his mentor. "Bill . . . convinced my
parents to audition me for an agent," Spencer says, "and he has provided invaluable help and advice to me over the years."

Jesse soon made some big strides in acting, landing a part as an
understudy in a Melbourne production of *The King and I*, and later as
Christopher Robin in a musical version of *Winnie the Pooh*, what he
calls his "first 'real' production." After that, Jesse won a part as Tiny
Tim in the musical *Scrooge*, but had to pass on that one for his first

break on TV — on the Warner Brothers series *Time Trax* (1994), a series about a futuristic law enforcement officer who uses time travel to catch criminals. "This was filmed over 10 days in Queensland," recalls Spencer, "and was great training about filming schedules, make up, costumes, and how many 'takes' it takes to put together a movie."

By the time he was ready for high school (or his schooling for "years 9–12" as they say in Australia), Spencer began attending Scotch College in Melbourne. While in his second year at Scotch, he auditioned for — and won — a role that would change his career. The role was as a young man named Billy Kennedy, on the Australian soap opera *Neighbours* — one of the highest-rated and longest-running Aussie shows of all time.

Neighbours chronicles life on a single street in a mythical Melbourne suburb called Erinsborough, and, in addition to Spencer, has been an early proving ground for such Australian greats as singers Kylie Minogue and Natalie Imbruglia, and actor Guy Pearce. Jesse played the Billy Kennedy character — who, just like in real life, had a doctor for a dad — from 1994 to 2000. Billy got up to all manner of teen hijinks, experienced "relationship problems" with several girlfriends and ultimately left the crowd on Ramsay Street to take an apprenticeship as a woodworker in Queensland.

In addition to being a fairly huge heartthrob among *Neighbours* watchers — especially ones who were teen girls — Spencer won several accolades while on the show, including the "Dolly Prince of Soap" award, as chosen in 1998 by the readers of *Dolly Magazine*, and being selected "King of TV" by readers of the Australian magazine *TV Hits* in 1999.

For his part, Spencer acknowledges just how important *Neighbours* was to his career, calling it "a once-in-a-lifetime opportunity" that gave him not only tremendous public exposure in his home country, but an excellent "boot camp" opportunity to participate in the making of a regular show.

"A daily soapie like this has incredibly high standards which are necessary to produce a show a day," he explains. "Weekly shows, which are at least a half hour in duration have an entire week to produce the show and to perfect everything — from lighting to the number of takes, but *Neighbours* has to produce a half hour program every day!"

After his success in *Neighbours*, Spencer went in search of glory in films, and in 2003, he found it, in triplicate. That year, he appeared in two feature films — the Australian biopic about champion swimmer Tony Fingleton, *Swimming Upstream*, alongside Judy Davis and Geoffrey

Rush, and *Uptown Girls*, with Dakota Fanning and Brittany Murphy. As well, Spencer had an important role in a made-for-TV flick in 2003, *Death in Holy Orders*, based on the P.D. James book. None was a huge success, but they did give Spencer some much-needed exposure to audiences in the Australia, the U.K. and the U.S.

And it was in the U.K. — in London, to be precise, where he was at one time the roommate of James McAvoy, of *The Last King of Scotland* fame — that Jesse found himself when he learned that he was going to be part of the *House* cast. "I had to go to USA immediately and begin a new life over there," says Spencer about winning the part of Chase. "It was a huge change for me."

After having gotten around the whole accent problem for his *House* audition, it was up to Spencer to master the intricacies of the Dr. Chase character so that it would seem convincing to the series' die-hard fans — not an easy task when many of them consider the young Aussie doc to be the least endearing of the Princeton-Plainsboro bunch. But as Jesse — who speaks fluent French — told interviewers Alain Carrazé and Jean-Marc Morandini on the Europe1 TV network, part of the secret lies in maintaining a little bit of mystery when it comes to revealing Chase's true colors.

"I think they [the *House* writers] kind of keep Chase more 'gray,'" he said. "He would side with House because he wants to stay on his side. He is kind of manipulative and wants to be forward too. But, on the other side, when he works with kids for example, we can see his soft side. The two facets are interesting and I would like to keep it that way."

Despite the challenges involved in playing the Chase character, Spencer will no doubt see his time on *House* as a very successful stint — if for no other reason than the boost it gave to his personal life, and the relationship he built with co-star Jennifer Morrison, who plays Dr. Cameron on the show. The pair, who were engaged over the Christmas holidays of 2006–07, but broke up before the following fall, have also starred in the quirky 2006 film *Flourish*, which Morrison produced.

But anyone who thinks that life as a glamorous Hollywood couple working on the same hit show is easy better think again, as Spencer told the interviewers from Europe1. "You work 11 to 14 hours every day when you're on set," he explained. "I mean mostly we just go to work. We work — it is as simple as that. We wake up, we work, and we get home. We get grumpy and we don't want to talk about the show."

For all his success on *House* — success that has brought him to ply his trade on a different continent than the one he started on — Spencer knows that it sometimes takes equal measures luck, skill, and level-headedness to get ahead in the acting game.

"It's tough in this industry — it doesn't matter whether one is auditioning for an advertisement or for a role in theater or television," he says. "You just learn to take the hundreds of knockbacks! All these people are looking for a certain 'look' for each job — the right age, height, hair type, size, etc., before they even consider any abilities — you learn not to get optimistic or disappointed!"

(CP/Picture Perfect)

"It was one of the great stupid decisions of all time."

— David Shore, on quitting his job as a partner in a Toronto law firm and driving to Los Angeles to pursue a career as a television writer

DAVID SHORE

You know you've made it as a big-time TV writer when you can get the characters on your show — which also just happens to be one of the highest-rated series in primetime — to mention your home town.

And that's exactly what happened in an episode of *House* in early 2007, toward the end of the show's third season, in a scene where Hugh Laurie's lead character barks at an airline employee about the details of a trip he was planning to Cambodia. "I don't want to layover in Frankfurt, Taipei, Singapore or London, Ontario," grumbles the good doctor. "That's why I asked for a direct flight to Phnom Penh!"

Only diehard *House*-watchers would have known that the reference to "London, Ontario" must have come directly from the pen of David Shore, the show's creator and lead writer. And, indeed, in an interview with James Reaney of the Sun Media service in Shore's home country of Canada, the writer confirmed it was true. "That was my doing," Shore said. "I literally just dropped the word 'Ontario' into the script."

Originally, the line, in an episode entitled "Fetal Position" (see page 311 for more details) had Dr. House making a reference to the more famous London — the one in England — as a place in which he did not want to end up being laid-over on his way to the Asian capital. (For the record, it's the same London, Ontario, that's the home town of director/writer Paul Haggis of Oscar-winning *Crash* fame.) But Shore changed that to the smaller London, his place of birth, just to add a little realism to the episode — and of course to get a plug in for his home town — noting that as House's head writer, he gets to "do a polish on all the scripts" before they are shot.

Now, while it might be a tired old cliché to claim that "it's a long way from London, Ontario, to Los Angeles," it's a cliché that has a truly literal application to Shore's career — mainly because, in 1991, he decided, at the age of 32 to make that long trip by car, heading to Tinseltown with a friend to try his luck at a career in writing for film and TV. And while such a venture is risky for anyone, Shore was gambling a lot more than most aspiring scribes who head to L.A. looking for fame and fortune.

That's because the life Shore was leaving behind included a high-paying (and prestigious) job as a partner and municipal and corporate lawyer in Toronto, Canada's largest city — one that paid him a huge (and reliable) salary. Of course, with things having worked out so well a decade and a half later on *House*, you might expect Shore to do a little 20/20 hindsight analysis, and claim that chucking law for Hollywood was all a calculated move, which worked out exactly as planned.

That, however, would be an approach that's completely antithetical to the writer's honest, uncompromising view of how things work in the TV world.

"It was one of the great stupid decisions of all time," Shore told a workshop at Canada's Banff Centre for the Arts in June 2006. "The smart thing to do would [have been] to write a little bit first and figure it out from there. . . . I went down there, I bought a computer, I started typing."

Those early typing sessions led, six months later, to Shore churning out a feature film "on spec" — that is, without a contract or commitment from a producer or studio, and simply hoping to sell it based on its merits. He passed it to some friends to read, and in the one week they took to look it over, he decided to write another spec script — this time for a TV show. "They read both of them," recalls Shore, "and said, 'hmm, maybe you should do TV.'"

Two years later, Shore got his first big break, securing his first paid writing job on an episode of the TV show *The Untouchables*. That job provided another important "learning experience" for Shore about the TV-writing world, one just about every scribe has to go through at some point in their career. When his *Untouchables* script was revised, rewritten, and rehashed into its final shooting version, Shore recalls that he could hardly recognize his original work. "What you come to grips with is you've got a lot to learn," he told the Banff audience. "Now I'm rewriting other people . . . but hopefully not quite that dramatically."

Still the gamble that Shore calls "stupid" did — in the end — prove to be anything but. Over time, Shore came to work — as both a writer and producer — on hit series like *NYPD Blue, Due South, The Practice, Law & Order* (for which he received two Emmy nominations, in 1998 and '99), *Century City*, and *Hack*, all of which formed a solid background for his own creation, *House*. "I've been lucky enough to get hired on some really good shows," he told the Banff audience. "Because if they'd offered me a job on a bad show back then, I would have taken it."

The story of Shore hopping onto an Ontario highway and heading south is one that holds a lot of power for the millions of people who hope to one day "make it big" in some form of entertainment, and who dream of one day abandoning the drudgery of their day jobs to work in a creative field that will also pay them lots of money. But it is important to remember that while his success does have a certain dream-into-reality quality to it, David Shore was into his fourth decade before he decided to make this break, and that he had managed to forge a pretty good career on the cutthroat Toronto legal scene before heading to L.A.

He was born on July 3, 1959 (just a few weeks after Hugh Laurie, as it turns out), and his household, in that now-partially-immortalized-on-TV city of London, was made up of his parents and his younger, twin brothers, Phillip and Robert, who are both now Aish HaTorah rabbis doing outreach work in Israel. In an interview with Frances Kraft of the *Canadian Jewish News*, Shore described his early life as having been spent in a "typical Reform-type Jewish household," adding that his personal religious beliefs do not play a big part in his creative work in writing and developing *House*.

"Generally television goes to great lengths to ignore religion, and I think that's really artificial," said Shore, who now belongs to a Conservative synagogue in L.A. "Even if someone's not religious, religion is a significant part of their life, especially at times of crisis." Within this discussion of the role religion plays on *House*, it might also be worthwhile to remember that Dr. Wilson, Robert Sean Leonard's character — and seemingly the only person in whom the irascible House can confide — is Jewish.

Shore attended Masonville Public School and A.B. Lucas Secondary School in London, and remained in his hometown to do his undergraduate degree at the University of Western Ontario. After that, he got his law degree from the prestigious University of Toronto Law School before entering private practice. Interestingly, he credits some on-the-job experience he gained in law as having helped him come up with the character of House those many years — and many miles — later in L.A.

"I used to be an attorney. And I would still be an attorney if I didn't have to deal with people," Shore told Mary McNamara of the *Los Angeles Times*. "I think human interaction is the most annoying feature of most jobs. So I started thinking of a doctor who hated patients."

But while it is one thing to have an idea for a main character and a show to base around him or her, it is quite another to actually be able to put that idea onto the small screen. Shore had been successful writing and developing shows for primetime — as we've seen, he had those two Emmy nominations for *Law & Order*, and his work on several other series like *Family Law, The Practice, Traders, Hack* and *Due South* (about a straightlaced Royal Canadian Mounted Police officer who solves crimes in Chicago — essentially, a Canadian-makes-good-in-the-USA story, not unlike Shore's own personal tale) had established him as one of the TV industry's go-to guys.

But in the ultra-competitive world of primetime TV, you're only as good as the project you have on the go, and Shore needed somebody to work with who could help him make his idea of a grouchy, patient-hating MD a reality. That somebody materialized, in 2003, in the form of Paul Attanasio, a veteran TV producer and series developer who had worked on NBC-produced shows *Homicide: Life on the Street* and *Gideon's Crossing*. Attanasio told Shore that he knew that NBC was looking to try to duplicate the success of their mega-hit *Law & Order* and to compete with the huge ratings of *CSI* on CBS. In other words, it was time to develop another "procedural" show — a show in which some kind of mystery or crime is solved during a (usually) one-hour time slot, and in which the "process" of the solution essentially makes up the plot.

But Attanasio — inspired by the regular "Diagnosis" medical column in the *New York Times Magazine* he enjoyed reading — wanted to take the procedural model into the medical realm, by turning a medical case into the "mystery" to be solved in each episode. When he approached Shore with the idea, the writer realized that it would be possible — with the help of a strong character, like the misanthropic doctor he had been thinking about, a character he has also likened to Sherlock Holmes — to change the procedural genre around a bit by having that lead character drive the action as much as the crime and crime-solving usually does.

But Shore and Attanasio quickly realized that loads of medical jargon, combined with a not-very-likeable doctor as lead character, did not exactly sound like the basis for the world's most compelling TV series. As Shore told the *Free Press* in his home city of London. "It's not about the medical stories as much as it is about a character who's so clever, philosophical, and ethical."

And in addition to all this, what the show really needed was some sort of hook — some way of drawing the interest, Attanasio and Shore hoped, of millions of viewers, week in and week out. "We needed a reason why people would find a nasty, antisocial doctor likable," Shore said in his *LA Times* interview. "So we gave him pain."

That pain comes in *House* episodes in the several forms — including the physical pain in the good doctor's leg that he tries to knock back with Vicodin pills while limping around with his trademark cane, and the deeper, psychological pain of seemingly not being able to form close relationships with his parents, his fellow doctors, and even his romantic interests.

Shore admits that the character trait of absolute — or, at least seemingly absolute — emotional detachment is one he has intentionally given to his lead character. "House is blunt because he literally wants to be shocking, he wants to shock people into action," Shore told the *LA Times*. "He stands by his belief that it doesn't matter what your motives are, what matters are the results. House does what he wants, and doesn't care what other people think. And he's not always right. I mean, he is, in the end, but he's wrong sometimes, on the way to the end."

Again, though, the equation of grumpy, pain-filled lead character plus medical intrigue still does not seem as though it would equal a successful, 21st-centruy TV series. Understanding that, Shore and Attanasio decided that there was one missing piece of the puzzle — and that piece was humor. Of course, at the same time David Shore was building a c.v. that included a number of popular dramas, Hugh Laurie was working away in the U.K. to become a successful comedic actor — bringing the perfect blend of the moody, unfriendly Dr. House and impeccable comic chops to the new series. "Hugh's comic timing absolutely fuels the show," Shore told McNamara. "We can give him the most outrageous things to say and he says them and somehow they're dark but they're also very, very funny."

As *House* became increasingly popular, reporters started seeking out Shore's wisdom on what makes successful TV script writing — or, put another way, how and why he thinks *House* has become so successful. Indeed, most of the interviews with Shore, who's firmly settled just outside L.A. in Encino, California, with his former-TV-producer wife Judy and three kids, that have appeared in print and online since *House* hit the air in the fall of 2004, have tended to be filled with quotes about the writer/creator's "approach to developing character" or his "unique way of framing dialogue." In short, these articles could easily have all been subtitled "David Shore's secrets of TV writing."

A good example of this approach came in May 2006, when Shore did an e-mail interview with John Doyle, TV critic for the Toronto *Globe and Mail*, a daily that bills itself the "national newspaper" of Canada. Explaining his approach to writing in general — and how he developed a toe-hold in the U.S. writing for dramatic series — Shore wrote to Doyle that while he was still practicing law in Canada, "I started thinking that I should move to Hollywood and be funny (turned out I was more dramatic than funny)."

Another example of the kind of insight the press was trying to get from Shore came in a June 2006 interview he did with the *Toronto Star*, another major paper in his home country. In response to TV critic Vinay Menon's request for a summary of *House*, Shore took the comprehensive approach: "I think it's a dramatic show, I think it's a character-driven show, I think it's a procedural show, and I think it's a comedy, all at the same time. And to make all of those things work at the same time can be a challenge."

By the end of the show's first season, *House* fans and TV critics were convinced that the show had many great elements — not the least of which was outstanding writing. But the Hollywood scene being what it is, it took a 2005 Emmy Award to really announce that Shore had arrived. (He was also nominated for a 2006 Emmy — but didn't win.)

The Canadian scribe captured the '05 Emmy for outstanding writing in a dramatic series for his episode on *House* called "Three Stories," the next-to-last installment of season one. The episode, which, as the title suggests, features three interlinked stories about patients suffering from leg pain — one of whom turns out to be House himself. The Emmy recognized both Shore's novel approach to telling the three stories, and the mysterious way it revealed details about House's life and medical problems. But much like his initial foray into TV writing, it turns out the whole experimental approach to writing "Three Stories" was a risk for Shore. "It was either the worst thing I'd ever written," he told the *Canadian Jewish News*, "or the best. I honestly wasn't sure."

The writer's acceptance speech at the Emmy's was classic Shore, making the connection between his personal life and his contributions to the script — and the show. "I want to thank Hugh Laurie for making me look like a better writer than I am," he said, "and my parents for making me happy and well adjusted enough to enjoy this. But I also want to thank all the other people who have come into my life and made me miserable, cynical, and angry because this character wouldn't be the same without them."

So what can Shore do for an encore? Well, one of the logical steps — and one tried by several writer/producers who have made it big on TV — is to aim to put his work onto the larger screen. But Shore says he's not interested in the movies, and for a very interesting reason. "The odd time that I get a chance to catch a movie, I frequently walk out realizing that I could have stayed home and seen a better story, better told, by just turning on the TV," he told the *Globe and Mail*'s Doyle. "Movies have too often become about the event while television is almost always about the story."

As well, Shore made a comparison between TV in his home country and in the U.S., as well as between TV and the movies, one that explained a lot about why he wanted to remain a television guy. "Canadian television so often fails for the same reason American movies so often fail: they're not controlled by writers," he said. "Now I'm biased on this one and there are obviously great, smart directors out there and great, smart producers but no one knows the story like the writer. American movies are controlled by directors; Canadian television is controlled by producers; American television is controlled by writers."

Clearly, the control Shore exerts over *House* has made it one of the great shows on the small screen today. And just as clearly, millions of fans are glad that he made that "stupid decision" — almost two decades ago — to stop being a lawyer and head to Hollywood to take a shot at TV glory.

SEASON ONE

1.1 Pilot

First aired: November 16, 2004
Writer: David Shore
Director: Bryan Singer
Guest stars: Robin Tunney (Rebecca Adler), Rekha Sharma (Melanie Landon), Maya Massar (Asthma Mom), Dylan Basu (Asthma), Ava Rebecca Hughes (Sydney), Kvarra Willis (Kid #2), Ethan Kyle Gross (Molnar/Internet-Research Patient), Candus Churchill (Substitute Teacher), Michale Ascher (Egg Salad Lady), Alana Husband (Tech), Janet Glassford (Reception Nurse), Andrew Airlie (Orange-Colored Patient)

Episode Differential

In many ways, the kick-off to the series is different from the episodes to come, but its shortcomings certainly didn't deter viewers from falling in love with the alienated — and alienating — Dr. Greg House (Hugh Laurie), or his pretty and witty band of diagnosticians. This first episode gives a good deal more background on its primary patient than later episodes will, before stepping inside the fictional Princeton-Plainsboro Teaching Hospital, which is filled with dramatic diffuse yellow light.

Rebecca Adler (Robin Tunney) is a 29-year-old kindergarten teacher who regresses into baby babble in front of her class, then seizes. She comes into the care of Dr. House by referral from his best friend, Dr. James Wilson (Robert Sean Leonard), head of oncology. The expected cause is a brain tumor — "boring," in House's opinion. But pre-empting House's reaction, Wilson — who has been repeatedly called the Dr. Watson to House's Holmes by creator David Shore and critics alike — has already claimed he is related to the patient: she's his cousin. Over the course of the episode, this is revealed to be false, but — with or without the viewer's knowledge — the most important theme of the *House* series has been introduced within the first seven minutes: truth.

"Everybody lies," House is fond of saying.

It is interesting to note that the first we see of House is not House the man, but his cane. A low shot from behind gives viewers a glimpse of Laurie's hip and hand-on-cane as he walks with Wilson, who carries the patient's file. In other words, the first thing we need to know about House is his disability. We will soon learn how it informs his personality. "People don't want a sick doctor," he tells Wilson, a defense for why he never wears a white coat. Is it also the reason House doesn't like to meet face to face with his patients, preferring to study them as though they are hypothetical, logical cases?

Eric Foreman (Omar Epps) is the new doc on the block in this episode. So far, his character, a neurologist, has been with House just three days to Dr. Cameron's six months (Jennifer Morrison), and Dr. Chase's one year (Jesse Spencer). "Dr. House doesn't like dealing with patients," Cameron whispers to Foreman just moments into their first diagnostic rap session, and so the audience encounters the first disagreement among the team — between Foreman and House. The two function as parallel characters, so much so that in a later episode Cameron will tease Foreman that they are starting to look alike, right down to the running shoes. What makes Foreman and House alike is their self-confidence, and their willingness to go out on a limb for what they think is right. Their emphatic nature is what makes them similar, but their disagreements are fundamental: Foreman believes that treating people is why they became doctors; House that treating illnesses is the reason. This basic divide plays into their approaches, dilemmas, and roles throughout the course of the series.

Only seconds later they disagree again over the tumor diagnosis. Foreman cites the med school credo of thinking of horses when one hears hoof beats, not zebras. "Are you in first year of medical school?" House asks tersely. He has no problem with humiliating his staff. If you had to work for the guy, you'd probably hate him, but as a viewer, one realizes that what House is doing is cutting through the niceties to get to the point. After all, lives are at stake. But Foreman impresses House by quick-stepping ahead using House's own logic, that if everybody lies, it's also probable that everybody screws up, and perhaps the patients' tests should be rerun. The exchange plays into the theme of trust, and that popular old adage "Trust no one over 30" in this case should be shortened to "Trust no one." The theme will continue later in the episode when House asks Foreman for a detailed patient history. What happened to the "everybody lies" philosophy? Simple: "Truth begins in lies."

But with Foreman and House in temporary agreement, and childlike nods from Drs. Cameron and Chase, the next conflict presents itself in the form of the sexy supervisor — Dr. Lisa Cuddy (Lisa Edelstein), Dean of Medicine. Cuddy is House's boss, but she's also his sparring partner — nothing he can say will phase her. These two specialize in sexual diminutives, and yet their respect for one another is obvious. In seasons one and two, an episode can barely pass without a comment from House on Cuddy's cleavage, possible undergarments, and her obvious desire for him. She fires back targeting his disability: cane/phallus comparisons, and quips that she's pretty sure she can outrun him.

With House as the exception, she appears to run the hospital smoothly, and even his taunts and deceits seldom shake her. She is the matriarch to his patriarch, and the two are constantly fighting for control. Now, she has pulled his power — all authorization, from MRIs to phone calls — until he makes up the clinic hours he's behind (they've been piling up for years). He yells, she deflects, and ultimately the formula for the show emerges, as House grudgingly gives in to serving the public hiccupers and snifflers in order to win back his MRI privileges and save his patient.

Most episodes feature a triptych of small-issue patients, and through House's discussions and examinations of these low-key sufferers something goes off in his brain and he has his "Aha" moment, leading him either to solve his lead case, or solve it temporarily — meaning, the patient is cured until the patient gets worse. The predictable nature of the show is part of its appeal. The clinic patients provide comic relief, either through their unusual illnesses, their common illnesses and their surprising stupidity about them, or through House's outright avoidance to see them.

The show isn't nice by any stretch of the means, but again, this is part of what draws viewers. While people don't want to think of their own doctors hiding in other exam rooms to watch *General Hospital*, everyone who works with others can relate to the "where do these people come from?" element of the show. Many would like to be as frank and dismissive as House, but tact and fear hold us back. The show serves as a work fantasy — House is the guy who always (or almost always) gets away with it. In this episode he shares his drugs with his very first patient (Vicodin, the painkiller House takes for his abscessed leg muscle), and offhandedly declares that the man's wife is having an affair. House hasn't written the man a prescription, nor has he examined him for the affliction the man claims to have (back pain). This behavior is typical for House. Information is often presented with abrasive tags like "you idiot," and "you moron," but House remains the hero because nine and a half times out of ten, he is right. We should all be so lucky.

We also get first glimpses into Chase's and Cameron's characters in this episode. Frequently the young doctors are asked to follow House's hunches. As they cease radiation treatment for Rebecca Adler's tumor, they're asked to explain rationale to which they don't necessarily subscribe. Dr. Chase, like his namesake, evades. Dr. Cameron is straightforward — to a point, holding back the information that Adler won't want to hear. In later episodes, we'll see this behavior repeated. Cameron can't stomach lying to patients; at the same time, she has a tendency to buoy their spirits when she oughtn't. In keeping with her girl-next-door persona, bad news is not her strong suit. She is eager to please and wants to be the bearer of good messages, not ill. She will always do what is right, unless it burdens her emotionally to do so. Chase is disgusted by the fostering of false hope, but Cameron stands by her actions, believing a false thing to be better than none at all, and again playing into the theme of falsity and truth.

Show creator David Shore has admitted the series was inspired by the writings of Berton Roueche (*The Medical Detectives* and *True Tales of Medical Detection*). In this episode and many others, the doctors leave the hospital to scout around for evidence of molds, toxins, allergens, drugs, pets that could pass a virus, and other clues. After checking out Adler's classroom and returning without leads, as the newbie, Foreman is asked to break into the patient's house. When Foreman shows surprise and opposition to the suggestion, House calls him on a piece of his past, naming names, showing that he not only knows of Foreman's teenage criminal record, he knows the specifics. House is all about the details.

When Adler's condition takes a turn for the worse, their previous guess obviously wrong, Foreman relents on the issue of B&E, and asks Cameron, "white chick," to come with. The show is known for its racial ribs, usually passed from House to Foreman, but the first race joke of the series belongs to Foreman.

The team hurries to find the true cause of their patient's symptoms, and now that they're all in agreement, there's just one problem: Adler no longer trusts them. There's that word again. She wants to go home to die. Through stubbornness that rivals House's own, she has forced his hand, and he must meet with her. This is an opportunity for the patient to diagnose the doctor — and also to fill in viewers, who may be thinking of tuning in again, of vital characteristics to watch for in upcoming episodes. The show is fond of long, introspective conversations between doctors and patients, which may force viewers to wonder if this is one of the best funded hospitals in New Jersey.

A bleak rain falls and House's shirt is the same indistinct green as the patient's, setting them up as parallels in this particular scene — he as one who has overcome, and she as one who refuses. She chastises him for hiding in his office because he doesn't like the way people look at him (an echo of his earlier conversation with Wilson), so how can he expect her to fight? House's argument is convincing, but not convincing enough. The patient requires proof, House informs the team. Trust isn't enough. The proof the patient requires lies in her thigh muscle, further setting her up as a parallel character to House.

The episode has multiple endings. One has to do with Cameron, who after talking to Foreman about his being hired for his juvenile record, has concluded that it's possible she's been hired for her looks. Confronting House, he admits, "Gorgeous women do not go to medical school." He hired Cameron not because of her beauty, but because her beauty gave him an indication of her hard-working nature and what was truly important to her. At the same time, he raises a question that provokes curious energy between them. The second ending has to do with Orange Guy, the man House questioned about his wife's fidelity. The man has since straightened out his carrot and vitamin consumption (and, we can only assume, his back pain), and his wedding ring has been removed. "The son of a bitch is the best doctor we have," Cuddy tells him behind closed doors. The third ending is the patient's happily-ever-after closer. She's obviously back on the road to healing as her entire class bursts in on her. The fourth and final ending is a confrontation between House and Wilson about the lie that brought the patient to House in the first place. We begin the episode with the two doctors in close proximity and conversation, and end the same way. When Wilson turns the question back on him, House claims, "I never lie." Proving his own "everybody lies" theory correct, one of his duped clinic patients arrives just then, demanding a refill for a placebo (candy pellets from the machine).

Highlight
House's rant about living and dying with dignity, the impossibility of the latter.

Support Staff
House's cane is a device for sexual innuendo. It's also an instrument that he uses to achieve power (beyond, of course, the ability to walk). He has a tendency to spin it or examine it while concentrating, as if it could tell him the answers, but he will cast it aside during tense scenes, such as when he needs the use of both hands to administer emergency procedures. In this episode, House asks Cuddy if she is going to grab his cane to stop him from leaving.

Exam Room
- House holds his cane on the same side as his injury — the right side. Most people will use the opposite arm for a cane, but as creator Shore has said, "some people feel more comfortable with a cane in the dominant arm, and that is acceptable."
- House reads *Gossip: Spring's Hottest People*. Sherlock Holmes was also a fan of pulps.
- House isn't as dressed down in this episode. Later, he's always in jeans.
- Wilson is sporting hair that's almost as long as Chase's. By episode two, he'll be clean-cut/traditionally doctorly.
- With the exception of Foreman, the diagnostics team holds House at less of a distance. At one point, Chase is standing behind House's desk, leaning against his shelves. At another, he is lounging in House's chaise. Cameron will also hold the precious and powerful white-board marker at one point, with-

out comment from House. Later, such actions will be seen as attempts to usurp his power, and will inspire witty remarks. However, there is one scene in this episode in which House decides to refill his cup, and the entire team follows him from his office into the larger room like a troupe of puppies.

- The card that the kids present their teacher has a dark twist to sublimate the happy ending. Its inside message: *We're happy you're not dead, miss Rebecca.*
- Already we see Dr. Cuddy fundraising and managing the hospital's income. In the scene with the Orange-Colored Patient, she mentions the money he puts into the hospital. This sets the scene for future episodes, including those that feature Edward Vogler, the billionaire who wants to run a hospital as a business.
- In later episodes, the diagnostics team will pose the question, "And if we're wrong?" House's answer will almost always be "He dies" or "She dies." In this episode, when the question is posed he answers with the softer "Then we learn something else." At the end, when he and Wilson are watching the medical soap, one of the characters on the small screen asks why they do this. The answer? "Because we're doctors. If we make mistakes, people die."

Other Themes

Respect — this theme begins with the tête-à-tête between House and Cuddy and the quoting of the Rolling Stones' "You Can't Always Get What You Want" lyrics. House starts it, and Cuddy follows up with a re-quote, ". . . but if you try sometimes, you get what you need."

The theme continues through to the patient, who asks Dr. Wilson if House is a good man. Wilson's answer leads her to question if one can be a good doctor without also caring about people. When Adler refuses treatment, the diagnostics team wants to override her decision by claiming the illness has made her mentally incompetent. House is firm that it is not the case in this situation. Wilson speculates that now that he has met the patient, she's not just a file. House respects her, and therefore, must respect her wishes.

Foreman and Cameron are both frustrated by the reasons they were hired, because it shows a lack of respect from House for their efforts to attend good schools, maintain excellent grade-point averages, and become good doctors. Cameron, in particular, craves House's respect, even in this early episode. "Kinda hard to work for a guy who doesn't respect you," she says.

Booboos

- When Foreman and Cameron break into Adler's house, he's wearing a full suit, but she's got on a revealing tank top. Is the slender 20-something doctor prone to hot flashes, or is it simply a matter of adding a little is-it-hot-in-here-or-what?
- Also during the break and enter, Foreman encounters a pet bed and says the dog has fleas. There's no animal to be seen, and at an earlier point it was revealed that the patient had had no visitors. Who's watching her dog?
- Adler goes suddenly blind after her talk with Wilson, but in the scene where she confronts House about his methods she plays the scene as if she can see, glancing at the rain on the window, challenging him with big eyes, and weeping emotively. She's refused treatments, so how can she see? Even if she can make out shadows, her gestures seem false.

What's Up, Doc?

- The tracheotomy in this episode is one of the most detailed (some might say gruesome) in the series.
- Afterwards, the bandages are positioned too high on Adler's throat.
- Fans have debated whether there would be tracheotomy tools in the MRI scan room because of the strength of the magnet used to take the scans. Others have posited that the tools would have to have no ferrous metal in them.

1.2 Paternity

First aired: November 23, 2004
Writer: Lawrence Kaplow
Director: Peter O'Fallon
Guest stars: Kylee Cochran (Young Mother), Alex Skuby (John Funsten), Scott Mechlowicz (Dan), Paul Ganus (Trainer), Robin Thomas (Dan's Father), Wendy Gazelle (Dan's Mother), Scott Hochstadt (Jake)

Episode Differential

"Paternity" begins mid-game on the lacrosse field — a Canadianism from the Ontario-born creator David Shore? Just before Dan, a 16-year-old, is hit hard by another player, he experiences double vision. Because of the technique, right away the audience is let in on the fact that the illness will not have been caused by the blow, or at least that there was an exhibiting symptom before it.

Following a new beefed-up credit series, which includes the Massive Attack song "Teardrop," the first shot is a close-up of the soles of House's shoes, crossed at the ankles, Nike swoosh clearly visible on the heel grips. He is reading a celebrity magazine and consuming a red lollipop — two of his favorite things. Wilson enters and House urges him to close the door quickly. He has five minutes until he's off, and explains that while a diagnosis would take 30 seconds, reassuring a concerned mother would take 25 minutes. "Yes, concerned parents can be so annoying," Wilson chides, a remark that carries some weight, given the episode's title. House pops his Vicodin, like candy, with his sucker still in his mouth.

As House signs out of clinic duty, he is set upon by Dan and his parents, who claim to have an appointment. House denies the plausibility of such a thing, but courtesy of the interfering Dr. Cameron, who has been answering his mail, they do. House takes an interest when he learns that one of Dan's symptoms includes night terrors. After House accuses Dan's parents of molestation (a trigger for post-traumatic stress disorder in a minor) and dismisses his case as ordinary, House spots a jerk of the boy's leg. He calls it a "myoclonic jerk," and, after a quick eye exam (in which House notices the boy's eye color is different from his father's), "What does the jerk tell us?" is the first question in the diagnostic brainstorm.

"Nothing good. The brain's losing control of the body. Can't order the eyes to focus, regulate sleep patterns, or control muscles," replies Foreman, who is true to his name in often being first to answer. House raises the eye color issue, and the two argue over false paternity statistics and place bets. House decides he wants to see the night terrors, leading to a scene in which House himself is the terror. Throughout the series, House will frequently play a death figure — in and out of the patients' visions — due to his abruptness about possible outcome, the course a body follows when it breaks down, and his acceptance of it. After an MRI, Chase is the first to guess at answers in the hope of pleasing House and gaining that invisible gold star, and Foreman, as in the pilot, the first to disagree.

Unlike Cameron in the previous episode, Chase is candid when delivering news of a diagnosis to the family. He candy-coats nothing, letting them know that they won't have a definitive answer for some time, but that if it is MS, yes, it *will* hurt. When Dan goes missing that night, the doctors believe he may be suicidal. Looking on the roof is House's suggestion — once he finally straggles in. He notes that some of the orderlies keep the door propped open in order to nip out for a smoke. It's interesting that in both this episode and the previous one, House referenced the habits of the larger hospital staff (in the pilot, he noticed the sniffling egg-salad sandwich maker), yet in the later "Babies and Bathwater," the ill maternity ward volunteer will elude him. House considers the patient's night wandering great news, as Dan's confused state doesn't fit with MS. Cameron suggests neuro syphilis, but in the end it is one of House's earlier clinic patients — the yummy mummy and her all-natural breast milk — along with some help from the staff's bet over Dan's paternity, that drives the parentage theme of the show and helps House arrive at their solution.

Highlight

Evil House as a night terror, standing over the patient, who begs to have his parents present, while House proceeds to mark and cut off his big toe, saying, "This is gonna hurt, Dan." Laurie plays this moment to perfection, equal parts natural and sinister. Note that he gets the patient's name right, a sure sign this is not reality.

Support Staff

When Cuddy asks House to ante up from his own pocket for the parental DNA tests, he lets the cane fall between them across Cuddy's desk. The shivery mock-sexual expression Edelstein gives back is priceless.

Exam Room

- The shoes House wears were Hugh Laurie's idea, beginning with the pilot episode. According to a *TV Guide* interview, in March 2007, the show's costume designer Cathy Crandall said, "He thought a man with a cane needs functional shoes, and since Hugh likes Nike Shox, we stuck with those." Apparently, the wardrobe department houses 37 pairs of size 12 1/2 Nikes just for House.

- If you pause on it, the letter Cameron has typed says that House is scheduled to clinic Monday to Friday 3–6 p.m. Yet in the previous scene, he was leaving at 4:00. She also makes him sound overly empathetic. Ha.

- His name on the letter is hand-printed. The writing is not particularly "girly," but perhaps girly enough for a man with a big cane.

- "Parents said?" Chase questions Cameron when the diagnostic team discusses night terrors. He raises his eyebrows, bites his pencil, and grins, pleased to have scored one over her, and cementing their relationship as one of sibling rivalry.

- House's piano is a Sohmer & Co., the company that invented the five-foot baby grand. We see the piano for the first time when we see House at home. The phone is ringing where it sits on the bench (the staff want to tell him they've literally "lost the patient") but House doesn't answer. He's too busy smoking cigars.

- House actually offers Foreman a cup of coffee and pours it for him. Foreman has been up all night rescuing wandering patients, but for House this is a rare act of common courtesy. Perhaps he is as empathetic as expert letter-writer Dr. Cameron has said.

- House propositions Cameron. When she says, "What about sex?" in reference to the patient, he fires back: "Well, it might get complicated. We work together. And I'm older certainly, but maybe you're into that." Fans of relationship developments should earmark this moment in their minds.

- Chase plays it safe and never bets on the paternity of the child. In contrast, House picks up $100 from Cuddy, $100 from Cameron, $200 from Foreman, and $600 from Wilson who went with double or nothing when House offered it as he collected Mom and Dad's coffee cups.

- In a later episode, House will encourage a false paternity, asking a pregnant wife who's too late to abort whether the husband and the boyfriend look alike.

Lies

- House and Wilson debate lying about leaving early versus simply hiding out.
- Chase jokingly suggests that in order to get the paternity test, he and Foreman could tell the family their son has Huntington's — "the whole family should be tested or they'll die."
- "The Boy Who Sued Wolf" references the Aesop fable about lying to get attention only to find yourself in trouble later when no one in the village believes you anymore.
- House lies to this lawsuit-happy patient, dangling gonorrhea test results. (Or is House lying?)
- Without their consent, House DNA-tests the parents' coffee cups.
- The patient's parents have lied to him for 16 years, and to his doctors, that he is their biological child.
- After House and the parents have played you're-more-in-the-wrong in Cuddy's office, House bemoans their behavior to his staff: "And the wrong treatment kills any hope of the right diagnosis. Why do people lie to me?"
- The patient acknowledges his parents' lie, but proves the lie doesn't always matter.

Booboos

- The lacrosse scene at the beginning has one reverse image in its midst. The word TARTANS on the jerseys appears in mirror image.
- When the episode starts Dan is playing for the Tartans. Toward the end of the episode, his team is called the Comets.
- Following the first brain surgery, Dan still has exceptional hair. He's wearing a small bandage, but it doesn't look as if much — if any — of his head has been shaved. Was the nurse really that concerned with keeping this Joe Average high school boy pretty?

What's Up, Doc?

Eye spy — this is two for two for actors who can't control their windows-to-the-soul. The patient's head is strapped to the chair but that hasn't solved the case of the roaming eyeball. In the scene where Foreman explains the retinal biopsy to Dan, he says, "See we go through the pupil. You won't feel it. The eye's been paralyzed." One of Dan's pupils is clearly dark, dilated, in contrast to his other, which is pale and blue. But under threat of a giant needle, the patient's still glancing off to the side. Sure, even fake needles are "scary as hell," to borrow Foreman's words.

1.3 Occam's Razor

First aired: November 30, 2004
Writer: David Shore
Director: Bryan Singer
Guest stars: Marco Pelaez (Hospital Pharmacist), Kevin Zegers (Brandon Merrell), Faith Prince (Becky Merrell), Alexis Thorpe (Mindy), Lauren Cohn (Jodi Matthews), Jason Stuart (Adam Brown), Ben Campbell (Jerry Morris), John Kelly (Robert Marrell), Joshua Wolf Coleman (Suburban Pharmacist), Beth Hall (Shelby Lever)

Episode Differential

The show opens with a scene of an idyllic college campus before finding itself inside a dormitory where Brandon is on the telephone exaggerating his cough in order to get out of work. After vigorous sex with his girlfriend, he passes out, staying true once again to the show's *Six Feet Under*–style format of opening with the victim. It should be noted that while this episode was aired third in the series, it was the second in terms of shooting schedule.

Following the theme, we get the usual debate between Wilson and House about why House should accept the patient. In the end they agree that it comes down to "a proximity issue" — House should treat this patient because this is the patient who is in their emergency. Proximity will be the subtle theme of the show; sex the more obvious theme, especially since it is one of the first images we're presented.

House's first patient is the woman who had a cold the previous week, and has brought in a paint chip to show the doctor the outdated color of her mucous. After an insult or two, House is surprisingly empathetic, volunteering tests for the woman who is going to lose her job and benefits. Why? She says she doesn't like to be told what to do. The doctor can obviously relate, as we'll see with his subsequent clinic patients — all of whom will prompt him to call for consults from Cuddy. It's House's way of deflecting the duty he least wants to do. Sore throat guy, the woman who jogged six miles whose leg hurts, and the young man with an MP3 player in an embarrassing location — all of these patients will be forced to wait for Cuddy, and in one case Wilson because he is closer. Again, proximity.

Brandon's symptoms worsen, and his girlfriend is concerned enough about him to boldly confront Chase in the crowded clinic, asking if she may have caused Brandon injury through her aggressiveness during sex. The exchange leads to a confrontation between Chase and Cameron. After she chews him out over not getting enough specifics, he coolly inquires, "Have you ever taken a life?" This is the first flirtation from his side toward Cameron. Anyone who has studied sexuality knows that attraction is based in large part on proximity, and this is what Chase is experiencing when he confides, schoolboy-style in Foreman, "She's weird, isn't she?" of Cameron. Exposure to a person increases likelihood of attraction.

Other proximal relationships are discussed in this episode, including House's treatment of Foreman. Unlike Chase and Cameron, theirs is a dynamic based on the negative. House doesn't want Foreman to stop thinking about the case, which is why he constantly dismisses his suggestions rather than encouraging him to keep thinking. Chase is still acting the role of the good son, defending House to Foreman. He wants to be the star pupil.

The growing number of symptoms is alarming, and House challenges his team who is convinced of Occam's Razor, that the "simplest answer is always the best." Early on, House raises the possibility that the wrong medication may have been administered, but without proof, they dismiss it. As in subsequent episodes, the team will strike on the right answer but doubt themselves in favor of other treatments. House's eureka moment occurs with Watson . . . er, Wilson, while he is waiting for a prescription refill for his Vicodin. However, it's the proximity of the patients in his clinic that really reveal the source of Brandon's condition. If Brandon, like these patients, hadn't seen a doctor for a minor ailment — his cough — he would not have been prescribed a cough suppressant and delivered by a fallible pharmacist a dose of Colchicine, sparking off an allergic reaction.

Highlight
Cameron's ecstatic spiel to a stunned Chase about what happens to the human body during sex. She is toying with him to the extreme. She knows it, we know it, and he would like to think it is something else entirely, as evidenced when he tries to ask her out at the end of the show and is cut off with a simple, "No." In this scene however, Cameron goes from describing how a woman can have an hour-long orgasm to "Hey Foreman, what's up?" so smoothly and sweetly it is chilling — and hilarious.

Support Staff
The cane gets left out in the cold on this episode — no big acting moments for House's wooden sidekick.

Exam Room
- Wilson seems to be smart-mouthing House more in this episode.
- In keeping with the close look at character relationships in this episode, following an exchange with Cuddy, Wilson reminds House that there's a fine line between love and hate.
- There's a shot of Chase reflected in the glass so that his image hovers overtop of House who is in his office. This technique was popularized by filmmaker F.W. Fassbinder and his cinematographer Michael Balhaus, who introduced it to Hollywood when he later worked there. It is an easy camera setup that implies distance between two characters. In other words, even when House's staff defends and supports him, there is something within his character that separates him from them.
- In the scene where Cameron spouts off about sex, Chase has already poured two coffees, without being asked, proving that Foreman is right: Cameron already has a sexual control over him.
- One question that might arise from this episode would be: Why would any caring parent give a medication to her son, knowing it might interact with his other treatment? It seems unlikely when her son has been so sick that Mom would bring her son his cough suppressant without first checking with his doctors. In an earlier scene, Chase and Foreman discuss the power that doctors have over the untrained. Be that as it may,

Mom does sneak in the medication. As they agree to put Brandon into the clean room, Foreman says, "If he gets a cold, he'll die." This would be fear enough for any parent, but it's more likely Mom had already given her son the medication.

- House needs to be reminded of his patient's name twice in the same scene.
- The format of this episode will be echoed by the season two episode "Clueless"; in that episode House is also convinced of the right cause for illness early on, but cannot find the proof he needs for treatment.
- "Working with people actually makes you a better doctor," Cuddy tells House, punching home the theme of proximity.

Lies

- Brandon lies to his employer so he can stay in bed with his girlfriend/fiancée.
- Wilson avoids lying when he is asked why he wants House to take Brandon's case. We've seen him lie before, but this time he levels with him.
- Cameron leads Chase on as a way to exert power. It's not a lie, but she definitely has ulterior motives.
- House lies when he tells the clinic patients they can't have any of his Vicodin. We know he is prone to sharing.
- The mother giving her son his cold medication is a lie of omission.
- The son not declaring that he has taken it seconds that lie.
- House pretending he needs consults for simple diagnoses is a falsity.

Booboos

- Fans have pointed out several mistakes of continuity. The F in fever written on the white board sometimes has a strike through it; other times it doesn't. Another continuity error has to do with Cameron's hair. When she talks to Chase about sex and how it makes her nervous, she places a strand behind her ear. Seconds later the hair comes loose, but only in the front shots. In shots from behind, it remains fixed.
- Fans have also pointed out the inaccuracy of the video games

on House's Gameboy. The sounds coming from the game do not match the real life sounds of *Metroid: Zero Mission*. Do I smell a booboo or a case of red tape?

What's Up, Doc?

The patient wouldn't recover so fast. According to experts in the field, the survival rate is incredibly low for sclerosing pan-encephalitis. In 2004, there were only 37 cases of the measles in the United States. Compare that to the pre-vaccine era; the National Institute of Health reports that before 1963 there were 500,000 reported cases of measles each year.

1.4 Maternity

First aired: December 7, 2004
Writer: Peter Blake
Director: Newton Thomas Sigel
Guest stars: Ever Carradine (Karen Hartig), Kenneth Choi (Dr. Lim), Benjamin Parrillo (Dr. Kubisak), Sam Trammell (Ethan Hartig), Cress Williams (Hospital Attorney), Dwight Armstrong (Charlie), Nate Torrence (Young Man), Jocelyn Jackson (Young Woman), Hedy Burress (Jill), Melissa Marsala (Lupino), Alexandra Bokyun Chun (Kim Chen), Madison Bauer (Soap Patient), Marc Menard (Soap Doctor), Shawn Carter Peterson (Male Med Student), Donna Stearns (Volunteer)

Episode Differential

Considered a tearjerker of an episode, "Maternity" opens with a shot of a baby. As the parents debate names, the infant begins to spit up *again*, we're told, and an obstetrician is fetched for assistance. The tiny child seizes in his arms. Later we'll realize that we've been looking at Baby Maxine, the child who will live. This episode marks the first death on the show, and a cruel one. The case comes to House by coincidence, and fate will play a key role in the episode.

Where normally they have to twist House's arm to make him take cases, Wilson and Cuddy both dissuade him. Cuddy accuses House, who thinks they have an epidemic on their hands, of reading into it what he wants. Both change their tunes quickly as three more infants fall ill with the same symptoms. Baby "Maxine" Hartig and Baby Chen-Lupino, and their respective parents get the starring roles.

With an over-the-top touch, the clinic echoes the maternity theme. Jill is a marathon runner who can't lose weight. Guess why! In spite of an implanted birth control, she's four months pregnant after a fling with an ex. Afraid of letting her husband know about the infidelity, she asks House to unknowingly test him for paternity. House encourages the false paternity, asking if the husband and the boyfriend look alike. "The most successful marriages are based on lies. You're off to a great start," he tells her. Will he still believe this by the second season, when marital lies is one of the season's ongoing themes?

As Cuddy shuts down the maternity ward and continues to scour the hospital, which House calls *her* baby, for environmental causes, House and his team treat the infants with antibiotics, blindly hoping to beat the virus. Twice Cameron has to give bad news to the Chen-Lupino couple, and twice other doctors step in. We've seen this behavior from Cameron before, but in this episode it becomes the focal point. When Foreman chastises her the first time, she tells him, "It's easier to die than to watch someone die." Sounds like she's speaking from personal experience.

As the rounds of antibiotics begin to cause kidney failure in the babies, House opts for the "therapeutic trial," the method of reducing the antibiotics, leaving one child to take one, and the second child to take the other. Leaving the fate of the babies to random chance, we see House again as both a death figure, and as someone who has made his peace with the notion of occasionally playing God. He doesn't look happy about it here the way he usually does when he toys with patients; he looks like it's his job.

Highlight

It's hard to choose a highlight for such a tense episode, but Hugh Laurie still manages to insert a touch of humor here and there. He tells the unsuspecting mother-to-be clinic patient Jill that she has a parasite: "Don't worry. Many women learn to embrace this parasite. They name it, dress it up in tiny clothes, arrange play dates with other parasites . . ." Jill still doesn't catch on.

Support Staff

House hands it to Cameron.

Exam Room

- Life is more important to House than TV. He leaves his doc-opera in progress to seek out sickly infants.
- Foreman really is House's fore man. When they team up, he and House are together on the baby hunt. Chase and Cameron form the other duo.
- In spite of Cameron's inability to lay it on the line for the Mommy-Mommy Chen-Lupino couple, she defends her choice to sugar-coat.
- We see a softer side of Chase as the Chen-Lupino baby dies and he continues to shock it with paddles long beyond reason. He can't give up on the child.
- "Make sure she does her job," House says to Wilson when Cameron attempts to wriggle out of delivering the news of the baby's death to its parents. It's a bastard moment to be sure, but it also shows us House's dedication to the job. He feels Cameron should learn to devote the same, even when it means having to complete the worst task possible. Shortly after, we see House with the infant's corpse, about to complete an autopsy, leaving the audience with a profound sadness and wondering which job is more difficult, explaining death, or dissecting it.
- Later, House calls Foreman into the elevator to ask if Cameron is okay, showing that he is human. Foreman challenges House's reasons for asking, and in the end, in contrast, is apolitical, answering, "She's fine." Notice that Foreman always protects himself — he never gets involved in drama if he can avoid it.
- At the end, House questions Cameron about her experience with death. She lashes out at him, and a moment later we see her standing at the top of the stairs watching the Hartig parents depart with their child. At this point, we don't yet know the role death has played in Cameron's life, and it's implied here that House may be right.

Lies

- Foreman informs the Hartig couple of the risks involved in choosing one medication for their baby. He calls it a "hail Mary pass." In contrast, Cameron glosses over the risks, and

says, "We'll know in 24 hours if it's working."
- The healthy mother-to-be, Jill, asks House to covertly test her husband for paternity while telling him it is for mono.
- House obviously does test him, because he gives the Jill the good news on her return visit.

Booboos

House takes on the delivery for his clinic patient specifically so he can use the obstetricians' lounge. When he's conducting the infant autopsy, he gives the date as December 2, 2004. Now when they ask, he says she's due in late March. "That's five months from now," is the response, a miscalculation.

What's Up, Doc?

- When Baby Maxine first starts spitting up, the parents say she hasn't eaten anything so there shouldn't be anything to spit up. When House presents the case to his team, he says the baby was 36 hours old when it started spitting up. Babies are fed not long after birth, so one fact or the other is wrong.
- When House and his team are brainstorming viruses that could cause the newborns' infections, they rule out the herpes virus family, but list cytomegalovirus as a possibility, which is a member of the herpes virus family.

1.5 Damned If You Do

First aired: December 14, 2004
Writer: Sara B. Cooper
Director: Greg Yaitanes
Guest stars: Elizabeth Mitchell (Sister Mary Augustine), Lucinda Jenney
(Sister Mary Eucharist), Taji Coleman (Tech), James Symington (Priest), Dakin
Matthews (Marvin/Santa Claus Guy), Ann Dowd (Mother Superior), Lori Rom
(Sister Mary Pius)

Episode Differential

Christmas at Princeton-Plainsboro is much like any other time of year,
except that the clinic patients include a trio of nuns, and Santa has diarrhea.
In the Christmas spirit though, trust and faith are the themes of the episode.

Sister Augustine arrives in clinic at 11:00, and House manages to
ignore the patient for an hour. Pius, the young nun who is with her,
believes the rash on Augustine's hands to be stigmata; Eucharist, the older
nun, thanks House for his secular diagnosis of contact dermatitis. He says
she's likely developed an allergy to dish soap, and gives her an antihista-
mine, which she swallows with her thermos of tea. She has an instant
reaction, and House is called back into the exam room, where he administers epinephrine. One cardiac arrest later, and he's arguing his case with
Cuddy, who believes he made a mistake, administering too high a dosage.

We quickly learn that Chase *hates* nuns, and that Cameron trusts
House implicitly. Foreman, in contrast, won't trust a man who can't admit
he may have made a mistake. Echoing the team's trust issues, Augustine
comforts her young friend Sister Pius who doesn't understand how they
can issue treatments when they don't know what is wrong. Augustine says,
"Trust, Pius, everything happens for a reason." We also learn that
Cameron doesn't believe in God, just House apparently. "You're not even
a little agnostic?" Foreman asks her, and it's a fair question, since with
Cameron's continual optimism, it's more what we'd expect from her. It's
the concept of a singular being she can't fathom. Chase, as he often does,
evades the question and turns his attention to the patient.

The lack of trust heightens over the course of the episode. House
opts to treat Augustine in the high-pressure oxygen room, and
Foreman is in clear opposition. "I am both amused and annoyed that
you think I should be less stubborn than you are," House says, revealing the dynamic between them that continues from one episode to the

next. The sister's faith in House is also waning; she questions the treatment as she is rolled into the oxygen tank. Foreman goes to Cuddy, and Cuddy comes in on the diagnosis, removing House from his own case.

This is one of the few episodes where we see House doubt himself. Wilson, who is like an extension of House's own conscience, catches him going through the syringe drawer in the exam room. It's later in the episode that House lectures Cameron about having faith in herself. After he discovers the nun's fig wort tea in combination with the epinephrine is what caused her to seize, they determine her condition is a long-term allergy, something Cameron proposed originally. "Take a lesson from Foreman," he says. "Stand up for what you believe."

The nun loses faith as they isolate her in a clean room, and we again see Chase as the dutiful son. He volunteers to pray with her. Later, after the team has discovered the source of her problems, her old IUD, and removed it, she gives Chase back a prayer, the story of the prodigal son, ironic considering how duty and rising to expectation play into Chase's personality in every other way.

Highlight

House flirts antagonistically with Sister Eucharist in the hospital's chapel. After pointing out that in under two minutes, she's expressed four mortal sins (anger, pride, envy, gluttony), he accuses her of a fifth (lust).

Support Staff

- Cameron has brought in candy canes. "What the hell are those? Candy *canes*," House emphasizes. "Are you mocking me?" Cameron being Cameron, she protests, taking him seriously.
- House leaves his cane behind when he goes into the clean room to talk Sister Augustine into having faith in him and remaining at the hospital. His cane is often a symbol of his manhood. Here, is it a symbol of his pride?

Exam Room

- Often House pops his Vicodin as soon as he senses stress or trouble. This time he takes it immediately after glimpsing three nuns in his clinic exam room.
- After House has been removed from the nun's case, Cameron

says to Foreman, "You did what you thought you had to." If
she had said, "You did what you had to," it would have been
a compliment and shown her understanding of his actions.
The single addition of the word "thought" expresses her
opposition clearly.

- Between the nun's admission and Cuddy taking over the case,
  House's sports jacket changes three times. Did she actually
  give him longer than 24 hours to find the underlying symptoms before removing him from the case?

- When House visits the convent, there is a shot through a pass-
  through window where we see him speaking to Mother
  Superior in the kitchen. A set of copper pots hangs above, and
  above it, on our side of the window, is a crucifix on the wall.
  The two in combination are exactly his patient's problem — a
  copper cross. This is mid-episode, and often upon re-watching
  one can find an obvious clue to the final diagnosis embedded
  in either the shots or the dialogue.

- Chase actually says the name of the episode within the
  episode. The expression, "Damned if you do, damned if you
  don't" was made famous by Eleanor Roosevelt who said,
  "Do what you feel in your heart to be right — for you'll be
  criticized anyway. You'll be damned if you do, and damned
  if you don't." Most of the characters are damned in some
  way in this episode: Chase for losing his belief, House for his
  possible error, Cameron for not holding true to her diagnosis
  even though she holds true to House. Foreman is the only
  one who isn't.

- Wilson says the nun's condition may be divine will. House
  says it's not his will, again ascribing an all-powerful status to
  himself.

- Wilson may think House is going to hell, but House has
  enough belief for at least one Christmas carol. He plays
  "Silent Night" on the piano for the final montage.

- In the closing moments, we see Cameron opening a Christmas
  present that has been left at her desk, and, though we're never
  given an answer, we want to believe it's from House — that in
  spite of his self-involvement, he is indeed capable of tender-
  ness and reciprocation.

Lies

- House didn't lie when he said he administered the right amount of epinephrine. He was telling the truth. But he does lie when Cuddy is looking for an admission of his negligence.
- Sister Eucharist tells Dr. House that Augustine makes things up.
- "You're a lousy liar, Dr. Chase," Augustine says after he reports that her pulse is fine. She's startlingly right. In every episode where Chase lies, the other characters have seen right through it, and so have we.
- House accuses Mother Superior of lying, and of all the sisters of lying because they've not been forthcoming about Augustine's past. Mother Superior explains that these are not lies, that they believe life begins they take their vows.

Booboos

Booboos are scant in this episode. An error of consistency is a lock of hair that escapes Chase's cap in the clean room during the intubation. Without being brushed away, he is tidy again.

What's Up, Doc?

The Internet Movie Database cites Dr. Foreman as referring to the patient's "eophinosil" count, and the word he's after as being "eosinophil" (a kind of white blood cell). In the special features on the season one box set, Jennifer Morrison leads viewers on a tour of the Princeton-Plainsboro hospital set and explains the difficulty the actors have with managing the unfamiliar medical terms, and especially of managing those words and writing on the white board at the same time. Chances are Omar Epps mismanaged this word.

1.6 The Socratic Method

First aired: December 21, 2004
Writer: John Mankiewicz
Director: Peter Medak
Guest stars: Stacy Edwards (Lucy Palmeiro), Aaron Himelstein (Luke Palmeiro), John Prosky (Dr. Bergin), Sonya Eddy (Sally), Pat Musick (Trina Wyatt), Lilas Lane (Terri), Veronica Leigh (Wendy), C. Xavier Drayton (Male Truant Officer)

Episode Differential

The opening scene gives us the symptoms of Lucille Palmeiro, the patient-to-be — leg pain/blood clots, and delusions and voices. We're also shown the method she's been using to treat them; her son slips her nips of alcohol to calm her and has likely been doing so since she was diagnosed the previous spring. As a social worker prepares the final papers for extending her disability checks, Lucille clutches her chest and collapses. Add to these a deep vein thrombosis as the credits come up, the nervous pacing of the 15-year-old son, and House is lowering his newspaper with interest.

Age and all the inescapable things that go with it, this is the theme of "The Socratic Method." The fact that the patient is only 38 with these symptoms is a big part of the intrigue. And as much as he'd like to avoid it, House must confront his own birthday. Similarly, Luke, the young son of a schizophrenic patient, must lie about his age, claiming to be 18 as a way to handle his mother and get what he needs from her doctors, social workers, and the world in general.

Within a minute in their first diagnostic session, House has ruled out the schizophrenia as a cause of the deep bone thrombosis (DBT). Unlike his other patients, he's also heading for this one's room right away. As we'll see in future episodes, House likes mentally unbalanced patients. Wilson and the team offer some clues as to why: he likes the way they think ("badly"), they don't lie in the same (boring) way as "normal" patients, and he loves the puzzle of their minds.

House, who's often in a rush to find answers, can be patient, we learn in this episode. He takes the time to understand Lucille's language. Sitting by her bedside, twirling his cane, he reminds her they're talking about meds, not the Mets, as she goes off on a tangent about baseball. "No one believes me," she says. He reassures her: "I do."

Birthdays enter the picture again with the first clinic patient, a mother and her daughter who've come into the office on a pretense of wanting a strep test. The mother really wants a doctor to explain why a sugarless cake and managing her weight are better for her daughter's birthday.

Tension escalates when House tells his staff to strike the psych meds so they can get a better idea of what's going on with Lucille. Foreman administers Haldol after she has a freak-out about him drawing blood, and spits in his face. Though upset with Foreman for sedating her, one thing House admits the Haldol has done though is to help them diagnose her vitamin K deficiency. House breaks rules to discover underlying causes, but he's not happy when it happens and accidentally works for someone else. Chase still believes it's alcohol abuse. He is adamant about it, revealing some personal experience.

To go along with the six packages of Jumbo Burger the team finds in Lucille's apartment, is a plot with more twists than a bendy straw. After appearances by both a liver tumor, and a child services agent, House finally puts it all together, realizing Lucille might not be schizophrenic after all. Both her actions, and her age, are his clues.

Highlight
Clinic patient number two, the man with incurable hiccups, is definitely the comic relief in this episode, especially as House instructs him to try slapping himself just a little harder.

Support Staff
- When the patient's son gets in his face about having sedated his mother so they could run blood tests after he's specifically asked them not to, House threatens, "I have a cane and I know how to use it."
- House compliments Cuddy on her outfit, he claims that it says, "I'm still a woman," then amends that it actually yells this. Cuddy comments on House's "big cane" and how subtle it is too.
- House hangs his cane on the wall beside the urinal while Cuddy confronts him in the men's room.

Exam Room
- This is the first time we've seen House order a Rueben — dry, no fries, hold the pickles, $5.80 with tax. He hands Luke a

bill and directs him to the cafeteria.

- "Don't lie to him, Limpy. Lively Lucy never lies to Lucas. Look what I do to him," Lucille shouts at House. It sounds like gibberish, but if you look at the words, it's her way of expressing her relationship with her son, and her way of asking House if she can trust him.
- Cameron introduces herself to Luke as Allison Cameron rather than Dr. Cameron. It seems a bit odd, especially given his age.
- Cameron is the first to remember House's birthday. She claims it was on a form she saw when going through his mail.
- What Lucas is reading to his mother is the poem "Her Praise" by William Butler Yeats. The first three lines of the poem, though they are not read on-screen, are: "She is foremost of those that I would hear praised. / I have gone about the house, gone up and down / As a man does who has published a new book . . ." Notice that it references a *house*, and also pacing, which is how the doctor of the same name met the boy who is now reading the poem.
- When Chase calls Cameron on her lie to get quick reads on the clotting studies, he ribs her, "Pretty fast. You promise to date the entire lab?" But it's also Chase's way of flirting.
- We see a shot of Wilson peering through an X-ray, nearly identical to the one of House that is in the opening credits sequence.

Lies

- When he is in the interview with the social worker, Luke mentions a younger sibling as being "the dependent," and he the older brother just helping out. There obviously is no sibling; he is the dependent.
- Luke claims to be 18 years old when in fact he's only just had his 15th birthday.
- Cameron tells the lab that the mother bled out two units and if it happens again, she'll die. In this way she secures the clotting studies they need faster. "If it had happened at home, she'd have died," Chase says by way of legitimizing the lie.
- "Everybody lies except for schizophrenics and their children?" Cameron asks when House doesn't doubt the patient's drug use. The question should be a statement since in this episode

it's true — or nearly. There's one thing the mother doesn't confess about.

- House tells Luke he can tell his age by looking at his X-ray. It's not even his X-ray.
- House proposes they shrink the mother's tumor, which they do. The whole team and Wilson is complicit in this one.
- House assumes the blame for Luke being taken from his mother by social services. He prefers the deception to causing a rift between the reunited mother and child.

Booboos

- Some fans have argued that the show runs in approximately real time. "The Socratic Method" isn't necessarily set around Christmas but it follows an episode that is. Although the exact date isn't revealed, House's birthday occurs within the episode. In the season two finale, "No Reason," House wears an admissions bracelet, which reads "DOB 06-11-59." It should be noted this is Hugh Laurie's actual birthday. The question remains, which birthday is House's? Some might argue that he's more of a Capricorn personality than a Gemini, but either way the timeline is a little funny.
- When House talks to Luke about his mother's vitamin deficiency, the lid on the tomato sauce bottle is alternately open and closed.

1.7 Fidelity

First aired: December 28, 2004
Writer: Thomas L. Moran
Director: Bryan Spicer
Guest stars: Dominic Purcell (Ed Snow), Myndy Crist (Elise Snow), Clementine Shepherd-Ford (Samantha Campbell), Brennan Elliott (Adam), Henri Lubatti (Head Chef), Endre Hules (Soup Chef), James Conkle (Young Boy)

Episode Differential

It's pretty easy to guess what the theme of an episode titled "Fidelity" will be. Strangely, this episode is one of the most faithful to a straightforward, through plot line.

Ed returns from a jog with his annoyingly nosy best friend — who has asked about his relationship with his wife, including how often they're engaging in sex — only to find his wife, Elise, still in bed and incredibly irritable. Some people are a little ugly in the morning, but they usually won't pop you in the nose for suggesting they get up, which is exactly what happens here. Realizing she has just cold-cocked her husband, Elise admits she needs help.

The case comes to House by way of Cameron. He's interested that she's interested, which is true of their relationship at large.

The clinic patient, a schoolteacher with "a heart of silicone," allows for plenty of boys-will-be-boys scenes. She's been having shortness of breath, but that's certainly not why House calls Wilson in for a consult. The sub-plot allows for even more discussions around the issue of fidelity, since House believes her husband has been dosing her oatmeal to reduce her sex drive. The breasts were a birthday present, but one he obviously didn't want — at the same time, one he doesn't want other men to have either. House actually suggests that this woman do what men have been doing for centuries: begin having discreet affairs.

Back to Elise: no tumors are detected, but the patient does begin to hallucinate ants crawling out of her skin. When House moves on to suspect African sleeping sickness, the team turns against him. They bat around their own diagnosis. In spite of her number one symptom, none are convinced of sleeping sickness because Elise has never been to Africa nor had a blood transfusion.

House being House, he remains in the lead even when there are no leads. There has been only one known incident where African sleeping sickness was transmitted by sexual contact. House decides that Elise must be incident number two. But why should he get his hands dirty asking about the sex lives of others? He sends his staff to make it perfectly clear to husband and wife that if they've been cheating they must come clean: her life depends upon it. College sweethearts, both deny any outside contact.

As Elise slips into a coma, it's confession time, but there is no confession to be had. House suggests that Ed sign off on the treatment, even though it is potentially fatal if Elise has been faithful. In an episode where fidelity could kill a person, we know that the only option here is failure. Elise comes out of the coma, but not before Ed makes it abundantly clear that he hopes she dies — so that he will know she never lied to him. Cameron cannot accept this behavior, and tells him so brashly.

Highlight
Cameron crying in the lab as House comes in. She is fixing the centrifuge, and House comments on how centrifuges always make him cry too. She reveals her true relationship with death, and we learn for the first time about her late husband.

Support Staff
Just the usual for House's right-hand man.

Lies
- Elise's infidelity.
- Elise's lie to the doctors about her infidelity.
- House lies about needing a consult from Wilson. Does he, does he really?
- House and Wilson discuss whether plastic surgery is a lie if everyone can tell they are falsies.
- The real reason Ed's jogging buddy has been asking about his marital relations.
- Wilson tells the truth about his own infidelities. He reveals that even at the time, he didn't lie about them.

Exam Room
- This episode, House's soap includes a joke credit roll, including names from the actual *House* staff: Marcy G. Kaplan

(Associate Producer, Co-Producer), and Cindy Carr
(Wardrobe, Set Decorator).

- Foreman and House discuss why House is always riding him, and then House continues to ride him — especially after Foreman sedates the already overly sedate patient. To a certain extent, this echoes "The Socratic Method," when House specifically told the staff not to sedate, and Foreman did.
- Chase's answer to the question of House always being on Foreman's case is a flippant "He's got a crush on you!" To a certain extent it's true — Foreman is House's favorite. Even if House is harder on him, he treats Foreman more like a man, where Cameron and Chase are always the children.

What's Up, Doc?

A doctor with mad skills like Cameron's wouldn't be sent out to deliver news of the illness to Elise's lover so that he can get himself checked out and on medication. But it makes for a more dramatic ending this way, as Cameron heads up the walk of a stately house only to be greeted by Ed's jogging buddy.

1.8 Poison

First aired: January 25, 2005
Writer: Matt Witten
Director: Guy Ferland
Guest stars: Roxanne Hart (Margo Davis), John Patrick Amedori (Matt Davis), Shirley Knight (Georgia Adams), Kurt Fuller (Mark Adams), McNally Sagal (Mrs. Miller), Molly Mankiewicz (Blonde Woman), Christopher Malpede (Math Whiz), Kenya D. Williamson (Nurse), Ulysses Lee (Chi Ling), Jim Lau (Chou-Young Ling), Linda Wang (Jen Ling), Andy Milder (Bus Driver)

Episode Differential

What will become the case of the poisoned pants opens in a classroom setting as Matt Davis attempts to get his teacher to allow him to go to the bathroom in the middle of an exam. Sniffing a cheat, she refuses, until he collapses in convulsions on the classroom floor.

This case comes to House by way of Foreman. But House won't accept the patient until Foreman admits it isn't human empathy that makes him interested but the medical data itself. This scene plays back on the conversation he and Foreman had in the pilot episode, in which Foreman believed they were there to treat the patient, and House that they were there to treat the illnesses. Whatever their differences, they both have the same objective: to get people well. This exchange is brief, and on Foreman's part half-hearted, but it sets up the dynamic that continues throughout the episode of House and Foreman as becoming more and more like one another. Foreman has even started to wear sneakers.

As always when it comes to a young patient, the first suspect is drugs. Matt's mom denies his use of any illegal substances, but the team rolls their eyes and inspects their home anyway. No drugs, but maybe some bad tomato sauce. They rule out bacterial infection, in favor of poison. Their next dilemma: which poison?

Another search of the patient's home turns up an empty pesticide can. Pesticides fit perfectly, but this time as Chase again prepares treatment, Mom interferes, claiming the can contained only orange peel oil because Matt was tending the garden specifically for his environmental science class. The team believes it's likely that Matt may have been cheating, using the pesticide anyway (note that this is the second time Matt's accused of cheating, the first being when he stands up in class). But Mom begs Chase not to inject her son with the hydrolase since the treatment would increase his toxicity if they are wrong. Once again, we see the theme emerging as one of trust. Mom trusts her son at all costs, and the hurdle in this episode is whether she can also bring herself to trust his doctors.

A second patient, Chi Ling, a student from the same school, is admitted with the same symptoms. With two houses to search, and a mom who won't sign off on any more treatments until the Centers for Disease Control gets back to her, the team compares acne creams and antiperspirants in their search for a likely suspect. Detergent seems to be the only thing these two boys have in common. It's not the cause, but it does lead House to take a closer look at their clothes.

Highlight

Clinic patient 82-year-old Georgia is experiencing a personality change with marked euphoria. House diagnoses it as a case of syphilis, leftover from the dirty '30s — but not before Georgia declares her newfound love for Ashton Kutcher, and oh . . . maybe Dr. House too! Wilson in the clinic reciting Georgia's love note to House aloud: priceless.

Support Staff

- "Maybe we should all pitch in and get you a nice cane," Cameron jokes when Foreman says the difference between him and House is that he isn't a pompous cripple.
- House twirls his cane while talking to the ever-fashionable Wilson about whether he washes new clothes before wearing. If we're to go by Wilson's response, the cane is a symbol of manhood once again. "Hey, I'm a man," Wilson states. "I don't have time for laundry. I'm saving lives here."

Lies

- Chase phones the patient's mom and pretends to be the CDC so she will sign off on the treatment the team wants.
- Matt admits to buying the new clothes in an attempt to fit in — it's the one thing he did hide from his mom.

Exam Room

- The writer is named Matt; the character is named Matt. Coincidence?
- House sends Cameron with Foreman on the initial search for the patient's drug stash. The implication is he trusts her not to do them.
- Chase loses Ms. Davis' confidence in his first examination of her son when he admits that "I gave my mum a little trouble when I was his age." She's not impressed with his admission of having done drugs even as a teenager. And why should she be? Considering doctors have such free access to drugs, who wants to know about their drug habits — past or present?
- During Matt's first in-hospital seizure, House hovers outside the glass window watching instead of entering the room to help — like the silent angel of death.
- We see the "princeton plainsboro teaching hospital" sign for the first time. So hip, it's all lowercase. Wonder who's managing their corporate image . . . ?
- Cameron is the first to raise the possibility of pesticide poisoning, based on Matt's symptoms, not any evidence. She's frequently the doctor to predict the proper diagnosis, and just as frequently abandons it.

- The clinic patient is an inverse of the primary patient: both feature mother-son dynamics. In Georgia's case, her son, who has brought her in, is a naysayer. In Matt's case, Mom is. Georgia's son dismisses everything his mother says. Matt's mom believes everything her son says, but doesn't want to believe anything his doctors tell her.

- Ms. Davis is upset that the doctors have the wrong answers, but she's not upset that they've obviously gone rooting through her home and garage for them.

- In this episode, House does what House does best: browbeats the patient's caregiver, in this case his mom, until she'll allow the treatment House wants to give. Paraphrasing the refusal-of-treatment form, House says, "'Besides, I enjoy controlling every single aspect of my son's life, even if it means his death.' Sign here, please. I brought a pen." He may be accusing the mom of being controlling, but it's exactly what he's doing at this exact moment.

Booboos

Ms. Davis says that the night before her son got sick they argued over his college interviews — he wanted to be himself, no haircut, ratty old clothes. Is this one of the fundamental contradictions of being a teenager — that Matt would care more what his peers think of him than what university administrators think? Or is it a plot hole?

1.9 DNR

First aired: February 1, 2005
Writer: David Foster
Director: Fred Keller
Guest stars: Brandy Norwood (Herself), Harry J. Lennix (John Henry Giles), Chloe Webb (Cora), Clint Baker (Tommy), David Conrad (Marty Hamilton), Mike Starr (Willie), Richard Sinclair (Doctor), Courtney Henggeler (Server), Victor Raider-Wexler (Judge Winter), Rif Hutton (Morris), Michael Oberlander (Ross), Dennis Howard (Chaplain)

Episode Differential

DNR — Do Not Resuscitate — refers to the patient, but it also refers to the past. As Foreman's old boss makes an appearance and attempts to win him back, we're reminded that Foreman hasn't been on House's staff very long. Essentially, we joined Princeton-Plainsboro when Foreman did. The struggle this time is not just between House and the patient, but House and Foreman.

House gets involved because John Henry Giles is a famous musician — a trumpet player who can no longer blow — previously diagnosed with ALS (amyotrophic lateral sclerosis or Lou Gehrig's disease).

House is keenly interested, but having completed his residency under John Henry's regular doctor, Foreman is the one assigned by Cuddy to lead the case. A fan of John Henry's music, House makes it his mission to bring back the man's breath — and the use of his legs — at all costs, even if it means disregarding the Do Not Resuscitate form he has signed, making an "attack" that will land House in court. Foreman proves once again that he's not afraid to stand up to House, arguing with him about his violation of his patient's rights.

In court, House shows he's not above playing politics to gain favor. He expresses concern for the the judge over the "clubbing" of his fingers and urges him to seek medical advice, distracting the judge from the trial and also endearing himself with his concern.

In the wake of the assault, John Henry's old doctor, Marty Hamilton, flies in from Los Angeles. In addition to being Foreman's old boss, Hamilton's the type of man House cannot stand. He's bent on proving him wrong, and at the same time curing the incurable.

Highlight

When House and Foreman argue methods of mentoring — Hamilton's versus House's. Foreman recounts the mistake he made with a patient and how Hamilton forgave it. House says, "He never said you were forgiven. I was there, he said it was not your fault." When Foreman replies, "So?" House goes into a rant that sums up the essence of why he and Foreman work so well together: "So, it was. You took a chance, you did something great. You were wrong, but it was great. You should feel great it was great; you should feel like crap that it was wrong, but that's the difference between him and me. He thinks you do your job, and what will be, will be. I think that what I do and what you do matters. He sleeps better at night. He shouldn't."

House has also summed up why even when his character is unethical, sexist, racist, and all-around bastardly, we continue to support him and tune in every week.

Support Staff

- House hands it to Chase before he intubates John Henry.
- He also throws it on the bed so he can wheel John Henry out of the room.

Lies

- John Henry hasn't told his manager about the session he's to play.
- House agrees only to treat the pneumatic symptoms. Right away, we know he'll overstep.
- There are two lies regarding the DNR. First, House violates the hospital agreement not to resuscitate. Second: "You assaulted that man," Foreman says, and House says he'll never do it again. Foreman challenges him that this is a lie, saying that he knows House will do it again.

Exam Room

- The character is referred to by both first names, "John Henry." The name echoes the story of the African-American folk hero — a steel driver, a man who works with the hammer and knows that it is his fate to do so from the time he is a baby. After the invention of the steam engine, John Henry faces off with the machine that is to replace him. He outperforms it, but eventually his work kills him. Similarly, this character feels there is little to his life without his work, and he recognizes the same dedication in House. It's also likely no accident that Giles rhymes with Miles, a real-life great jazz trumpet player.

- Foreman writes on the white board this episode.
- House is served, and hands the papers directly to Cameron.
- John Henry's manager carries a bag from the popular music shop the Princeton Record Exchange, located in Princeton, New Jersey.
- When House is in court, Wilson is sitting directly behind him. He leans forward, almost like the angel on House's shoulder. We frequently see Wilson act as House's conscience. He's the "I know I should" voice in House's head that House obviously doesn't have. Here, we see the relationship manifest in a single moment.
- This episode is the first time first names are used as a form of mockery. In a later episode, Cameron will use first names to manipulate "Robert" and "Eric." Here, House and Foreman's old boss use them as a way of knocking one another down a rung. "Say 'hi' to my friend, Jimmy," House says, a recess-style introduction between Hamilton and Wilson.
- At the end of the episode, John Henry has been able to abandon his wheelchair. He walks out of the hospital with only a cane, emphasizing his similarity to House's character.

1.10 Histories

First aired: February 8, 2005
Writer: Joel Thompson
Director: Daniel Attias
Guest stars: Paul Sklar (Cop #2), Smith Cho (Julia), Leslie Hope (Victoria Madsen), Ogy Durham (Chris), Charles C. Stevenson Jr. (Walter), Troy Robinson (Cop #1), Patty Onagan (Girlfriend), Tomiko Martinez (Tall Girl), Brandon Brocato (Phil), Bonnie Perlman (Mom), Farrah Skyler Greye (Nurse), Suzanne Ford (Mrs. Whitney), Kevin Moon (EMT), Larry Clarke (Officer Gilmar), Leslie Karpman (Jodi)

Episode Differential

When House plays sick from the clinic, Cuddy forces him to guide a pair of medical students through the practice of taking patients' histories. At the same time, a homeless woman's own mysterious history is distracting the team from what should be an obvious diagnosis. Apparently, a picture is worth a thousand words.

The homeless woman, who shall later be introduced as Victoria Matson, talks her way into a rave in an abandoned house. As the party is being busted, Victoria goes into spasms, which is how she finds her way to Princeton-Plainsboro, and eventually to Foreman, who's skeptical she's not just faking her way in for a free meal — even after she seizes. Given Foreman's laissez-faire attitude, Wilson turns to House. House is always willing to work if it will irk. Curious to know why Wilson's so interested and why Foreman's so not, he steps in.

In spite of his reluctance, Foreman winds up the main man on the case. He breaks the rules to get her through faster for an MRI, using another person's name and appointment. Before the MRI can occur, however, Cuddy shuts it down — the patient has a surgical pin in her arm that the MRI would have magnetically torn from her body. Until they know who the patient is and what her history is, they cannot proceed. This puts Foreman out beating the street, using the patient's sketch as a map, bartering his best jacket away to the homeless in exchange for information. The all-knowing House just leans back and waits, sure they'll get a name and a medical file by tracing the surgical pin. Foreman manages to find the patient's home, a box full of bats. Strangely, even though in other episodes we saw the team considering lunch meats and improperly canned foods as possible road signs to disease, Foreman doesn't pause to consider that their patient sleeping with flying vermin might be a clue to her condition.

Several diagnoses, and an escaped-then-returned patient later, the team is dealing with a fatal case of rabies. Foreman can't give up his search for Victoria's history, a complete about-face from when she arrived.

Highlight

When House is sifting through Victoria's drawings, a shocked med student says, "You're reading a comic book." House fires back: "And you're calling attention to your bosom by wearing a low cut top. Oh! I'm sorry. I thought we were having a 'state the obvious' contest. I'm competitive by nature."

Support Staff

When the two medical students under House's tutelage come back with different histories for the same patient, House smells a rat — a lying patient. The girl is fabricating her history because she has no memory. To prove this to his students, House holds up the cane for the Korsakoff patient to see the second time he goes into her room, and she walks into his trap, using it as part of her story.

Lies

- House lies, very feebly, about being too sick for clinic duty.
- Foreman lies to get Victoria in for an MRI quickly.
- The cop initially lies about tasering the patient.
- The patient with Korsakoff lies to all three of her medical examiners.

Exam Room

- This isn't the first time Foreman pre-judges a patient who is disadvantaged, and it won't be the last. As we saw in "The Socratic Method" when Foreman sedated the "schizophrenic" patient because she was giving him a hard time, Foreman will always put himself first and protect himself, even if it means cutting corners on the patient's care. Here, if he had his way, the patient would have been discharged and he never would have been bitten. Normally, Foreman is very empathetic, but he does have a natural survival instinct, which makes him occasionally callous: he knows that the disadvantaged are often more desperate, and therefore less predictable.

- The *House* staff often has fun with naming. Victoria's comics reference Kaplow's Pawn Shop. Lawrence Kaplow is the show's writer/producer.
- House tells the med student he's competitive by nature. It may not be just a good line; proving other doctors wrong is his motivation for taking on many of the cases he handles.
- Lisa Edelstein gets the line that states what we've all been thinking since the pilot in terms of these doctors playing detectives (no matter that we love them for it): "You are a doctor; do what doctors do. Pick up the phone, dial 911 and a cop on the other end does what cops do and finds the missing person! I assume the rest of you have doctor things to do."
- It's surprising that House has known Wilson as long as he has and has only just discovered this piece of personal information about Wilson's brother, especially considering House's nosiness and the kind of personal sleuthing he is always doing.

Booboos

Taser guns are illegal in New Jersey.

What's Up, Doc?

- To bring Victoria's fever down, she is placed in a tub of ice water, an act she sees as torture, with House once again being envisioned by a patient as a sinister figure. House uses the word "hydrophobia" to describe her fear of water. "Aquaphobia" is the proper word. "Hydrophobia" is another name for late-stage rabies, based on the inability to swallow and the tendency to salivate.
- The shot to the stomach we see Foreman getting for rabies hasn't been used since the mid-1980s. Standard shots these days use a much smaller needle and are given to the buttock and arm.
- Foreman gets bitten and has symptoms within hours. His hand wouldn't be tingling for several days. If he were getting the rabies shot after nerve symptoms were present, there'd be little point.
- These days, surgical pins usually are made from non-magnetic metals. Victoria ought to be able to have her MRI without fear of damage (as should John Cho's character in "Love Hurts").

Pacemakers, of course, are another story. If she had one of those, she really wouldn't be able to have that MRI.

1.11 Detox

First aired: February 15, 2005
Writers: Lawrence Kaplow, Thomas L. Moran
Director: Nelson McCormick
Guest stars: Marco Pelaez (Pharmacist), Akiko Morison (Anesthesiologist), Maurice Godin (Dr. Hourani), Amanda Seyfried (Pam), Nicholas D'Agosto (Keith Foster), America Olivo (Ingrid), Mark Harelik (Mr. Foster)

Episode Differential

In "Detox" House faces his biggest enemy — himself, without medication. Cuddy bets him a month off from the clinic in exchange for him lasting one week without his Vicodin. Only problem is a teenager's life hangs in the balance.

After a fake-out opener where we believe a 16-year-old girl and boy are about to finally "do it" (with their clothes on?), we see them grab the car keys and hit Dad's Porsche instead. A bit of careless driving and blood-coughing-up later, the Porsche is wrecked. Keith is admitted to Princeton-Plainsboro several weeks later, still bleeding internally.

The internal bleeding, coupled with hemolytic anemia, which is uncommon in 16-year-olds, sends the team to conduct a battery of tests. Chase is the boy wonder this episode, suggesting they remove fluid from Keith's eye in the hope that it will cause movement and break up the blood clot, which is what happens. House, who is suffering his own hell without his Vicodin, would have left the eye alone to concentrate on Keith's vitals. Chase is commended.

House has a far-out theory that it may be the rare hepatitis E, which he's determined to treat. Seldom does Cameron disagree with House, but she does here, claiming to the rest of the team, "This is a mistake." Foreman goes one step further, saying, "This is a lawsuit." Only the dutiful son, Chase, remains, pointing out that House is often right about long shots. Cameron believes the boy's symptoms point to lupus, or at least that it is more likely, and she is torn about carrying out House's treatment. She doesn't want to lie, and Foreman instructs her not to.

House is looking like the drug addict he is. He's broken his fingers with a pestle to distract himself from the pain of his leg. He confronts and insults Keith's father as his son lies dying, and even Cameron can't hide her disgust at his behavior. Foreman has attempted to restore House to normalcy by slipping him meds, urging him to save the boy and worry about his own problems later.

A shaky House commands his team to dig up the dead cat Jules, and we see him performing the necropsy as Keith is prepped for surgery to receive his new liver. House storms into the O.R. with a termite, commanding the surgeon to cease the transplant. As if his ungloved and unmasked entrance itself wasn't enough, and the brandishing of the termite also not enough to get the results he wants, House spits on the operating table. Keith's father is furious and is the first next-of-kin to physically assault House (there will definitely be others in episodes to come). As she so often is, Cameron is the only doctor who still has even a shred of Mr. Foster's confidence. When she says, "I think you should trust Dr. House," he gives in, and tells them to let the liver go to another patient.

Even without his pain pills, House has solved the case. Naphthalene poisoning, due to an infestation of termites, killed Jules the cat, and also infected Keith.

Highlight

Even though he's not at his prettiest, this whole episode is a Hugh Laurie fest. It's a toss-up between House's quietest and loudest moments: the ever-skeptical House who is rendered pleasantly speechless by a woman massaging his hand, and the no-holds-barred House who interrupts the liver transplant.

Support Staff

House slams it on the table during his discussion with Wilson about whether or not he's changed since first going on Vicodin. House claims all of his symptoms are signs of getting older and crankier.

Lies

- Cameron is expected to lie to the patient's father, or at least to persuade him toward the treatment for hepatitis E. She begins to, but in the end she doesn't.
- House lies when he tells Wilson that he closed his hand in the car door.

- Wilson is withholding information — it was actually his idea that Cuddy make the bet with House to go off his medication.

Exam Room

- House's desktop is suddenly metal, very handy if one is planning to smash one's fingers upon it with a blunt object. In the other episodes, it is a glass top, which would not work in this scene.
- After House bursts into the surgery, bug in hand, and spit a-flying, the O.R. nurse says, "We can't do this surgery now." The exasperated surgeon declares, "Ya *think?*" as if it is the stupidest most obvious statement he has ever heard. The show frequently scripts medical staff stating the obvious (for the benefit of the general viewership), then has other doctors tease them for speaking in laymen's terms.

Booboos

- In an homage to countless film driving scenes where the actor looks too long at the passenger, *House* finds perfection. Keith's girlfriend is weaving, zipping along at 30 over the speed limit but as soon as he coughs blood on the rear-view he has her full and devoted attention — not enough that she would pull the car over though.
- House acts as though he doesn't understand when the masseuse Wilson has brought in for him grips his hand firmly and speaks Spanish. Surprising considering his usual knack for languages; Spanish is one of the easier languages to learn because it is phonetic. Portuguese and Spanish are similar, and House has just read an article on sleeping sickness from a Portuguese medical journal in "Fidelity." And wait . . . doesn't House speak Spanish to Alfredo's mom in the later episode "Humpty Dumpty"?

What's Up, Doc?

House refers to the "necropsy" he performs on the cat as an "autopsy." But an autopsy done on an animal has its own word. This could be a boo-boo, or it may be just another example of the show using the simplest terms to avoid confusing the wider audience.

1.12 Sports Medicine

First aired: February 22, 2005
Writers: John Mankiewicz, David Shore
Director: Keith Gordon
Guest stars: Scott Foley (Hank Wiggen), Bryan Singer (Himself), Meredith Monroe (Lola), Art LaFleur (Warner Fitch), Salli Richardson-Whitfield (Sharon), Deirdre M. Smith (Carol Moffatt), Timothy McNeil (Patient #2), Sean Everett (Patient #4), Richard Swaidan (College Student)

Episode Differential

Major league baseball pitcher Hank Wiggen comes into the hospital's care like a home run. Even tight-laced Wilson is basking in the celebrity glow, having his baseball card signed.

Kidney problems coupled with bone loss point to steroids, and the fact that Hank gained 25 pounds while in Japan also seems to point to steroid use. Hank's urine comes back negative, but House points out that steroids can hide from tests. One thing can't hide . . . shrunken testes. House prescribes lupron, assuring the still-protesting ball player and his wife that it won't hurt him. Only problem is, it will.

In an episode where the dialogue is packed with sports metaphors (and testosterone), it only makes sense that the staff's lives should revolve around sports too. House reveals himself to be a monster truck fan. Strangely Wilson is too — but not enough to accompany House on his evening with the best tickets money can buy, tickets so good House says they have to sign a release in case of death. Looking for a buddy to accompany him, House turns to the last person you would expect to see in the midst of a truck rally: Cameron. A romance isn't budding yet, but we know it may be when Cameron asks if it is a date.

When Hank's kidneys begin to fail, his wife is adamant about donating hers. "We're a match," Lola declares to House, as if love is strong enough to make it so. Love is strong enough apparently, except that it's also gotten in the way just a little — Lola's pregnant. She is delighted with this information until House explains that she can't be both pregnant and Hank's donor. In one of the few scenes where House shows sensitivity, he leaves her alone to ponder her choice and discuss it with her husband.

The team manages to keep Hank alive after a suicide attempt, and when House confronts him about it, Hank reacts with emotion.

Heatedly, he fumbles his urine receptacle and House winds up getting "peed on," a minor incident that leads him to the proper diagnosis. He runs into Lola in the hall, and when he tells her that he thinks she should keep the baby, she embraces him tearfully. House realizes she has no sense of smell. When House combines this final symptom, which is hers, with her husband's, he can see the answer. It takes two to make a thing go right.

Highlights

This intro takes the trophy. As cringe-inducing as it is, Hank Wiggen's arm breaking is one of those scenes you could watch on repeat. Favorites that follow closely behind: when House pulls the sheet off Hank, exposing him, and says, "Hypogonadism. Isn't that a great word?" and when House asks Cameron to the monster truck rally, clarifying, "Exactly, except for the date part."

Support Staff

House breaks out the fancy cane for the monster truck rally.

Lies

- House suspects Hank of lying about his drug use. He is, but not the kind House expects.
- Wilson lies about having to speak at the conference. Truth is, he's already cancelled.
- House puts the patient on lupra for his steroid use. Cuddy confronts House saying, "You put him on lupra . . . And you told him it was like milk?" When House confesses, she says, "Is there any way in which that is not a lie?" House's only defence: "It's creamy."
- When pressure is put on him, Hank does come clean about his steroid use from five years before.

Exam Room

- Bryan Singer, *House* producer and the director of *X-Men* and *The Usual Suspects*, makes a cameo as the director of Hank's anti-drug commercial.
- Hank Wiggen draws his name from Henry Wiggen, a character written by American novelist Mark Harris, best known for *Bang the Drum Slowly* (1956). His Wiggen character was also

a baseball player, a pitcher for the fictional New York Mammoths.

- House orders his coffee black no sugar in this episode. In other episodes, we see him add sugar. Is the doctor watching his weight? Or does he just jones for sugar on certain days?
- The plot line of Foreman dating the pharmaceutical rep gets dropped pretty quickly. In "DNR," Dr. Hamilton asked Foreman if he was seeing anyone and if it was serious. Foreman answered in the affirmative, perhaps setting up this scene. But we'll only get this glimpse of Foreman's apartment before the show moves on.
- This is the first mention of Stacey — and House's romantic past. We don't meet her yet, but we know that House is capable of love. Interesting that this information is introduced just as he is taking Cameron out.

Booboos

- In the opening scene Hank breaks his right hand, but the X-ray shows a broken left hand.
- When Chase, Cameron, and Foreman are out having a drink, Foreman leaves his cell phone unattended. A message comes in, and Cameron picks it up to see who it's from. She has just taken a sip of her beverage, which is half full. A few seconds later the level of her beverage is three-quarters filled.
- Hank's name is "Wiggen" on his baseball card, but at one point House says "Wiggens": "Hank Wiggens stole your pills."

1.13 Cursed

First aired: March 1, 2005
Writers: Matt Witten, Peter Blake
Director: Daniel Sackheim
Guest stars: Tracy Middendorf (Sarah Reilich), David Henrie (Tommy), Nestor Carbonell (Jeffrey Reilich), R.J. Root (Sam), Jack Walsh (Ozzy), Alejandro Patino (Cabbie), Abbey McBride (Blonde), Dennis Bendersky (Davey), Daryl Sabara (Gabriel Reilich), Patrick Bauchau (Dr. Rowan Chase)

Episode Differential

If a sub theme of *House* is distressed father-son dynamics, then "Cursed" sets the theme with its story of a high-powered father, his divorced wife, and their son whose illness could undo the father's carefully groomed image.

The episode opens with a group of 12-year-old boys entering an unoccupied mansion for some under-aged beer and cigarettes. Gabe is less sure about the lost boys' behavior and gets doubly freaked out when an Ouija board is produced and says he will die. At home a week later Gabe's mother finds him in bed still with a fever he's had for days. She takes him to Princeton-Plainsboro.

Cuddy informs House that he's taking the case, which is tentatively considered to be a kind of pneumonia. As House guesses, Gabe's wealthy businessman father is a hospital donor. It's one of the usual reasons Cuddy brings House cases. House is intrigued once Cuddy describes the papular lesions on the boy's arms. When Gabe's father (who also lists fighter pilot on his c.v.) shows up and berates his ex-wife, the staff, and even his son, Chase immediately takes Gabe out of the room so they can talk one-on-one about his symptoms, but mostly about overbearing fathers. In a mirror of the episode's main case, Chase's own father, Rowan, a world-famous rheumatologist, shows up. As the two haven't spoken in years, Chase is mystified at his presence but apathetic to his father's communication attempts. A sleuthing House soon learns that Rowan is near the end stage of terminal lung cancer and is in America to see Wilson for a consult. In a decision that House is conflicted in making, he keeps this knowledge from Chase.

Rowan is brought in to consult — much to Chase's annoyance — and suggests an autoimmune disorder (he is, after all, an expert). House then remembers Gabe's father angrily rattling off rare diseases that only occur in South Asia when he ranted about the attention — or lack thereof — that his son's case was getting. Putting this together with the father's numb wrist, House diagnoses both as having leprosy. Gabe's father confesses that he wasn't a fighter pilot, but spent several years following a guru in India, something he's just not proud of now that he's a businessman. The episode closes with Chase seeking out Rowan to offer a father-son drink, only to discover Rowan is already preparing to leave. They have an awkward goodbye that Chase doesn't realize may be his last moment with his own father.

Highlight
When Chase investigates the attic hideout, the boys mistake him for a cop. When the cops do show up, all Chase's suaveness goes out the window, which is where he must go too. Chase quickly follows the boys down the tree, landing on his butt.

Support Staff
As he's about to look in the microscope, House hands it to Chase.

Lies
- Gabe was someplace he shouldn't be; he only reveals it to Chase when his parents are out of earshot.
- Gabe's father wasn't a pilot.
- Gabe's father was in India for two years.
- "He's just a liar," Gabe says of his father, which leads to a "He loves you" argument from Chase. Lying is cancelled out by love.
- Chase Sr. says he's there for a conference. House reveals that he's not registered.
- House makes a lie of omission by not telling Chase the true reason for his father's visit. But he's true to his promise to Chase Sr.

Exam Room
- This episode it's a glass board, not a white board. The board changes several times throughout the series.
- The similarity of the names should go without saying: Robert Chase and Rowan Chase. Ruh-roh, two pompous docs starting with *R* under one roof.

- Chase says it's been 15 years since his parents' divorce, 10 since Mom died. He also reveals her alcoholism, a predilection for gin and tonics. Knowing Chase's adolescent care-giving role makes it easier to envision him heading for the seminary.
- House brings the elder Chase in on the diagnosis for his own amusement, but he's not cruel. He's willing to play Solomon, saying that both their diagnoses could be right, with one triggering the other. For House, he's also unusually torn over the death dilemma — to tell or not to tell.
- Once again, we see Wilson acting as House's conscience as they discuss whether House should tell Chase that his father is dying.
- True to other episodes, the show gives us a hint early on, with the elder Dr. Chase mentioning the true illness only 10 minutes into the episode and House mocking him for the suggestion: "Maybe if we were in Calcutta."

Booboos

- Chase says the house looks like it was built in the '60s. The house certainly doesn't look it.
- Chase Sr. doesn't have time for a drink? It seems like he'd make time. Flights to Australia aren't cheap, but Dad should be able to afford to miss just this one.

What's Up, Doc?

Just in from Australia, Chase's father suddenly has a New Jersey license to practice medicine? He says he's the one who extubated Gabe.

1.14 Control

First aired: March 15, 2005
Writer: Lawrence Kaplow
Director: Randall Zisk
Guest stars: Ron Perkins (Dr. Simpson), Chi McBride (Edward Vogler), Sheila Cavalette (Anesthesiologist), Joshua Miller (Ricky), Andrew Borba (Mr. Van Der Meer), Sunny Mabrey (Jenny), David Joyner (Cardiac Surgeon #2), David Castellani (Boardmember #2), Vivian Bang (Robin), Sarah Clarke (Carly Forlano), Dar Dixon (Don)

Episode Differential

Some fans gripe at the introduction of Vogler, the pharmaceutical CEO who takes over Princeton-Plainsboro. While it seems like a narrative stretch, House having a nemesis makes him suddenly a little less godlike, and helps shape the show into areas of rich character depth.

Carly, a young executive is giving a rush presentation to her board about expansion plans. Just after the start of the meeting, her leg seizes. She clears the room and pages her put-upon assistant.

In an excellent parallel, at Princeton-Plainsboro Cuddy is also announcing news to her board: the news of a 100 million dollar donation to the hospital courtesy of Edward Vogler, a self-made CEO of a pharmaceutical corporation. The stipulation? He's the new chair of the hospital. In a hallway shot where Cuddy and Vogler are assessing the hospital, Vogler sees House for the first time and takes an instant disliking. For his part, House notes that Vogler will be using the hospital as a free lab for his drug trials. Playing upon the theme of control, Cameron, tired of having her opinions relegated to the back of the room, unabashedly tries "soft positional bargaining" to manipulate her teammates.

Once admitted by House, Carly begins to show signs of possible cancer. Carly refuses to have a simple test done, which makes House suspicious. After Carly worsens, House consults with the team, and looking over all the previous tests House notices that Chase screwed up an MRI, scanning the wrong leg. Chase is given a merciless verbal lashing with the admonishment that his mistake could kill the patient. Visiting her room while Carly sleeps, House notices slash marks on her upper thigh (as anyone ever examined by a doctor can attest to, it's a major blunder of the show. The slash marks would be noticed within minutes). When he finds Ipecac syrup in her room, House's diagnosis of bulimia is confirmed. She's killed her heart with the dangerous purgative. To get her on the top of the transplant list, he has to lie about her bulimia, a psychological condition that could keep her from getting a new heart.

House and Vogler have had several run-ins, ostensibly over whether House should wear a lab coat or not. When Vogler visits House's office the two men flat out admit they don't like each other. This intensifies when Vogler sits in on a tense transplant committee meeting where, despite Cuddy's suspicions, Carly's placement is approved. After the successful surgery Vogler visits House in his office placing a bottle of Ipecac on his desk. Vogler says a nurse found it in Carly's room but House is suspicious that it was Chase who sold him out.

Highlights

During an office confrontation with Vogler, he turns off House's iPod, which is cranking out The Who's "Baba O'Riley." After their terse exchange, House turns his iPod back on but instead of The Who's stadium-sized riffs drowning out Vogler, it's a jaunty rendition of "Hava Nagila."

Also in this episode, Cameron spontaneously confronts House about whether he likes her.

Support Staff

As he frequently does, House slips into drum major mode, twirling his cane while examining the symptoms on the board.

Lies

- The kid in the clinic with the "dumb" dad. The dad is lying about not being able to talk after House doses him, but he does confess to House by blinking. House lies too — by not reporting it.
- House lies to the transplant board by avoiding the question as long as possible of whether there's something he's not telling them about the heart recipient.
- House says he doesn't like Cameron. Is it a lie? He leads her on, he toys with her, he occasionally returns her gestures of kindness. It's hard to say.

Exam Room

- In another of his grandstanding Christlike moments, "I have healed you," House says to the mute.
- As if this line wasn't enough, Vogler says to House, "Tough being a doctor. All that power. Power to play God."
- House tells the mute that yesterday he would've said the man had to give the money back. What changed between one day and the next? It's a kind of workplace sabotage. With the hospital swimming in money, and someone at the top of that money that House doesn't respect, he feels no qualms about cheating. He cheats twice this episode — with this clinic patient and with the heart transplant.
- House says he's been through three regime changes. He's been working under Cuddy for eight years, as we'll find out in the next episode, so he's talking board and figureheads.
- This is the episode that Chase really begins to get his hate-on for House. In contrast, Cameron gets her love-on for him.
- Even in his deception, Chase is doing what House would do. He's going through the patients' things for clues. The only difference is that this time he wasn't ordered by House to do so.

Booboos

- Lisa Edelstein's Boston accent comes to the forefront of the transplant committee drama on the word "disqualify."
- People in hospitals are expected to wear hospital gowns for a reason — because they make for easy exposure and quick examination. It's unlikely House would be the only one to flip back that hospital gown. Since that's where her symptoms began, they would examine Carly's thigh muscle — likely her whole thigh, not just the conveniently unscarred portion.

What's Up, Doc?

- Contra Cuddy, clinical trials don't "save thousands of lives." Nine out of 10 new drugs never make it to the market because they don't save lives.
- "She'll outlive us all," the doctor says coming out of surgery. Chances of survival in heart transplant patients have definitely gone up, and women have higher survival rates, but his statement is still an exaggeration. According to a CBS News

broadcast in 2006, Tony Huesman is the world's longest living heart transplant patient, surviving 28 years after his surgery. So even if Carly gives Tony a run for the money, it will only bring her 32-year-old character up to 60. She still won't be eligible for the McDonalds' senior citizen discount, but then again, a Big Mac and Ipecac probably aren't the best combo.

1.15 Mob Rules

First aired: March 22, 2005
Writers: David Foster, John Mankiewicz
Director: Tim Hunter
Guest stars: Chi McBride (Edward Vogler), David Burke (Everhardt), Danny Nucci (Bill Arnello), Joseph Lyle Taylor (Joey Arnello), Greg Collins (Marshal Brady), Ingrid Sanai Buron (Kimberly), A.J. Trauth (Henry)

Episode Differential

Vogler and House's hate-on continues to fester as House is forced to treat a government patient who's hiding much more than just his mobster past.

In a hotel room a mobster named Joey is eating his dinner, surrounded by federal agents. Bill, his lawyer brother, is trying to convince Joey not to rat out his associates and go into witness protection. Now stressed out, Joey lights up a cigarette only to have Bill swipe it from his mouth, reminding Joey that he's just quit. When Joey stands up he suddenly collapses and lapses into a coma.

Cuddy and Vogler are meeting about hospital finances, specifically, House's department, which Vogler points out only treats one patient per week. House enters only to be told that the federal government demands that he treat Joey. House wants to fight it on principle, *and* because Vogler also tells him he has to do it, until Cuddy informs House that he will have to get his own lawyer. House acquiesces in the first of several compromises, bent rules, and barters in this episode.

When Joey wakes up, Vogler is informed by someone on the team that the patient is ready for discharge, and House is furious, not only at the leak but that Vogler would override him. The point is moot when Joey is brought back to the hospital in another comatose state. Tests show strangely high levels of estrogen in his body as well as evidence of

Hep C, something Joey may have picked up in prison through sex or tattooing. When Chase delivers the news to Joey's brother Bill, the lawyer slaps Chase. (Save for House, Chase will be the series' most physically abused character.)

Visiting House, Bill is assured that while they have to treat Joey for the Hep C, it won't go on his chart. As a reward, House is presented with a restored hotrod. Wilson tells him that he can't keep it, but House and Wilson nonetheless find time for a Jersey joyride. While they're treating the Hep C, Joey's other symptoms continue to flummox the team. It's only after a third session treating a slacker teenager's infant brother for objects stuck in his nose that House clues in. Looking at the infant's grasp of concepts (he put a toy cat in his nose, followed by a toy policeman and fireman to "retrieve" them), he realizes that the estrogen isn't a symptom, it's just too much estrogen. Taking the symptoms apart, House diagnoses the comas as due to a metabolic disorder (both comas occurred after Joey ate steaks late at night), the Hep C from prison, and the estrogen from "Male Flame" — an herbal aphrodisiac marketed to gay men and sold on the same website where Joey buys his anti-smoking lozenges. Bill now has to admit that his brother is gay and only wanted to enter witness protection so he could be himself with a new name in new place.

Back in her office, Cuddy informs House that Vogler was going to axe the entire department but she was able to stall him by threatening that she knows what all the hospital's "secrets" are. The catch? House has to fire one of his staff members.

Highlight
Even fans of Jesse Spencer have to admit: it's fun to watch Chase get cuffed. A close second might be House's response to whether he'll also get cuffed when delivering news, "That would be a new one, hit me so hard his brother turned straight."

Support Staff
Just can't keep that cane away from the white board. They're always hanging around together.

Lies
- Joey has been living the straight life, and letting his brother pretend he's not gay.

- One of the team members tells Vogler the patient is ready for release. All of them believe he is, but no one confesses.
- House makes a lie of omission by leaving the Hep C off Joey's chart.
- It's not a lie, but it is deception that House takes Foreman off the case so the other staff will think that House *thinks* Foreman ratted him to Vogler about the transplant committee lie.
- Chase says he didn't do it, and that House can trust him. He doth protest too much.

Exam Room

- House wears his lab coat once he realizes what's at stake. He's happy to taunt Cuddy in front of Vogler, but, eventually, even House realizes where the line in the sand is drawn.
- Joey is referred to as 35 when he's admitted, but 30 by the diagnostic team. Considering the actor Joseph Lyle Taylor (who has appeared on multiple episodes of *Grey's Anatomy, CSI,* and *Law & Order*) was born in 1964, he's maybe a bit too old to pass for either age — although the stress of being an in-the-closet mobster might age a person just a little.
- Cameron confides in Chase about her conversation with House about her feelings. He is callous, and doesn't understand how she could like him. Don't forget, it was only nine episodes ago (in "Socratic Method") that Chase was flirting with Cameron, asking her if she promised to date the entire lab in exchange for fast test results, and only 12 episodes ago (in "Occam's Razor") that he was saying, "She's weird, isn't she?" to Foreman, who knew that he meant exactly the opposite.
- Cameron takes Chase into her confidence this episode; House takes Foreman into his.
- House calls Cameron "my girl," even after her admission of feelings for him last episode. Such a cold player. He doesn't mean it. And thankfully, she doesn't buy it. Later, he says that because she's "cuter" her test results count for more than Chase's. Poor Chase, jilted and bested.
- When they discuss hemlock, Cameron says, "It grows wild by the highways out here," reminding us that she's not from there originally. The philosopher Socrates is the most famous victim of Hemlock poisoning.

- Cameron continues to be the good news girl, telling Bill "He's awake . . ." as his brother comes out of his final coma.
- House takes Wilson's advice this episode, wearing the lab coat and letting Vogler make the call to the government when the time has come for the patient's real release.
- "Good morning," House says to his team as though they are children in a classroom. His greeting comes right after telling Wilson he's promised to fire one of them.

Booboos
- With so much at stake, why does Bill care whether Joey is still smoking? It seems like he'd have more pressing concerns. It's a red herring to convince us that one brother is poisoning another to keep him out of court, but once we discover the truth, it doesn't really work on the rerun, does it?
- Joey has prison tattoos, but gets an MRI. There's no issue raised about it in this episode but wait for season two's "Acceptance" . . .
- Cameron drinks coffee in the lab. Next to all that expensive equipment?
- House has *Metroid Prime: Hunters* on his Nintendo DS, but fans point out that the sound effects are wrong again.
- House calls the car a '65 Corvette but Wilson refers to it as '66 in a later scene, saying, "The '66 came with a shut-up button."
- Chase is pretty chummy with Bill, saying they've got a "whole barnyard down in the basement." It's not been very long since Bill slapped him.
- In the clinic with the nose-packing baby, House sets the final toy down on a tray beside the others so that cat, cop, and firefighter are lined up together. These are separate visits so wouldn't the brother have taken the toys home with them? That would certainly make it hard to capture this scene, which leads House to his Eureka moment.

1.16 Heavy

First aired: March 29, 2005
Writer: Thomas L. Moran
Director: Fred Gerber
Guest stars: Chi McBride (Edward Vogler), Rose Colasanti (Cashier), Cynthia Ettinger (Mrs. Simms), Ramón Franco (Mr. Hernandez), Karen Goberman (Mrs. Ayers), Teddy Lane Jr. (Mr. Conroy), Susan Slome (Mrs. Lucille Hernandez), Jennifer Stone (Jessica Simms), Alyson Morgan (Clementine), Austin Leisle (Seth), Alec George (Classmate #1), DJ Evans (Classmate #2), Bryan Fabian (Classmate #3)

Episode Differential

While this episode explores the issue of body image, House pits his team against one another, and Vogler gets ready to throw his weight around.

On a private school yard, a group of kids are exercising with their gym teacher, when Jessica, an overweight girl, begins timed skipping, much to the cruel delight of her classmates. As the gym teacher pushes her to finish, she falls to the ground. When the teacher listens and hears no heartbeat he calls paramedics, telling a disbelieving receiver that one of his 10-year-old students has had a heart attack.

At the hospital, House takes the case to his team. Ten-year-olds, even morbidly obese ones, don't have heart attacks. As they're about to go start their battery of tests, House casually tells them that Vogler is forcing him to fire one of them. This starts a round of infighting and bickering while the team tries to test Jessica. Chase believes it's all the fault of her weight and lifestyle. Cameron and Foreman defend Jessica, saying it could be caused by any number of issues.

Vogler begins to surreptitiously interview the team members, asking them whether they are happy with House, and whether there's anything Vogler can do for them. It's during this that we discover positively that Chase is the mole, giving Vogler updates on what House is up to. Even so, Vogler reminds Chase that his status is precarious, should some other team member start to feed Vogler information on House.

Jessica begins to bleed from sores that erupt on her chest, which the team diagnoses as warfarin-induced necrosis. If that's the cause, they'll have to amputate Jessica's breasts. In a last-ditch effort, they struggle to find another cause until House thinks that maybe the obesity in itself is a symptom. When he notes that Jessica is short for her age yet both her parents are tall, he concludes that she must have a pituitary condition causing both the obesity and the sores.

After curing Jessica, House goes to Vogler with a plan, one Cameron proposed — a pay cut across the board to forestall any firing. No dice, Vogler replies. It was never a matter of money, but rather to see if House would follow orders. House readily offers up Chase's name but Vogler vetoes it, with the episode ending with his command to "pick someone else."

Highlight
Chase saying that the one thing he seldom sees in America are children eating apples or riding bicycles.

Support Staff
It's surprising by the end of this episode that the cane isn't the only staff House has left.

Lies
- Jessica lied to her schoolmate, telling her that her mom gave her the diet pills.
- She kept her diet-pill consumption secret from her mother.
- The clinic patient, Lucille Hernandez, has been lying to her husband as she cheats on him — not all of their children are his.

Exam Room
- Chase shows his fat phobia in this episode and Foreman admits that he was a little heavy as an adolescent. Chase also openly mocks Cameron as they discuss the social pressure to stay thin, pointing out that it's easy to believe everyone should be happy with how they look when personally one weighs only 90 pounds. It's a cruel taunt because of its truth; is Chase still smarting from the fact that she likes House?
- Foreman asks if House is playing a game with them by telling them one will be fired by week's end. He references the show *Punk'd*, which stars Ashton Kutcher, who will be referenced twice this season, and again in season three. Maybe one of the writers of the show has a burning crush on Kutcher?
- Once again, House makes a doormat of Wilson. He manages to get a free meal simply by responding "Together," when the

cafeteria cashier asks how to ring it up.
- Right on schedule, House pops his pills after sending his team out to find the ones their patient wasn't supposed to be taking.
- As usual, Foreman is the first one House turns to for a second opinion — this time over whom to fire.
- House is all over Cameron this episode — but not in the way she'd like. He leaves her to prove her own innocence (rather than proving her guilt) in the case of the warfarin and whether or not she made a mistake and gave Jessica too much. She points out the number of times she has stood by House and winds up calling him a "misanthropic son of a bitch." Does House hear her on a deeper level? It's her suggestion, after all, that he takes to Vogler.

Booboos
After proper diagnosis, Jessica manages to drop 30 pounds *in one week?*

What's Up, Doc?
- Warfarin is given orally; rarely is it injected.
- Vogler may be chairman of the board, but he's in no position to wander the hospital looking at patients' charts.

1.17 Role Model

First aired: April 12, 2005
Writer: Matt Witten
Director: Peter O'Fallon
Guest stars: Chi McBride (Edward Vogler), Bobbin Bergstrom (ICU Nurse), Joe Morton (Senator Gary H. Wright), Missy Crider (Susan), Elizabeth Karr (Hostess), Dominic Oliver (Reynolds), Sahar Bibiyan (Clinic Nurse)

Episode Differential
House runs up against hope when he treats a black presidential candidate and Vogler adds a new twist in his hospital version of *Survivor.*

At a Democratic Party fundraiser, Senator Gary H. Wright vomits and collapses after a speech. At Princeton-Plainsboro, Vogler asks House to take on the case. To sweeten the deal he also offers House a way out of firing one of the team — if he gives a speech extolling the virtues of one of Vogler's new drugs at a cardiologist's conference. While House suffers through the idea of sacrifice, the team examines the senator and eventually discovers toxoplasmosis, a fungal infection mostly seen in only HIV-positive patients with full-blown AIDS.

Senator Wright demands a new HIV test. He claims he has never indulged in risky behavior. Moved by the Senator's firm belief, House orders a new test, much to Wilson's surprise, and the test comes back negative. While HIV is ruled out, the senator comes down with more opportunistic infections as his white cell count disappears and the team shifts their focus to leukemia. However, the senator's near-death state means House can't perform the diagnostic test.

Strange viral test results point House toward the now-intubated senator's tongue scar, which Wright had previously tried to explain as a childhood accident. Interrogating the patient, House discovers that Wright had childhood epilepsy.

While following up with the much healthier senator, House asks why he would run for president when he knows he won't win. "I assume you think you have to win every fight," the senator asks rhetorically. It's that line that sends House to the conference. With all his coworkers in attendance, House begins to give a lackluster reading of the press release before he attempts to leave the stage. Vogler forces him to go back where House freestyles on pharmaceuticals and patents the companies use to gouge patients. In the audience, the team shrinks back in horror before leaving.

Highlight

Just the word "Sexsomnia" is enough, although the first scene with the clinic patient is also pretty good. House tells her she was pregnant, and she says, "I haven't even been on a date." He answers, "Since it's physically impossible to have sex without someone buying you dinner." His solution to her immaculate conception problem is that she start a religion.

Support Staff
- "Afternoon delight, she just loves the hardwood," House says of Cuddy, holding up his big cane.
- He also slaps it on the senator's bed table before depriving him of oxygen and forcing him to confess to his lie.

Lies

- The senator hides his childhood epilepsy behind a fake swing set/tongue-biting story. House sees through the story from the beginning, but doesn't realize the epilepsy part until later.
- House originally tells his team that Vogler saw the error of his ways and repented. It isn't until Cameron finds a press release while sitting at House's computer that his team knows about the deal he and Vogler struck.
- Foreman and the senator discuss lies and whether black politicians lie less than white ones. The senator says they do, because they're less likely to get away with it.
- "Lie to me," the senator tells Foreman in a later scene when Foreman tells him a procedure will hurt. Foreman invents a bad lie, and the senator spits, "You can't lie for beans."
- The clinic patient says she's not having sex. House says either she's lying or he's wrong. They're both right — she's unaware of her sexual activity.
- House believes the senator is lying because he's tested positive for HIV, but denies any gay activity.
- The first HIV test lied. It was a false positive.
- Chase tells the truth about feeding information to Vogler.
- House tells the audience the truth about Vogler's new drug.

Exam Room

- Cameron compares House to God when she asks him if he knows why people pray to God. He points out that she doesn't believe in God, which she acknowledges before saying that she thanks House because it means something to her to be grateful.
- "That's great, but just so you know, I've never made a tree," House responds, referencing the 1913 poem by Joyce Kilmer.
- This episode marks the second time Cameron has declared her hatred for sports metaphors. (The first was in "Poison.")
- For one of the first times, House believes someone. The senator stirs him with his speeches. He points out that House may take chances, but not necessarily on people. House runs a second HIV test, and we're given the impression that he might even be considering taking a leap of faith with Cameron.
- House asks Wilson why he hasn't put the moves on her, and Wilson responds, "What makes you think I haven't put the

moves on her?" gaining the upper hand with House *for once*. House's look tells Wilson (and us) everything we need to know. But by the end of the episode, it won't be enough to see it through.

- Twice this episode House asks Cameron "why?" — once, why she likes him, the second time why she is leaving. The answers are remarkably similar, and both times she approaches him only to have him shun her. The first time, in the lab, she walks up close to him and he walks away, leaving her standing there. The second time, at House's place, she extends her hand, but he won't shake it or even look at her for that matter.

- In absolute irony, House is playing "High Hopes" on piano when Cameron comes over to his house to quit — that song about an ant moving a rubber-tree plant, and impossible acts that are made possible through belief.

1.18 Babies and Bathwater

First aired: April 19, 2005
Writers: David Shore, Peter Blake
Director: Bill Johnson
Guest stars: Chi McBride (Edward Vogler), Ron Perkins (Dr. Simpson), Kenneth Choi (Dr. Lim), Michael Goorjian (Sean Randolph), Marin Hinkle (Naomi Randolph), Reggie Jordan (Anesthesiologist), John Berg (Dr. Prather), S.E. Perry (Officer Davis), Guy Camilleri (Heyden Brown), Kevin Brief (Officer Angle), Diane Sellers (Gail Friedman), Veronica Brown (Female Boardmember), Michael Simpson (Andrew Kaplan), Natalie Shaw (Rachel Kaplan)

Episode Differential

House's team breaks apart as he contemplates whether he may have pushed Vogler too far. But just like House, he pushes it aside as much as possible to try to save a patient.

Naomi, a late-term pregnant woman, is driving her slightly tipsy husband home from a night out. She begins to black out and swerves to the side of the street. A police cruiser pulls up and demands that she get out to perform sobriety tests while the husband protests. Naomi slumps to the ground, passing out.

At the hospital, Foreman examines Naomi, telling her it doesn't seem to be neurological. After, he meets up with Chase who asks if he has seen House or Cameron yet. Cameron, as they'll learn, has quit in act of useless sacrifice. In House's office we're given a comical dream sequence where he gives Vogler the news of late-stage cancer. Terminal. We're tipped off that it's a dream when House walks without a limp.

Chase thinks Naomi has pre-eclamsia, a deadly condition for the fetus. House orders tests while he continues hiding out at the clinic. While there, he treats the infant of a raw food enthusiast couple and notes that their baby's weight has gone down and it has pneumonia. House admits the child and lectures the parents but later Cuddy will call child protection services and have the parents barred.

Naomi is told they must C-section her child early and start treatment for cancer. She wants to hold out for several more weeks to give her child a better chance. As she reveals to House — or rather, as he deduces — though her current husband doesn't know, this wouldn't be her first child. Years ago, she had a daughter who died in infancy and that's why she doesn't want to birth prematurely.

Vogler convenes the hospital board to put to vote the revoking of House's job. When Wilson is the lone abstainer, Vogler asks him to leave the room so they can vote on his dismissal. Dejected, Wilson goes back to his office to start packing where he encounters House, who wants to know what clinical trials for cancer may be going on at the hospital. House lies, glossing over the fact that she will just have come out of a C-section. Vogler discovers the lie and takes Naomi off the trial while he and House have a final blow-up in the lobby.

Naomi is prepped for surgery but won't make it off the table. House goes into the hallway to have a talk with the husband and tells him he has to make the worst choice he'll ever make — to save at least the child's life. The husband consents to the C-section and Naomi dies. In an episode where House's job is on the line, we see why Wilson and Cuddy are willing to defend him selflessly.

Stopping Cuddy on her way to another board meeting, House asks her to follow up on the raw food couple's child. During the meeting Vogler again puts to vote the termination of House. All agree except for Cuddy. Vogler asks what changed her mind since the previous day and she responds that House saved two lives. This time, Vogler votes to dismiss Cuddy. This time he's gone too far and the board votes against Vogler, who leaves, along with his 100 million dollars.

Celebrating in House's office, Cuddy walks in and downs a glass of champagne. She admonishes the boys that they should be mourning. A few jobs were saved, but the hospital did lose millions of dollars.

Highlight
House is cocky as ever. After Vogler tells him that he'll destroy him, House replies, "So that's a 'no' on us being squared away. . . ."

Support Staff
- In his dream, House walks without a limp.
- House doesn't have it with him in the O.R. or in the waiting room when he talks to Naomi's husband.

Lies
- House lies in order to get Naomi into a clinical trial — he omits the fact that she's pregnant.
- Naomi lies about it being her first child.

Exam Room
- House searches for sugar in the diagnostic office. He can't even make himself a proper cup of coffee without Cameron. Does the big tough doc have abandonment issues?
- The clinic patient runs parallel to the Diagnostic department's patient in that she is an already born but still underdeveloped baby. Similarly, Cuddy has a clinic patient with hemorrhoids — a common side effect from pregnancy, even though in this case she's examining the rear of man.
- The obstetrician who appears in this episode also appeared in "Maternity."
- Jennifer Morrison doesn't appear in this episode, but her name does in the opening credits, letting us know that her hiatus is only temporary.

Booboos
When the cop is questioning Naomi in the opening sequence, her arm changes positions between shots. It goes from being on the steering wheel to down by her side.

What's Up, Doc?

- As medical fan site Politedissent.com points out, "Dr. Chase suspects that this is pre-eclampsia (sometimes called 'toxemia of pregnancy'), but seems not to notice that she is missing the three cardinal signs: edema in the feet, high blood pressure, and protein in the urine."

- Politedissent also points out that it's convenient the MRI crash cart was equipped with terbutaline — a drug not normally included in a crash cart.

- According to Andrew Holtz's *The Medical Science of House, MD*, patients and their partners seldom have to choose between the life of the mother and that of the fetus. Most times when the pregnancy is at 27 weeks, it is fairly safe to start cancer treatment without substantial risk to the fetus. Aggressive chemotherapy has been used on pregnant cancer patients who are in their third trimester, including radiation, provided the beam can be directed to limit the fetus' exposure. The most dangerous time to conduct chemo is early in the pregnancy. During the second month, the fetus' major organs are developing. In these cases, a termination is usually the answer.

1.19 Kids

First aired: May 3, 2005
Writers: Thomas L. Moran, Lawrence Kaplow
Director: Deran Sarafian
Guest stars: Stephanie Venditto (Brenda), Mark Bloom (Doc #1), Geraldine Singer (Woman), Tim Haldeman (Mature Man), Skye McCole Bartusiak (Mary Carroll), Diego Clare (Dawson), Erin Foster (Second Applicant (Dr. Petra Gilmar)), Dylan Kussman (Mr. Carroll), Rhea Lando (Teammate #2), Lindsay Pulsipher (Teammate #1), Ben Jelen (First Applicant), Cindy Lu (Nurse), Eric Cazenave (Doc #2), Kelly Kirklyn (Mrs. Carroll), Eddie McClintock (Coach), Shari Headley (Third Applicant)

Episode Differential

In the post-Vogler world, House goes through the motions of replacing Cameron (and gives us a glimpse of what he'd be like during speed dating) while also handling an epidemic and a young patient who may be sick for entirely different reasons.

At a swim meet, 12-year-old Mary is preparing for a high dive. Though sickly, she makes the dive but upon surfacing there's no applause, nothing. While she dove, a judge dropped to the ground from, what we'll learn very soon, is bacterial meningitis.

At Cameron's apartment, House asks her to return. Citing the intense "weirdness" between the two of them, she declines. House is then paged away by the developing meningitis epidemic from the swim meet that's landed at Princeton-Plainsboro. Once there, Cuddy demands that he join the rest of the staff in assessing the attendees' exposure.

While taking patients, House happens upon Mary, who, with neck pain, fever, and a rash, has all cardinal symptoms of meningitis. When House is intrigued by the difference in her neck pain (side to side as opposed to the classic up and down), he wants to take her out of the meningitis pen for further testing. After pleading with Cuddy, he gets a one hour reprieve. The catch here is that because of the epidemic, none of their medical imaging gadgets are available, and they'll have to do lumbar punctures and bone marrow collection in places varying from hallways to morgues.

When initial tests prove inconclusive, Cuddy sends them back to examining the outbreak patients and the boys continue the differential while taking temperatures and feeling neck glands. House is given another brief reprieve when he's told that his interviews for filling Cameron's position are starting to show up. House starts the interviews with Wilson present to make sure the process isn't a complete nightmare for the applicants. Wilson, who can barely keep his own head clear of House's swings on the best of days, isn't very good at ensuring this. First up is a kiss-ass hipster who went to Johns Hopkins, like House did, and likes music, like House does. House baits him along only to crush him with an indictment of both his meaningless rebellion and Chinese character tattoo. Also notable is a sassy and brassy Jewish female doctor who manages to one-up everything House can throw at her. When Wilson exclaims that she's perfect, House notes that her shoes aren't sensible — a sign of her insecurity — and Wilson realizes that House isn't ready or willing to replace Cameron.

An impromptu (and improbable) head scan using an ultrasound shows that Mary is bleeding into her brain. A concerned Cuddy has an operating room ready in minutes. When the surgery proves inconclusive,

House is at a loss until he notices that only the girls from Mary's swim team have visited her. None of the boys. Thinking the problem may be related to her traveling and her "mature" lifestyle, he uses the ultrasound, this time on her abdomen. He shows Mary her fetus. House's diagnosis is TTP, a rare multi-system disorder that can present during pregnancy. He presents her options as abortion or treatment.

In a last-ditch effort to bring Cameron back to the team, House returns to her apartment. This time, Cameron has a deal for him. She'll return, if House goes on a date with her.

Highlight

House and Wilson banter after the perfect Cameron replacement leaves the interview. House says, "The eyes can mislead, a smile can lie, but the shoes always tell the truth," to which Wilson responds, "They were Prada, which means she has good taste." House's most witty comeback: "They were not Prada. You wouldn't know Prada if one stepped on your scrotum." Wilson's response doesn't indicate that he would mind such an act: "Okay, well . . . they were nice, pointy."

Support Staff

- Cameron points out that his cane is new. House says it's slimming.
- House uses it to knock on Cameron's door.
- House turns on the taps in the bathroom with it for the boy who needs Raisin Bran.

Lies

- Does Mary lie about being sexually active? Or without Cameron present, did the staff not take a proper history?
- House is lying when he strings the tattooed interviewee along.
- House says that the perfect candidate has shoes that tell the truth.

Exam Room

- Between the title of the episode, the coach saying she's "mature," and the patient saying she's more emotional than usual, we have our hints to choose from right upfront. We get another hint when House encounters grunting in the men's bathroom. House asks the noisy stall occupant, "Good lord, are you having a bowel movement or a baby?" This phrase really ought to clue us in, especially when we're not expecting a 12-year-old to emerge from the stall.

- In this episode, interviews for Cameron's position structurally take the place normally filled by clinic patients.
- "That's our Hitler," Wilson yells when the perfect candidate leaves the interview. He's referencing *The Producers*.
- Foreman and Cuddy see the same patient this episode: Foreman before House steals him to deal with Mary, and Cuddy when House approaches her for an O.R. and a surgeon.
- "Under New Jersey law, you're the boss," House tells his 12-year-old patient when asked if he's going to tell her parents about her pregnancy and subsequent abortion. This gave many fans pause, but it's true: New Jersey courts threw out their parental consent/notice law.

Booboos

- The coach says she's mature, but most coaches and teachers see through their charges' tough acts and know they are vulnerable.
- What hospital conducts interviews during an epidemic? If it's a quarantine area, they wouldn't be bringing people into it.
- House and the boys hide in the men's room for their consult, but as we've already seen at Princeton-Plainsboro, there really aren't any gendered spaces. Cuddy entered the boys' bathroom in "The Socratic Method" when she was looking for House, and if you aren't going to observe separate male and female change rooms, why worry about the tinkler? Yet, somehow, Cuddy is avoided.
- When Foreman does a sonogram of Mary's brain, she comes out of her absent seizure. The probe he is using switches from the left side of her head to her right between shots.
- Many fans believed that we were being led toward the conclusion that the coach was actually the father of Mary's child. There's the shoulder massage at the beginning of the episode, the fact that he calls her "mature," that he's on the road with her 24-7, and that no other boys present themselves. The writers should have thrown in a small clue early on, like the vague presence of some of her 16-year-old male teammates watching her dive.

What's Up, Doc?

There are two white board inconsistencies. We see "intercranial" bleeding listed — which would mean bleeding between skulls. Later, it's corrected to "intracranial" — within the skull. House also misspells "hemorrhage" as "hemorrage," which is corrected the next time we see the board. But hey, even doctors make mistakes. Who says House always won his spelling bee?

1.20 Love Hurts

First aired: May 10, 2005
Writer: Sara B. Cooper
Director: Bryan Spicer
Guest stars: Stephanie Venditto (Brenda-Nurse), Marco Pelaez (Pharmacist), John Cho (Harvey Park), Mark Brown (Dr. May), Kristoffer Ryan Winters (New Guy), Elizabeth Sung (Marilyn Park), June Squibb (Ramona), Matt Malloy (Aubrey Shifren), Keone Young (Clyde Park), Christina Cox (Annette Raines), Peter Graves (Myron Chase)

Episode Differential

With Cameron returning (and closing in on her quarry), this episode presents with the black humor and risk-taking that will add an edge to all following episodes.

In the clinic, Harvey Park, a nervous young Korean man played by John Cho (best known for his role in *Harold and Kumar Go to White Castle*), is waiting and holding a cup of what appears to be urine. When he runs into an agitated House, spilling the fluid over him, House exclaims, "Who walks around with an open jar of urine?" Harvey turns around in terror. When House is told that it was just apple juice and that he should go back and apologize, he finds him only to see Harvey stroking out.

Now with the onus of scaring the patient into stroking, House takes the case. The team wants to do an MRI to find the source of the stroke but Harvey has a metal plate in his jaw from a car accident years ago. With Cameron back on the team, the talk also turns to the terms she secured from House before rejoining Princeton-Plainsboro. When it's revealed that the term was simply one date, the word spreads around the hospital, and everyone is giving his or her advice. Wilson cautions Cameron about the strange morass that is House's heart.

Cameron notices something wrong with Harvey when he seems to enjoy a neurological test that involves poking needles into his muscles. This is confirmed when his only visitor, Annette, is caught strangling him. Chase stops the team from calling the cops, revealing that Annette is a dominatrix, whom Chase once met at a fetish party — much to the shock and laughter of House. Harvey and Annette have a consensual S/M relationship, and now the team starts to look at trauma as a cause of his stroking — something Chase had suggested before but not pursued because he didn't want to out Annette (or himself).

Though Harvey said his parents were dead, House suspects something is up, and manages to have his team track them down. Shamed at their son's lifestyle, they haven't spoken to him in years. House badgers the parents into consenting to surgery on Harvey's brain.

House finally figures it out (jaw infection) and it's date time. It starts off nervously, like any other date. But, thanks to House's charming personality, he proceeds to tell Cameron that she's only interested in him because he's damaged. A second date isn't scheduled but the episode ends with House looking at a photograph and looking to a past that may come back to haunt him sooner than he thinks.

Highlights

Chase and Cameron investigating Harvey's kink-rich apartment together. Chase lingers a disproportionate amount of time over Harvey's S/M gear, prompting snark and indignation from Cameron.

Or House, Wilson, and a clinic patient who doesn't want to go back to work, as they discuss House's date with Cameron, the clinic patient acting all buddy-buddy with them. "Do her, or you're gay," the patient says.

Support Staff

"I think she likes lame," Wilson says to House of Cameron pre-date, fully intending the double entendre.

Lies

- Harvey and his "friend" Annette lie about his parents being dead.
- Harvey and his "friend" Annette lie about their relationship — she's really his dom.

- Chase withholds information from the team. He knows the woman with Harvey is a dominatrix.
- House tells Harvey's parents their son is dead in order to get them to come to the hospital.
- Clinic patient Ramona asks House to lie to Myron, to give him a weaker prescription and tell him that it's better for his heart.
- Ramona lies to Myron to make him see House.
- Ramona and Myron are not married to one another. They never say that they are though; this is an assumption House makes. They are however engaging in the deception of an affair, and lying to one another about how much sex they each want.
- The dom sneaks in as a nurse to see if Harvey's alright.
- The team sneaks the dom in to see Harvey when she's already been banned.

Exam Room

- Right up front we get the foreshadowing that kink will lead to cure, in the title, and also when House tells Wilson, "He peed on me. I'm not into that." More foreshadowing comes when House says to Harvey, "You seem like a regular kind of guy who'd forgive another regular guy." Later, he'll call Harvey a perv.
- When Cameron returns, she and Foreman embrace warmly, but there's no hug for Chase.
- The always-oblivious Chase will point out, "He's so old," of Cameron's House crush. She'll respond, "And you're so young." In spite of his reservations about her choice, he'll also instruct her to "jump House," since she shouldn't expect to be handed anything.
- Chase is a long ways away from his seminary days, admitting to his love of very kinky girls — or one girl, anyway.
- Foreman counsels House against dating Cameron. He likes Cameron, as we can tell from their embrace upon her return, but he doesn't want a workplace romance. He advises House to be a jerk so she won't continue to fall for him. Note that it's his advice House ultimately takes.
- While in Cuddy's office, Harvey's parents, Mr. and Mrs. Park, mention the name of their lawyer as they attempt to call him.

Maybe there's more than one Mark Lerner, but it's the name of a fairly famous lawyer from London, Ontario — show creator David Shore's hometown.

- House shows his fears for the first time — as he gets ready for his date with Cameron. As always, Wilson is his confidant and support.
- For a man who's only going to shoot his date down, House goes all out: donning a complete suit with tie done up to the collar, and buying a corsage for the lady. The only thing he doesn't do is shave. One has to wonder: How does he keep that beard perpetually at four days' growth? He must shave sometime or else he'd have more facial bush.
- House uses the word "damaged" to describe himself. It's the same word he used about her in the pilot.
- In the final shots, we see House looking at a photograph. Later, we'll deduce that it's Stacy.

What's Up, Doc?

As mentioned in "Histories," most surgical pins are now MRI-friendly.

1.21 Three Stories

First aired: May 17, 2005
Writer: David Shore
Director: Paris Barclay
Guest stars: Sela Ward (Stacy Warner), Stephanie Venditto (Brenda), Bobbin Bergstrom (Nurse #2), Nicole Bilderback (Caring Student), Carmen Electra (Herself), Andrew Keegan (Rebellious Student), Josh Zuckerman (Keen Student), James Saxenmeyer (Late 30s Man), Andi Eystad (Volleyball Player), Ingrid Sanai Buron (Nurse #3), Brent Briscoe (Farmer)

Episode Differential

More than the season finale that follows, "Three Stories" is the highpoint of House's first season since it tells us about House's past using a unique narrative structure while also showing us the most outrageous thing House has done yet — teach, at a teaching hospital.

Walking through the clinic he's waylaid by a patient who demands to see him. It's Stacy — lawyer and the major ex of House's life. She's remarried and her husband is sick with a mysterious disorder that she knows only House can solve. He hedges on any commitment to looking at the case and goes to class.

With an intimidating stare, House broods at the front of the class of young doctors. He begins to present three cases of leg pain that will result in a patient being discharged as a drug addict, and leave another near death. From his lecture, the narrative will intersect through House's unreliable narration, which mixes symptoms, patients, and results back and forth. While fans point to links between this episode and executive producer Bryan Singer's *The Usual Suspects*, the narrative device of false flashbacks harkens back to new wave classics like Alain Resnais *Je t'aime Je t'aime*, and even as far back as Alfred Hitchcock's 1949 film *Stage Fright*.

According to House, a farmer presents with a bite, a volleyball player with a sore leg, and — though it's hard to be sure, thanks to House's back and forth narration — Carmen Electra as a golfer/male drug addict with intense pain that only subsides when a syringe of morphine is grabbed from the equivocating doctor's hand and self-injected.

As House explains, the volleyball player has nothing wrong with her, but because of an overly caring doctor (a narratively handy Cameron), the patient is put through a painful and unnecessary test. The farmer is treated for a snakebite, which only causes an allergic reaction and sees his leg injury worsen into full necrosis. When House tells this patient that he will die, the farmer is more concerned about his dog than anything else. This tells House that the dog bit the farmer (and was carrying a necrotizing bacteria). Moments like this (being close to death), House explains to the class, focuses the patient's mind on what really maters. The dog will be put down, the leg will come off, but he'll live.

Switching gears, House reveals that the volleyball player was really ill with a tumor on her leg. Treatment will be successful. The drug addict however is actually ill: muscle death, from an infarction. House reveals that the patient diagnoses the same himself, after other doctors had wandered around leg pain diagnosis. Even then, he reveals, it's too late and surgery has to be performed to remove damaged tissue and possibly the entire leg. It's here that the dramatization changes and we're shown a clean-shaven House as a Princeton-Plainsboro patient.

It's also here that House's debate with Wilson over whether to treat Stacy's new husband intersects with the climax of his diagnostics lesson. The flashback now includes Stacy at House's side over five years ago. Cuddy and the surgeons want to remove the leg. House believes that they can clear the blockage and he'll survive the pain and possible heart attacks even though his system is bloody with dead matter. While suffering through that, House asks to be put in a coma while recovering. While he's under, Stacy (as his medical proxy) and Cuddy decide to remove his leg muscle to save both his life and most of his leg. As House presents this, the class debates the ethics of the decision. As we guess, it does not matter that Stacy saved his life, House never forgave her and it ended their relationship. As House ends the class, he accepts Stacy's husband as a patient.

Highlight
Apparently the entire episode, as it won not only an Emmy but was cited when the series won a Peabody award.

Supporting Staff
We learn how House got his.

Lies
- The farmer doesn't come clean about the dog-bite.
- Stacy reassures House as he's put under, knowing she is going to sign off on a procedure he doesn't want the second he's out.

Exam Room
- It's ironic that House was initially dismissed by doctors for drug-seeking behavior when in fact he was on his way to crippledom.
- The team has never heard the story of how House lost his leg muscle. It may be the end of the season, but if we think about the timeline, none have worked for him very long.
- House tells the class about the visions he experienced when he had no heartbeat. In response to a question from former Christian Foreman, House says, "There's no conclusive science. My choice has no practical relevance to my life, I choose the outcome I find more comforting." Cameron incredulously asks, "You find it more comforting to believe that this is it?"

The line might have made more sense delivered by Foreman or Chase. Cameron has previously said she doesn't believe in God. Perhaps she believes in an afterlife without a monotheistic figure, but her concern still seems misplaced here.

Booboos

- One of the patients is described as a golfer; later we find out that patient is House. Perhaps he can't play anymore, but have we ever seen him interact with anything remotely related to golf? He watches a lot of television, but strangely no PGA. And while he finds many tricks to do with his cane, swinging it like a golf club isn't one of them. He does have a golf-style cap that he sometimes sports though. Still, most golfers are golfers for life so it's surprising he's tuned into baseball, basketball, wrestling, and monster trucks, while golf is noticeably absent from his life.
- House hasn't only been brilliant since he began popping Vicodin. As far as we know, doctoring has been his sole career path. He may have diagnosed his own symptoms with no help from Princeton-Plainsboro, but why did it take him three whole days?
- Many fans thought this episode was such a zinger it should have been the season finale. "Honeymoon" pales in comparison, and might have been better saved as a kick-off to season two.

What's Up, Doc?

- House knows which venomous snakes are common in New Jersey, but can't tell the difference between a snake bite puncture and a dog bite?
- Amputation screw-ups do occur. House writing, "Not this leg," on his leg is actually common before a surgery.

1.22 Honeymoon

First aired: May 24, 2005
Writers: Lawrence Kaplow, John Mankiewicz
Director: Fred Keller
Guest stars: Sela Ward (Stacy Warner), Currie Graham (Mark Warner),
Mark Holmes (Ambulance Driver), Revital Krawetz (Woman)

Episode Differential

After the previous episode's experiment in storytelling, the show is back
to its formulaic nature — although it begins with the strangest date on
the show yet.

In a restaurant, House and Stacy are waiting for her husband Mark to
show up. As they parry back and forth about whether he will show up
(he's missed two appointments at House's office), Mark arrives, surprised
to see House. It's about as bad as first meetings can go. As House nastily
baits Mark and vice versa, Mark drinks his beer, insisting he's healthy.
Within seconds, he passes out. An ambulance arrives. House had dosed
Mark's beer to get him to the hospital for an examination, and called the
ambulance ahead. Good thing the driver had excellent timing.

At the hospital, all test results are vague and inconclusive. Cavalierly,
House orders a lapromatomy (basically, exploratory surgery). Growing
obsessed with proving the stubborn and disbelieving Mark ill, House
spends the night scanning the surgery footage. He notices subtle tremors
in his intestines. The team leans toward Alzheimer's, rare at Mark's age
but a possibility. House sends Foreman and Chase to investigate Stacy
and Mark's home, even though we'd expect this might be something he'd
like to do himself.

House suspects AIP but to test for it, he must induce an attack, something that may be life-threatening. House wants to go ahead and test, as
does Stacy, but Mark resists. Much in the same position she was in at
House's bedside, Stacy makes the same judgment call, and House acts as
her proxy, jamming the cocktail into Mark.

The test comes back positive and Mark can be treated but it means
he'll be a patient at Princeton-Plainsboro for some time. Cuddy asks
Stacy to come on as hospital counsel during Mark's treatment. She
accepts on the condition that House agrees it's okay. When asked, he
nervously does. The final shot of *House*'s first season finds him at home

trying to walk without his cane — as if he can just make the intervening years since he lost his muscle (and Stacy) disappear. When he falters, the soundtracks cues up the Rolling Stones' "You Can't Always Get What You Want" in an echo of the pilot episode. An overhead shot follows a Vicodin into his mouth.

Highlights

"The woman you used to live with?" Cameron says, asking if the patient's wife is who she thinks she is. "That's her Indian name," House replies without missing a beat. "On her driver's license it's 'Stacy.'"

The Woman He Used to Live With also comes out swinging when House confronts her about her feelings and she says, "What's your point? That I'm still in love with you? That I should abandon my dying husband and we should head to Rio?"

Support Staff

Perhaps out of agitation at being around his ex, House fiddles with it a lot this episode. He taps it on the floor while they talk. He uses it to play with the blinds, rests it behind his head, and eventually, throws it onto his couch as he attempts to walk without it.

Lies

- Stacy lied to Mark to get him to meet her for dinner: she didn't tell him House would be coming.
- House drugs Mark's beer, then assures the other diners that they have nothing to worry about unless they ate the veal.
- Cameron questions why they're taking a case where House believes the patient's wife over the patient himself. "What happened to 'everybody lies'?" implying that Stacy could have motives. "I was lying," House says.
- House pretends he's giving up on doing the test without consent, then jabs Mark on his way by.
- House tells the truth to Wilson when he says: "Some part of me wants him to die. I'm just not sure if it's because I want to be with her or if it's because I want her to suffer."
- Cameron says she's happy to find out that House is capable of love — even though he couldn't love her. Is she, is she really?

Exam Room

- House is mixing his booze and his meds again. "Pay no attention to the suspiciously empty bottle," he tells his team after staying up all night looking at Mark's surgery.
- Just as the Ob-Gyn department has a better lounge, they also have better equipment. The monitor House steals to get a better look at Mark's insides comes from the Ob-Gyn.
- When House wheels the monitor, he's walking without his cane since he has the stand to support him.
- Have you noticed that Stacy is always "Stacy Warner" or just "Stacy"? For an atmosphere where last names are commonly used, and with House not really thrilled with her marital status, you'd think that someone would wind up calling her by her maiden name at least once. Cuddy, Wilson, and House have all known her much longer than she's been married.
- House brings Stacy a cup of coffee while her husband is in surgery. He's even remembered how she used to take it, "double milk, no sugar," except that time does march on and she now likes sugar. This is the only time we've seen House bring a coffee to anyone. He does pour a coffee for Foreman once, in the diagnostics room when Foreman has obviously been up all night ("Paternity").
- We find out that Stacy moved in with House one week after their first date. Obviously he took more emotional risks then. They were together for five years.
- Always the death figure, "Time marches on," House says when Mark experiences paralysis in his extremities. It also refers to the conversation he had on the roof with Stacy about how "Something always changes."
- As always, when House attempts the test without Mark's consent, Foreman is the one to stand up to him first, then Cameron and Chase join him. Chase is the last member to stand up to House, confirming House's prediction that "The Aussie will run like a scared wombat if things turn wild."
- A single shot of House in the lab after his team departs with the diagnosis tells us how hard it was for him to take this case, and to violate Mark's choice.

Booboos

What's Stacy doing in the lab, having a heart to heart with Cameron about her romantic relationship with House? What's Stacy doing in the lab at all? And with a coffee!

What's Up, Doc?
AIP can be diagnosed from urine samples, but it's in the urine constantly, not just during attacks.

SEASON TWO

2.1 Acceptance

First aired: September 13, 2005
Writers: Russel Friend, Garrett Lerner
Director: Daniel Attias
Guest stars: Sela Ward (Stacy Warner), Joseph Williamson (Dr. Bruce), Mustafa Shakir (D Vontray), Jody Millard (Prison Guard), LL Cool J (Clarence), Michael Dietz (John Clift), Michael J. Gonzalez (Carlos), Bryce Johnson (James), Adrienne Janic (Dr. Vivian), Tony Ross (Emmitt), Christie Lynn Smith (Cindy Kramer), Warren Davis (Kent), Anesha Ndiaye (Darriene), Marshall Bell (Warden)

Episode Differential

"Acceptance" begins with a prisoner selecting his last meal. The shot lingers on LL Cool J, who plays the character of Clarence, the inhabitant of the next cell, and the next in line for this honor. After being let loose in the exercise room, Clarence hallucinates the four people he killed before he passes out.

House is on the case of his own accord. He's interested in this one in spite of — or perhaps because of — Cuddy's objections, and indeed the objections of his entire team, who don't believe it is worth their time to "save" the life of someone who is scheduled to die anyway. Season one left off with Cuddy asking for House's permission to hire his ex, Stacy Warner, to do legal for the hospital. This episode seems to pick up almost where the last left off. As House peers in on a meeting between Stacy (who is still nearly always referred to by her first name) and Cuddy, House wastes no time in popping his first Vicodin of the season, letting us know exactly where his stress/pain levels are.

This episode deals largely with his acceptance of Stacy's new role in his life. It is not the role he would like. The two are both allies and adversaries — twins of a sort, and they dress like it. The first scene shows them both in blue open-collared shirts. Normally House sports a T-shirt beneath his, but here he doesn't. Later in the episode, they're twins again, but in the negative: both wear brightly colored, casual T-shirts, and jackets; one white, one black. House and Stacy struggle with whether they can trust one another. He uses her to land the patient in the hospital, but she loses her faith in him as soon as she realizes she's been used.

Foreman struggles with his acceptance of having to treat a death row prisoner. Just as in "Histories," the episode dealing with the homeless woman, Foreman faces his own prejudices against the disadvantaged. Usually, Foreman is the do-the-right-thing doctor, but this time he makes no effort to stabilize the patient because he sees it as a band-aid solution. For most of the episode, he believes the convict created his own situation. Cameron points out that the death sentence is racially motivated with black convicts 10 times more likely to receive it. At this moment, the writers are speaking through her character. She doesn't care any more than Foreman does for this case. She spends the episode dealing with her inability to accept a terminal cancer diagnosis for a woman with a cough, a routine patient she picks up when House dumps his extra clinic hours off on her (hours that, ironically, he picked up in a barter with Cuddy that allowed him the inmate's case). The crux of the episode is that a woman with a cough will die in a few months regardless of how the doctors treat her, but a man on death row will be cured so he can return to die.

Highlight

It's a toss-up between Laurie saying, "Ruh-Roh," in Scooby Doo voice as Cuddy catches House admitting the death row inmate to the hospital, and the scene where Cool J/Clarence clobbers his hospital bed, ripping its arms off and yanking a tube out of his own throat because he's thirsty.

Support Staff

- House has to surrender the cane to the warden.
- House uses the cane to stop the elevator door before it closes symbolically between himself and Stacy. "Can I trust you?" he asks. "You used to," she replies.

Exam Room

- Cuddy's password is partypants, *really*. A wink to Lisa Edelstein's past as "Lisa E"?
- This episode contains more lines relegating the diagnostic team to the role of House's children than any other. "I love children, so full of hope," House says of Cameron's initial refusal to see cancer for what it is. When Stacy lingers outside the team's office, House closes the blinds on her and says, "What? Mommy and Daddy are having a little fight. Doesn't mean we've stopped loving you." Similarly, when Chase uses the mnemonic MUDPILES, House replies as if Chase is a boy who has requested to play in them.
- House begins his possessiveness of the white board, disarming Cameron of the marker when she attempts to use it.
- House adds "Dead Man Dying" to the top of the white board in between scenes.
- Foreman has a tattoo on his wrist that Clarence notices. In the season one episode "Kids," House refused to hire a fellowship interviewee who had a tattoo in the same place. Did House not notice Foreman's or did he think it was authentic rebellion, unlike the interviewee's?
- In Coma Guy's room, House eats a sandwich that looks remarkably consistent with his particular order of a Rueben, no pickles, from the season one episode "The Socratic Method." Although he ate Cape Cod chips in the pilot, here he has Lays plain. He's not willing to share them with Wilson until Wilson points out that if Stacy can't trust House, he can't use her. Realizing he needs Wilson for such observations, House offers the bag.
- After Wilson points out the larger trust required for House to win Stacy back, the doctor on the TV soap House is watching says, "We were gonna be with each other forever."
- There are two rich Aussie swipes in this episode, one regard-

ing yachting, the other, "Are you just playing polo?" when House calls Chase to check up on his work.

- "I could've hit that," House tells Clarence of Cameron. But he doesn't say it with regret.
- House is still toying with Cameron though. He taunts her sexually, saying, "Oh no, now you've left your entire body in my chair. What does that mean you want?"
- Cuddy points out that House seems to believe everybody lies except death row convicts. In this episode, it's true. The prisoner never lies.
- This episode is the first time Cameron opens up to anyone but House. She confides in Wilson about her husband and his cancer. Wilson tells her it's not worth it to make friends with dying patients.

Lies

- House lies to Stacy, who believes he has clearance from Cuddy to admit the death row prisoner.
- Cameron lies to her patient, Cindy Kramer, when she asks, "Should I be worried right now?" Cameron tells her she works for one of the best diagnosticians in the country and that they're pouring all their energy into figuring out what's wrong. House doesn't think there's any figuring to do. When it comes to telling patients they're dying, Cameron is as yellow-bellied as Chase is the rest of the time.
- House doesn't lie to the patient, but he does give the patient alcohol under false pretenses.
- Cameron lies when she tells House she's over him. It may be a new season, but the time lapse has only been long enough for Cameron to color and curl her hair. It was only one episode ago that she was asking Stacy about him.

Booboos

- Cuddy begins the episode with an assistant. Is he only good for one joke? He never appears again.
- In "Mob Rules," Joey has prison tattoos and gets an MRI — with no heavy-metal prison ink being sucked out of his skin. Looks like that's a special complication reserved for death-row Clarence.

- It looks like House opens the bottle of alcohol twice in his final scene. The cap has already come off when he gazes upon the five stages of dying that are written on the X-ray light box. When the shot cuts back to him, he's still removing the cap.

What's Up, Doc?

As Andrew Holtz points out in his book *The Medical Science of House, MD*, there is a drug hospitals use that will do the same thing as alcohol. Of course, that's not nearly as dramatic as watching Laurie and LL Cool J down generic whisky shots from urinal sample cups in order to counteract the copy toner the suicidal patient consumed.

2.2 Autopsy

First aired: September 20, 2005
Writer: Lawrence Kaplow
Director: Deran Sarafian
Guest stars: Stephanie Venditto (Brenda), Hira Ambrosino (Anesthesiologist), Gwen Holloway (Neurologist #2), Jewel Christian (Pam), Randall Park (Brad), William Jones (Dr. Murphy), Eamon Hunt (Neurologist), Sasha Embeth Pieterse (Andie), Jonathan Fraser (Salesperson)

Episode Differential

The camera pans around a young girl's room while she's getting ready in the morning. She's Andie. She's plucky. The room is like most other children's rooms except this one is stocked like a pharmacy. While dancing to Christina Aguilera's "Beautiful," Andie — who is dying from cancer — is putting on her wig. She gives herself one of her morning injections, and looking in the mirror, she begins to hallucinate with a crack of the glass and the shaking of the walls.

At Princeton-Plainsboro, a miserable House is suffering from hay fever when Wilson trails him in the hallway. As Andie's doctor, Wilson doesn't believe the hallucinations have anything to do with her cancer, which is in remission. House is pretty open about how unimpressed he is by cancer kids — the main point of the episode being that he really does trust no one — but he does take the case to the team. Right away the dynamic has been set-up: the super-adult young person dealing with death versus the juvenile House, so weak he cannot even cope with his sniffles.

No one can see anything odd but House insists that her oxygen saturation is off by one point. He orders a round of tests against his team's wishes. While Chase preps Andie for a scan, she tells him she has never kissed a boy. She asks if Chase would kiss her before she dies. After struggling with it, Chase gives the nine-year-old a chaste kiss on the lips, proving he is not always looking out for himself and showing his character's compassion. With nothing concrete coming back from the tests, Foreman — showing his House-like cynical side — suggests syphilis. While debating whether Andie could be sexually active, Chase reveals the kiss moment, becoming the butt of House's jokes for the rest of the episode and earning a truly scornful look from Cameron.

Throughout the episode House is challenged for the first time by not only the patient (with Andie's steadfast acceptance of her fate) but by Wilson, who knocks him down with genuine disgust at House's glib approach to her treatment. House shows the audience how caring he can be though, when he gives Andie her own decision about when to die. Chastened by the life and death talk with her, House decides to go through with a radical plan. He'll kill Andie, medically at least.

As a sister episode to the season opener, "Autopsy" also examines the blurry question: when is a life no longer savable? Instead of focusing on a death row convict, the show presents us with young girl who is a terminal cancer patient. The magic of *House* as a show is that it gets its cynicism and eats it too. Like a Chuck Palahniuk novel, the series takes great pains to remind us that illness and death are like a marble thrown by blind fate, striking any of us by chance. Still, in Andie's case, with only a year added to her life by House's bold, questionable treatment, we're reminded that even one year is worth fighting for.

Highlight

The scene where Andie asks Chase to kiss her is remarkably tender; it's also a harbinger of Chase's inability to make proper romantic choices.

Support Staff

- House tosses it to Cameron as he's trying to leave the clinic.
- Holds it aloft when he says to Wilson, "And I'm not terminal, merely pathetic. You wouldn't believe the crap people let me get away with."

Lies

As House discovers, Andie's bravery isn't a put-on or a show. Nor is it a malfunction. It's real.

Exam Room

- House is under the weather due to seasonal allergies. He's also the member of the staff that gets sick the most often — illnesses both real and faked.
- No stranger to over-medication, House maxes out the Benadryl.
- Add Yiddish to House's long list of languages. While he may not actually speak it, he can spiel off as many phrases as he needs to.
- House brings bagels for the team. We'll see the big brown bagel bag again in season three. Obviously, they're a morning favorite. Also, it shows that while House may steal food from Wilson, he understands what will win his team's respect on a daily basis. As a leader, he must provide.
- Chase and Foreman nearly switch roles in this episode. Chase has faith in the little girl, where Foreman doubts her as much as he would any patient, proposing she may have syphilis.
- When he argues with Andie about a kiss, Chase says that he is 30.
- Cameron hears the abnormal valve. Foreman sees the clot. Chase doesn't win any points with House this episode, though he does win points with the patient, which speaks to his bedside manner, not just his dreamy bedroom eyes.
- House listens to "Nessun Dorma" from Puccini's *Turandot*, performed by Bruce Sledge.
- This episode may get the award for the most "Yikes!" clinic patient ever featured — a self-circumcision. Thankfully, the viewing audience isn't shown.
- When they "restart" Andie, Foreman sees the clot on the MRI but House doesn't. House says it's good enough for him that Foreman has seen it. Some fans think this is an indication that House's respect for Foreman and his trust in him is growing. But of the group, House has always respected Foreman the most. He's willing to believe Foreman, particularly now, possibly because without his catch, they would have no answers left.

- On the strength of this episode, writer Lawrence Kaplow won the Writers Guild of America Award for Writing of an Episodic Drama.

What's Up, Doc?
- The expanded team for Andie's "restart" uses a metal bolt to fasten her to the table; at the same time an MRI is being used. As we've seen before on the show, metal and MRIs should never meet, and some fans have debated the logistics of this scene. However, some MRIs are designed to be used with surgical equipment. The show's credits list "Polestar-N20 Intraoperative MRI system."
- In addition to the bolt-resistant MRI, fans on the website Politedissent.com also questioned whether the cancer patient would have lost her eyebrows or just her hair. According to their dialogue, because scalp hair grows faster, it is also more susceptible to treatment. It is therefore accurate that Andie may still have her eyebrows.

2.3 Humpty Dumpty

First aired: September 27, 2005
Writer: Matt Witten
Director: Daniel Attias
Guest stars: Sela Ward (Stacy Warner), J.R. Villarreal (Manny), Charles Robinson (Robert), Ignacio Serricchio (Alfredo), Christine Avila (Luisa)

Episode Differential
While *House* never consistently pulls off *Six Feet Under*–like fake-outs with its introduction scenes, this episode does. Jogging through her neighborhood, Cuddy heads into her yard. She asks her handyman, Alfredo, if he's going to finish the roof in time for her dinner party that evening. He replies that his asthma is acting up and he needs to go home. Nonplussed, she goes inside. While drinking water in front of her kitchen window Cuddy begins to choke. After a few seconds of portentous music, Alfredo falls from the roof with a crash in front of the window.

House takes the case immediately because it has come from Cuddy, but he lets her know right away that it's not because he cares, asking if he gets bonus points for pretending that he does. House makes a snide remark about Cuddy not having been a real doctor in 10 years. Stacy tells her not to enter Alfredo's room, afraid she'll wind up taking responsibility for the accident. Cuddy isn't accustomed to being told what to do, and we see what happens when she isn't in control *and* cares too much. It's a near-lethal Cuddy cocktail.

Twin B&E scenes, with investigations at both Alfredo's apartment and Cuddy's house, lead to two different diagnoses. Finding black, fuzzy aspergilla growing under Cuddy's sink (but not before rooting through her underwear drawer), House thinks a fungal pneumonia is the cause. At Alfredo's apartment, Cameron finds a rat dead in a trap underneath Alfredo's bed. For her, along with Alfredo's scarring, his illness is a streptobacillus, an infection caused by rat bites.

At the hospital, the team and Cuddy debate, with fungal pneumonia seeming more likely. The unfortunate thing is that the treatment could destroy Alfredo's kidneys, which eventually happens. When neither diagnoses pans out, House moves to amputate the handyman's necrotic hand. Cuddy refuses, saying it will end his chances at work. House thinks that's lousy rationale for medicine and engages Stacy to force the surgery.

Even during surgery to remove the hand, Alfredo's fingers on his other hand begin to show the darkening signs of rot. House suspects endocarditis, a condition where the heart shoots out bursts of bacteria to the body's extremities. The cause? Parrot fever, or psittacosis, even though Alfredo doesn't own a pet parrot. Asking Alfredo's mother in flawless Spanish — to the shock of everyone else — House demands to know where else he works. The mother doesn't know. On a tip from House, Cuddy and Foreman head to a warehouse district and into an illegal cock fight arena where they see Alfredo's younger brother filling in for his ill sibling, handling the bird cages.

Alfredo is diagnosed but with a missing hand he's not put back together again, and Cuddy confronts the fact that as an administrator she's lost her edge as a doctor.

Highlight

While searching through Cuddy's underwear drawer, House deadpans to Chase, "Oh my God. She's got pictures of you in here. Just you . . . like some sort of shrine." To which the gullible Chase responds, "You're kidding me."

Support Staff
- The cane gets the usual treatement: House leans his chin upon it and hangs it from the white board.
- He twirls it twice in this episode.
- He hangs it on Alfredo's bed while taking his temperature.
- He and Cuddy discuss what an amputation would mean for Alfredo, a blue-collar worker, how it would be different for him. House says, "What can't work as a cripple?"

Lies
- Alfredo lies about feeling better; he continually tries to get out of bed to go back to work.
- Alfredo lies about his other job.
- House lies to the clinic patient about the medication he's prescribing. He tells him he's giving him the white Republican meds, but gives him the one that has been marketed toward black Americans. Even though Foreman tried to prescribe the same drug, he is infuriated with House's condescension.
- House lies to Chase about the "shrine" in Cuddy's drawer.
- House withholds the fact that he can speak Spanish — or enough anyway to suit his purposes.

Exam Room
- "Mexico playing Argentina on TV?" Cuddy asks Alfredo, stereotyping him as a soccer-watching lay-about. As will be revealed, he's anything but. It's not the first time the show has negatively portrayed Latin characters and it won't be the last — but here it also plays into this show's themes of assumption and white privilege.
- We see Cuddy's house for the first time. In addition to an elaborate spice collection, she has quite the variety of knives, hinting that Cuddy (or possibly someone she's hired) likes to cook.
- In contrast to House's place, Cuddy's home is decorated brightly.
- We see her drink from a water bottle that is Fiji-shaped, even

though the brand never shows.

- Cuddy and House reverse roles this episode. Cuddy has a tendency to become reckless when she cares too much.
- Alfredo's admittance band has the surname Astacio on it, and Dr. House — not Cuddy — as his physcian.
- "All this from falling off my roof," Cuddy says when she sits in on the diagnosis. It's the first clue that his symptoms aren't all from falling off her roof.
- House buys lollipops at a newspaper stand, and is also sucking on them during an earlier meeting with Wilson and Cuddy. He's sucking one when he walks out of the hospital with Foreman and Chase. He also puts sugar in his coffee this episode. Hope he has a good dentist.
- "The first casualty of this case is her sense of humor," House says, to which Wilson replies, "That's weird, nothing funny about almost killing a guy." It's another bit of foreshadowing. Alfredo has fallen off her roof, but at this point, the prescribed protein C hasn't done its nasty work yet.
- The clinic patient parallels the themes of race and privilege in that he doesn't want to take the "African-American targeted" drugs — from either Foreman or House.
- It's revealed that House and Cuddy were both at University of Michigan, at the same time.
- We learn that House has been fired by four hospital administrations.

Booboos

- Cuddy may be the Dean of Medicine, but she's not an emergency medical technician. While she might ride in the ambulance, she wouldn't be permitted to take over Alfredo's care there.
- The blood on Cuddy's tank top is closer to red paint in color than it is to blood.

What's Up, Doc?

- Fans have pointed out that the neck brace Alfredo wears in the ambulance is not on correctly.
- Fact: There have been fewer than 50 cases of human infection of parrot fever since 1996.

2.4 TB or Not TB

First aired: November 1, 2005
Writer: David Foster
Director: Peter O'Fallon
Guest stars: Joram Moreka (Father), Hansford Prince (Bogale), Andrea Bendewald (Cecelia Carter), Harry F. Brockington IV (Dahoma), Ken Weiler (Jerry), Mary Wickliffe (Mandi), Ron Livingston (Dr. Sebastian Charles)

Episode Differential

It's hard to hate a selfless western doctor trying to save the lives of millions of the poorest on the planet, but House makes a go of it nonetheless.

As a plane lands at a sub-Sahara African village, tuberculosis expert Dr. Sebastian Charles emerges with boxes of TB medication as the villagers swarm around, welcoming him. The greeting is cut short as a young boy falls to the ground with a collapsed lung. The opening cuts to a pharmaceutical company in New Jersey where Sebastian is presenting the boy's case (his lungs were chewed through by untreated TB) as an example, trying to get more medicine donated. During the presentation, Sebastian becomes feverish and collapses while someone shouts, "Isn't anyone here a doctor?" It comes off comedic in a big-pharma board room.

In Cuddy's office, the case is given to House, where he explains his distaste for grandstanding doctors. "The nameless poor have a face, and it's a pompous white man," he observes. In some ways then, this episode continues last week's theme. Back at the team's table, Sebastian wanders in (hospital-gown clad) and asks to sit in on the differential. Irking House further, Sebastian is insistent that he has TB and — making House scream ever louder — the team agrees. House suspects rightly that Sebastian will use the positive diagnosis of TB as an opportunity for a press push. He makes it a mission to prove Sebastian wrong with a series of cardiac tests (including a tilt table stress test with House at the controls).

During all this, Cameron and Sebastian begin flirting, with him telling her to come to his clinic in Africa, that it will change her life. It's logical that the do-good character of Cameron would be intrigued by this patient, but it should be noted that her character is frequently used for minor romantic drama and humor in ways that the other characters on the show (even other female ones such as Cuddy) seldom are. Wilson's marriages get little more than one-liners, Foreman's pharmaceutical romance quickly dissolves, and Chase's character is really only used to service Cameron.

While House has a temporary diagnosis of a PR abnormality (the patient will need a pacemaker), Cameron goes behind House's back to administer a skin test to confirm TB. When the test comes back positive the hospital attempts treatment but Sebastian refuses and indeed calls a press conference to announce he'll refuse the medicine that is denied to millions worldwide who can't afford it. House sulks, retreating to his coma patient's room with Wilson, watching the press conference unfold live. Noticing that Sebastian is becoming disorientated and that with the hot lights, he should be turning red, House charges into the room declaring that Sebastian is about to go into cardiac arrest. Thinking there is a problem with his insulin, the team believes he has an invisible pancreatic tumor. It's confirmed after a calcium tolerance test and Sebastian concedes defeat and accepts treatment for the TB as well.

As he's packing for his trip back to Africa, Cameron hands Sebastian a six-month supply of TB medication. He slyly suggests she can deliver the next shipment and she slyly refuses, suggesting that her heart still lies closer to House. Up above on their patio, Wilson and House muse about whether by saving Sebastian's life House is responsible for also saving the lives Sebastian saves.

Highlight

After having Foreman cover for clinic under his name, House has been ordered to apologize to an overanxious woman who believes she has breast cancer. Apparently, Foreman was dismissive. Not wanting to reveal the ruse, House runs into the woman at the clinic, literally. He acts the part of the cripple and gestures apologetically, making sure Cuddy is listening from the other side of the glass as he apologizes.

Support Staff
- House uses it to shove Sebastian's cell phone down the toilet.
- House uses it when he stomps the foot of the woman to whom he's supposed to apologize.

Lies
- Foreman wears House's nametag to clinic during House's scheduled shift.
- When House spots Cuddy together with his/Foreman's patient, he covers the House-Foreman mix-up by speaking of himself in the third person. This allows the woman to believe that

Foreman is House without raising Cuddy's suspicion.

- House knows Sebastian has TB, but is unwilling to confirm it.
- House steals a steak from the cafeteria by covering it with his salad.
- When *Newsweek* calls seeking information about Sebastian, House mouths off and then says, "Yeah, you can quote me." He spells out Cuddy's name.
- Sebastian says he feels well enough to take the stairs. Ten seconds later, he's tumbled to the landing, taking Cameron with him and pinning her.

Exam Room

- House trades in his regular Nikes for Converse this episode.
- When *Newsweek* phones, the phone displays the time as 1:53 and the abbreviated date is September 7, 2005.
- Cameron isn't going to learn a thing from her topple down the stairs with Sebastian. She'll get pulled over by a patient again in season three's "Que Será Será." This one may have caught her unawares, but you'd think she'd know better by then than to let her patients overexert themselves before discharge.
- Wilson misses his mouth when eating trail mix. Granola boy continues the scene without missing a beat.
- Normally the episodes air in fairly real time, meaning that holiday episodes have aired alongside their actual holidays. This episode is dated to September but airing in November.
- There's a reference to Chase's father in the present tense. The last time Chase's father appeared to us was in "Cursed," which was set in January 2005. At that point, Chase's father had three months to live. Fans have puzzled over the timeline, as well as Chase's age, which he gives as 30 in "Autopsy," to the little girl, but 26 in season one's "Cursed," to Wilson.

Booboos

- Fans have pointed out that Sebastian's pill cup contains different pills than what he pours out onto his tray.
- As House apologizes, his cane is in his right hand as per usual. In his left, he carries his backpack. Later, as Cuddy watches, the items are reversed.
- House and Wilson discuss the Nobel Peace Prize. Nobel Prizes

are awarded in Stockholm, but the Peace Prize specifically is awarded in Oslo.

What's Up, Doc?

The TB diagnosis is dropped before the show can get into the type he might have, i.e. infectious. No X-ray is done to confirm the skin test, and Sebastian continues to wander all over the hospital, which is fine, assuming he doesn't have infectious TB.

2.5 Daddy's Boy

First aired: November 8, 2005
Writer: Thomas L. Moran
Director: Greg Yaitanes
Guest stars: Bobbin Bergstrom (O.R. Nurse), R. Lee Ermey (John House), Diane Baker (Blythe House), Brian D. Johnson (Taddy's Boss), Jon Hershfield (Timekeeper), Mackenzie English (Katrina), Brian Chase (EMT), Matt McKenzie (Dr. Fedler), Wil Horneff (Taddy), Clifton Powell (Ken Hall), Vicellous Shannon (Carnell Hall)

Episode Differential

It's always a grim episode of *House* when the patient doesn't make it, but "Daddy's Boy" allows for the introduction of House's own "history" as well as exploring paternal dynamics.

A father and son exit a restaurant. The son, Carnell Hall, has just graduated from Princeton. His father, a hardworking scrap yard owner, admonishes him to go easy at the graduation party that night. Carnell assures him that he will, but on the jump cut to the bar Carnell is seen downing shots like an underage girl at Senior Toads. He suddenly experiences electric-like shocks, which throw his body to the ground in a series of frightening seizures.

Wilson catches the case first but brings it to House when all his tests prove inclusive. All usual suspects for shocks are ruled out, leading the team to suspect a latent infection of some kind. Meanwhile, Cameron witnesses House having a tense phone call with his mother. Digging further, as Cameron is always prone to do when House is involved, she discovers that House's parents will be in New Jersey for a stop over and that he's begging off dinner reservations through any excuse he can find. Over the course of the episode, we'll learn that House is close with his mother — but can't lie to her — and distant from his father, simply disliking him all-around. Devoted Laurie fans will have realized that this is an almost inverse dynamic to his own real life. As mentioned in chapter two, his mother largely ignored him but he shared many common interests with his father.

Thinking there's something more than what his patient is telling him, House fishes out of Carnell the secret trip he made to Jamaica with his rich college friends over spring break. House — in what is a series standby explanation — thinks Carnell smoked pesticide-laden weed and prescribes pralidoxime to clear out the toxin.

During an investigation of Carnell's friends from the trip, Cameron interviews "Taddy" at his new internship and discovers he has a groin rash. It's thought to be nothing as no one else has similar symptoms. Carnell, however, is still having shocks and his immune system is shot. House is dumbfounded until Taddy is brought into emergency, having started vomiting blood. Ripping off Taddy's pants the rash has blistered out and House asks if he slept with Carnell in Jamaica. Shocked, Taddy replies, "I'm not gay," with House snapping back, "I didn't ask if you were gay, I asked if you had sex," showing with a single line, the complex social dynamics the program's writers understand and are willing to explore on network television.

In the midst of the exchange, Taddy reveals Carnell's father's occupation — something Carnell and his father have hidden until now. Cue the House "brain flash" and he's off to confront Carnell's father. Dad reveals that he found a unique-looking plumb and made it into a key chain to remind Carnell where he came from. The device was an improperly disposed probe for checking weld strengths: Carnell has received the equivalent of 10,000 chest X-rays.

A tense exchange in the cafeteria occurs between House and his father (a retired air force pilot) starting with House's motorcycle, which, his father points out, looks odd parked in a disabled parking spot. After, when Cameron redoubts her interfering, Wilson offers up that House is a disappointment to his parents. Not understanding what he's getting at — House is a world famous doctor after all, what parent wouldn't be proud? — Wilson points out to Cameron that their son is miserable.

Highlight

While Cameron examines Taddy at his New York office after hours — an examination of his groin that looks suspicious from another angle — she darts up as Taddy's boss enters the room. Taddy blurts out that it's okay, "She's a doctor." His boss then asks if "the doctor" can leave her card on the way out.

Support Staff

- House passes it to Wilson before he mounts his motorcycle. Wilson passes it back, and House twirls it, snapping it into place on a holder on the bike.
- House uses it to dramatically sweep back the curtain to Carnell's room.
- We also get a cripple comment from Wilson: "You know what I figure is worse than watching your son become crippled? Watching him be miserable."

Lies

- Carnell lies to his father about his vacation.
- Mr. Hall lies to his son about his mother's death.
- Both Carnell and his father lie about what Dad does for a living.
- House lies to Wilson about needing the money for a "car."
- House says he can't lie to his mother, and in fact, goes to great lengths to ensure that he is busy, but telling the truth.
- Wilson lies to House about canceling the group dinner with his parents. He takes the check House offers in exchange, but reneges.

Exam Room

- Wilson has lent House money to buy a new car. House has a new ride, but it's no Volvo like Wilson's.
- House also has a new leather jacket, which Cameron can't help but comment on with some derision. Just when you thought she was into bad boys.
- The motorcycle love is one that House shares with Laurie, and, as stated earlier in this biography, it's another example of the character elements that Laurie brought to the role independently. It fits with House's rakish and risk-taking

personality, but it also draws on Laurie's own life skills.

- House's new game system is the Sony PSP.
- We learn a bit more about House's background this episode — what his parents, John and Blythe House, expected of him, that there are no real big secrets, he simply doesn't like his dad. . . . Note that House's mom's name is synonymous for happy — Happy House.
- Cameron shows her curiosity by attempting to orchestrate a meeting of staff and family. In payback, House compares her to his father. Is it the similarity between them that keeps House always at arm's length from Cameron?
- When House has dinner in the cafeteria with his parents, a despicable pickle is visible on his plate.

Booboos

Unless the father just started working in the scrap yard, he would know about the dangers surrounding things that wind up there. He wouldn't have given the son such a talisman.

2.6 Spin

First aired: November 15, 2005
Writer: Sara Hess
Director: Fred Gerber
Guest stars: Sela Ward (Stacy Warner), Julie Quinn (Matthew's Mother), Patrick Roman Miller (Maintenance Man), Kristoffer Polaha (Jeff Forster), Austin Whitlock (Matthew), Nathan Kress (Scott), Scott Kradolfer (Matthew's Father), Drew Garner (Blind Man), Currie Graham (Mark Warner), Taraji Henson (Moira), Alanna Ubach (Dr. Louise Harper), Tom Lenk (Allen)

Episode Differential

House has torn down a sports icon before, but "Spin" adds a new spin to the procedure with an overly honest, overly doped athlete. This episode shows how far an athlete will go to win, and also how far House will go to win Stacy back.

Opening at an exhibition cycling race, a family tries to catch the riders on the turn-around so their son can see his hero, Jeff Hastert. While running, the young boy begins wheezing, setting us up for the second fake-out of the second season, when Jeff collapses causing a pile up and flurry of dust and broken bikes.

Bored with the prospect of diagnosing a pro athlete as being on steroids in 30 seconds, House isn't interested in the case but accepts when Jeff admits to taking everything imaginable — except the deadly "Epo" (erythropoietin, a synthesized protein that causes increased red blood cell production and is almost guaranteed to cause strokes). While House believes Jeff, Cameron finds his doping — when weighed against the expectations of his fans — to be despicable.

No athlete, House meanwhile competes with Stacy's husband Mark — even going so far as to try to join his group therapy as a way to undermine his confidence. When this tactic doesn't work, House resorts to other measures, not least one which, like the next play in the disease plot (a leak), establishes a more subtle theme than that of competition. Wanting his own extra edge, House breaks into the office of Stacy's counselor, securing all the information he needs to step up his attacks on Mark and get Stacy back. The act immediately turns the viewer against House; but its drama is too appealing to resist.

When the media is tipped off that Jeff may have cancer, Stacy demands the entire team's cell phone records to determine who leaked it. Because of the good girl's vocal opposition to Jeff's cheating, the suspect is, of course, Cameron — but it turns that Jeff's voracious manager has planted the leak herself, hoping a cancer rumor would not only deflect accusations of doping but increase his sponsorship pull. House also accuses Jeff's manager of secretly giving him Epo, which would explain all his symptoms. At a loss when Jeff doesn't get better, House wonders if "normal" is not normal for an athlete artificially enhancing everything about his body.

Highlight

House injects Jeff with Tensilon to relive the symptoms of his condition and commands, "You are healed! Rise and walk." When Jeff responds, "Are you insane?" House declares, "In the Bible, you just say 'Yes Lord' and then start right in on the praising." After Jeff does indeed walk, House then reveals the Tensilon is diagnostic and "Only works for five minutes." When the patient collapses on the floor House continues, "or less."

Support Staff

- A bored House uses it to start a domino experiment across his desk, toppling CDs, books, and other items until, at the end of the line, his Vicodin falls into his waiting hand.

- He cocks it like a gun, making a reloading sound, when he thinks he's found the answer.
- House uses it as an excuse so the janitor will let him in to the therapist's office.

Lies

- Jeff admits to using drugs. He doesn't lie about that.
- The manager originally tells the press that what's wrong with Jeff is as likely to be acid reflux as drugs.
- House lies to get into the therapy session.
- House claims to want in to the therapist's office to retrieve his cane.
- The manager did make the call to the media to leak the cancer diagnosis.
- House accuses her of doing more than that, but she's telling the truth — she didn't mess with Jeff's doping.

Exam Room

- Normally House only pulls out the Mommy-Daddy lines around his staff, but this time he speaks to Stacy as if he and she are the mutual children when Cuddy enters the room.
- House was excited about treating an athlete from major league baseball ("Sports Medicine"). Is his reluctance to take Jeff's case an indicator of where cycling falls in his list of favorite sports?
- House pops his own little helper while Jeff admits to blood doping, saying that he does what he must to make him better at his job. Oh, the comedy.
- Stacy and House gear up for a combative flirtation that will provide the plot arc for season two. Other characters are often used to point out House's flaws so that viewers won't have to. This episode Stacy cautions him about having his only female employee complete his clerical work, saying it is one step away from sexual harassment.
- Only six episodes into the new season, House asks Cuddy if she can get rid of Stacy. Make note that Cuddy did give House a choice before she hired Stacy.

- Chase is the only team member who thinks that cheating can be acceptable. While Foreman disapproves of the cyclist's doping, he believes that those who put their faith in athletes deserve to be deceived. Cameron is livid at Jeff's deceiving children with his greatness. Meanwhile, Chase claims that issues aren't always black and white. The stance fits with Chase's own turncoat nature, but it goes against his seminary background. We can't help but wonder: how did this guy ever follow testaments carved into stone tablets?
- Looking at the imaging for Jeff's MRI, Cameron implies to Foreman the athlete deserves all he's getting. It's a cold side to Cameron we haven't seen much of yet.
- House steals Wilson's plain Lays potato chips in the cafeteria, but allows Wilson to keep his sandwich. House also alludes to his call-girl habit, as they discuss Stacy and Mark's relationship and whether or not they have serious marital issues. An inveterate thief, House ends by helping himself to some of Mark's apple pie. We know what he'd really like to help himself to.
- Stacy calls House and Mark "Noel Coward and Oscar Wilde in the third grade," both gay British wits.
- Once again, House compares himself to God.
- Care for some coffee with your sugar, House?
- House really knows no bounds in this episode. We see him take on Mark in the most juvenile and aggressive ways, stopping at nothing in his attempt to dupe/overpower the man whose life he saved only a short time ago.
- Cuddy is logged on to DocMixer.com and we hear her talking to a prospective date on the phone.

Booboos

- It makes for a funny scene, but no responsible doc would ever tell the patient to rise and walk. After all, when he collapses only a few minutes later, he's at risk of injuring himself. But that's okay, because we all know this is TV, a wonderful fantasy.
- Similarly, House would never be able to yell, "Nurse, clean-up in aisle four," unless he really *did* want that harassment lawsuit on his hands. House constantly belittles what the nurses do, maybe because in *House*land the diagnosticians do what

nurses normally would — TB skin tests, drawing blood, etc.
- The therapist would never let House into a session with Mark, knowing they have bad blood between them. House has been working for the hospital long enough (eight years), and the therapist is familiar enough with his leg damage and all-around damaged persona, that she wouldn't allow it to carry into a group session.
- Similarly, it's a bit weird that Stacy sees the same therapist, especially considering she's worked for the hospital only a short while. Seems like a woman of her age and her career would have already had a trusted therapist whom she'd been seeing for a while — off-site.

2.7 Hunting

First aired: November 22, 2005
Writer: Liz Friedman
Director: Gloria Muzio
Guest stars: Sela Ward (Stacy Warner), Hamilton Mitchell (Infection Control Officer), Currie Graham (Mark Warner), Wings Hauser (Michael Ryan), Matthew John Armstrong (Kalvin Ryan)

Episode Differential

An early highlight of season two, "Hunting" gives the show a needed jolt of sass, sex, and intrigue as House hunts a rat (and Stacy), and Cameron faces death and a naked Chase simultaneously.

The episode opens on Wilson and House leaving his building, where Kalvin, an HIV-positive gay man who's been trying to get House's attention for weeks, confronts them. He claims his T cell count is up but he continues to get sicker. House reiterates that Kalvin has full-blown AIDS, end of story. As House and Wilson leave, Kalvin grabs House's cane, which he uses to push Kalvin away. Kalvin falls backwards against a car and goes into sudden anaphylactic shock. He's definitely House's patient now.

At the hospital, the team runs down possibilities of opportunistic infections while Kalvin flirts with Chase. When Chase is deemed "Cute . . . and sensitive," the declaration receives a noticeable eye-rolling from

Cameron, whom Kalvin has also sized up as someone who doesn't have much fun with life. Later, while examining Kalvin, Cameron receives a spray of potentially lethal blood in her eyes and mouth when he begins coughing. While the public health officer deems her likelihood of sero-conversion to be small, she's put onto prophylactic treatment and scheduled for a series of HIV tests.

As Kalvin slips into cardiac failure, he tells Cameron to tell his father that he's sorry. For House, it's a clue, since gay sons on their deathbeds are usually never the ones giving apologies. In spite of her opposition to drugs only one episode ago, Cameron has taken Kalvin's advice about having more fun. Obviously some of Kalvin's confiscated crystal meth has made its way home with her. She's cranked, horny, and playing loud dance music when Chase arrives. He finds her with hair teased out, almost possessed looking. It takes him only a second to assess the situation and ask if she's high. She attacks him, pushing him against the wall with kisses, and ripping off his clothes. The next morning House diagnoses her "hangover" as something more than a hangover and within minutes, outs Chase as having taken advantage of a co-worker high on meth.

House's own romance has been heating up. Armed with private information about Stacy (that she still has feelings for him, that she and Mark aren't having sex, and that he's not doing the dishes), House insinuates himself into her life while Mark attends therapy. House shows up at her home and pointedly starts doing the dishes while helping Stacy hunt down a rat. We know of course that House is the rat this episode, but that doesn't stop us from rooting for him just a little.

At the hospital, Kalvin's father has arrived from Montana and while the two aren't speaking to each other, House not only finds out what Kalvin feels sorry about (he couldn't donate a kidney to his now deceased mother because of his HIV) but also suspects that the father's cirrhosis and Kalvin's heart condition are linked by a parasite common to wild animals.

In an episode where everyone (except Stacy) is behaving like a wild animal, House takes the opportunity to goad dear old Dad. When the father cold cocks House, he hits back with a precision cane strike to the liver. As the father goes into anaphylaxis, the diagnosis is made. The episode closes with father and son reuniting over the end music, but not before Cameron takes Kalvin to task for "recruiting" her into a life of fun that's anything but.

Highlight

Without a doubt, when Cameron "taps" Chase. He rips his shirt off like he's been waiting to do so for the entire season. Similarly, a hopped-up Cameron is quite a sight.

Support Staff

- House and Kalvin fight over it; House lets go and Kalvin falls, sparking his attack.
- House uses it to lift the toilet seat in Stacy's house, to further the distance between Mark and her.
- House raises it to kill the rat, but doesn't strike.
- House uses it in a liver blow on Kalvin's dad after baiting Dad to punch him.

Lies

- House lies about liking to do dishes, having changed, and all the other sensitive crap he lays out for Stacy like a rat trap.
- Stacy lied about smoking — back when she and House were together, she tried to keep it hidden. And she's lying about it now with Mark.
- Cameron steals some of Kalvin's meth, but admits to it pretty quickly. Of course, she'd be a fool not to since she goes into work when she's still coming down.
- Kalvin says getting HIV was the best thing that ever happened to him. He means it, but as Cameron points out, it's an awfully lonely hospital stay.

Exam Room

- The number on House's place couldn't get more Sherlock Holmes — it's 221B. Holmes' was 221B Baker Street.
- We get a reference to House and Wilson as a couple when Kalvin comes by House's place asking for treatment. There are arguments galore about whether Watson (Holmes' Wilson) was a partner to Sherlock in every sense.
- As House so often does, he takes his Vicodin while discussing someone else's drug use, in this case, Kalvin's.
- Unfortunately, there are no references to Lisa Edelstein's 1980s performance, *Positive Me*, even though this episode feels designed for one.

- Fans have pointed out that the wall calendar in Stacy's kitchen is from 1975.
- Cameron's HIV predicament, House's own hunting of Stacy, and her attic rat's symptoms take the place of any clinic patients.
- We're introduced to Steve McQueen, House's new favorite rat.
- We see a more tender side of House this episode as he apologizes to Stacy for pushing her away. We also see that he's been a cataloguer of other people's quirks and habits for many years . . . he knew how many cigarettes she was smoking while they were breaking up, even though she hid the act from him.
- The song playing at Cameron's is "Crystalline Green" by Goldfrapp — believable. Cameron looks like she could be a Goldfrapp girl.
- "Come on, Chase — don't turn into a good guy on me now," Cameron says. It's funny, because she's nailed Chase's personality in one line. His life philosophy vacillates between "goodness and duty" and "every man for himself."

Booboos

An excellent catch in terms of the show's logical errors was made by SciFiGeekNJ on the site www.housemd.guide.com: "How does a man who can't walk leave the toilet seat up?"

What's Up, Doc?

You'd think they'd be taking more precautions around Kalvin — before and after the coughing incident.

2.8 The Mistake

First aired: November 29, 2005
Writer: Peter Blake
Director: David Semel
Guest stars: Sela Ward (Stacy Warner), Stephanie Venditto (Nurse Brenda), Greg Winter (Chuck), Sammi Hanratty (Dory), Kate Enggren (Mrs. Ayersman), Adair Tishler (Nikki), Licia Shearer (Clinic Patient), Ryan Hurst (Sam McGinley), Kevin Moon (EMT), Sterling Beaumon (Boy Magician), John Lafayette (Dr. Schisgal), Allison Smith (Kayla McGinley), John Rubenstein (Dr. Ayersman)

Episode Differential

When Japanese director Akira Kurasawa made his 1950 film *Rashoman*, telling a story of a crime several different ways through several different characters, he couldn't have known the impact its narrative experiment would have — even all the way to television in 2005. "The Mistake" opens on a tracking shot through the backstage of an elementary school talent show. Kayla, a young single mother, preps her daughters for a routine. She returns to her seat to watch the show only to start writhing in abdominal agony.

After the credits, however, a title card tells us "Six Months Later," the first and only time we'll have this kind of open. Often there's a slight time lag between the victim's flare up and when they arrive at Princeton-Plainsboro or come to House's attention, but normally these time indicators are written into the dialogue, and are only a few weeks.

Kayla, the mother from the introductory scene, is dead and while Stacy prepares for the disciplinary hearing, the backstory is shaped and reshaped by different tellings. It begins with Chase being sent to do a pelvic examine to confirm Becet's disease in Kayla, after pissing House off by spilling his Vicodin. The story within a story or the as-told-to technique allows for many playful moments: Chase omits the spilling of the Vicodin when talking to Stacy because she says it's not important — until she realizes the patient switched hands between Foreman and Chase. Then we're shown the dramatized missing scene.

Chase administers a 24-hour skin test and tells Kayla that any doctor can look at the results the next day. Kayla returns to see Chase standing in the clinic lobby on the phone. As we learn later, after several different versions of this meeting, Chase has just been told of the death of his father, whom (thanks to House) he didn't even know was ill. Distracted, Chase looks at the skin test and tells Kayla to book an appointment with rheumatology. Ironically rheumatology was his father's specialty.

When Kayla turns back for what doctors know as the "door-knob question," or the embarrassing symptom turnaround, Chase, in his distraction, doesn't fish out what it is she wants to say and lets her go. Later that day, Kayla returns to the hospital through emergency, vomiting blood. The team attempts to cauterize her stomach ulcers but it is too late — an ulcer has perforated, leaking stomach acids into her gut and causing permanent damage to her liver. That's two different mistakes and two different versions and we're only 10 minutes in.

Kayla's brother Sam, a pushy New Jersey kind of guy demands that the team let him donate half his liver. When the hospital counsels against the transplant, House badly bribes and then blackmails a surgeon to perform the operation. The brother pays a friend at a lab to rush the necessary tests. As we'll learn later, this is another mistake. The surgery goes well with both patients recovering, but on a follow-up visit it's discovered that Kayla is rejecting the liver. During a heated exchange between House and the brother — after noticing old, cheap tattoos on his arm — House accuses him of having hepatitis. House announces he may have given his sister liver cancer. With a rejected liver and a barring from the transplant list, Kayla is told she'll likely die. She accepts the news stoically, knowing that her rejected liver was a clue that has now saved her brother's life.

On Sam's follow-up visit, Chase pulls his own turnaround, telling the brother, "I killed your sister." He says that he should have asked her if there was anything else wrong but he was drunk and hung over. Of course, he wasn't. But his sympathies have gotten the better of him and — either showing he truly possesses the guilt of a Catholic or else that Chase is so turn-coat that he will even turn against himself — he is driven to self-sabotage.

The question is: what version will he tell to the disciplinary committee? House, with his own version of events, tells Chase to tell the truth. In the end, Chase is suspended for a week but House, because of the blackmail allegations, has been "sentenced" to having his department supervised for a month by . . . Foreman. Like a simple lesson in quantum physics, for every mistake in this episode a new, possible, subjective reality was presented.

Highlight

Stacy says, "What are you hiding?" House replies, *"I'm gay.* Oh, that's not what you meant. Does explain a lot though . . . No girlfriend, always with Wilson, obsession with sneakers."

Support Staff

House twirls it as he waits to hear from the committee.

Lies

- Chase lies to Stacy by omitting details — such as writing Kayla a prescription, and the reality of the telephone conversation he was having when Kayla interrupted.
- Stacy lies to Chase to get away for a few minutes (that she gets cranky when she skips her coffee) to try to fish further answers out of Cameron, Foreman, and House about Chase's mistake.
- Foreman reveals that Chase tells patients a phony story about having his tonsils removed in order to bond with them; Chase still has his tonsils.
- House lies to the clinic patient when he attempts to scare him into securing medical insurance. He tells Cuddy the patient only has a cold, and now insurance.
- Sensing House is attempting to cover for Chase, Stacy attempts to get further answers from Cameron, who won't disclose.
- The brother, Sam, fudged his tests and hid his hepatitis.
- The surgeon has been cheating on his wife and lying about it.
- Chase lies to Sam, saying he was hung over.

Exam Room

- In the opening sequence, Kayla references Aretha Franklin growing up in Detroit. Franklin was born in Memphis, Tennessee, and moved to Boston, and Chicago, before Detroit became her home. It was there, at the age of 14, that she signed her first record deal.
- Sally Ayersman is the name of the girl who has been teasing Kayla's daughters. Kayla mutters that she'll key Sally's daddy's new convertible. Later, Ayersman is the surname of the surgeon House attempts to bribe, and his wife ends up keying his con-

vertible after she gets an anonymous tip about his cheating.

- House and Wilson are playing a game with quarters. Frequently in storytelling, quarters are used to symbolize choice, the idea of making a decision with a coin toss. In this episode, we see the consequences behind some of those momentary decisions — House's and Chase's.

- Chase bonds with the patient during her pelvic exam. It seems an unlikely time to have a personal conversation, but they talk about her mother's death, and also his mother's alcoholism.

- When House and Wilson do their mid-episode walk-and-talk, Wilson points out that the fact that he never met Kayla doesn't exculpate him; it inculpates him. If we think of this in the same terms as a regular case, this conversation is the clue for the audience as to the outcome. Wilson says outright that House is responsible for everything that happens in his department.

- House and the lollipops again: lollipop, lollipop, oh lolly lolly lolly . . .

- House also challenges Stacy this episode about her anger, telling her, "You're mad at me for letting you know what I did because you liked where things were going." She doesn't deny it.

- We see House in this episode being what he is and is always trying so hard to prove he is: a boss. This time we see him do it well. There's been bad blood between Chase and him before, but this is no time for it to cloud his judgment. Can we assume it's not just the guilt of letting Chase get that off-guard phone call, but also a dedication to standing up for his team that leads House to tell the story as he does in the hearing?

What's Up, Doc?

Chase is still wearing his gloves in the midst of performing a pelvic exam on Kayla, when he flips through her medical records. Pretty standard to peel off the gloves and dispose of them properly before handling anything else.

2.9 Deception

First aired: December 13, 2005
Writer: Michael R. Perry
Director: Deran Sarafian
Guest stars: Patrick LoSasso (Do-Gooder), Larry Weissman (Fat Man), Xhercis (Imelda), Nell Rutledge (Hailey), Bru Muller (John), David Desantos (ER Doctor), Peter Abbay (Cab Driver), Rod Britt (Teller), Cynthia Nixon (Anica Jovanovich)

Episode Differential

So what does House do for fun? Besides monster truck rallies, apparently he also enjoys the sights, sounds, and (at least in New Jersey) smells of off-track betting.

At an OTB on a snowy night House encounters Anica — an obvious racing junkie — at the kiosk. They flirt in the manner that House appreciates best; she puts him down. After the race begins Anica collapses to the floor in a seizure. House calls out, "Isn't anyone here a doctor?"

With no signs of fever and with strange bruises and anemia, House thinks Cushing's but, as set up in the last episode, Foreman is in charge for the month and he suspects alcoholism. When House takes Anica's history — a series first, with a form even — and flirts even more with her, she reveals that she's "had" Cushing's already.

With an MRI proving inconclusive and the team squabbling under Foreman's leadership — Cameron burns from not even being considered to lead the department for the month — a more detailed scan shows a mass on Anica's pancreas. When Cameron has Anica sign the consent form for the biopsy she nonchalantly signs it without even asking about the procedure. It's behavior that Cameron thinks is consistent with Munchausen's syndrome (faking illness for attention).

Cameron and House jockey for control of the case while Foreman complains to Cuddy about House driving him nuts. Cuddy dangles the possibility that the position could be permanent. Cameron the Righteous then surreptitiously leaves a bottle of Rifampin in Anica's room with a fake "dangerous" label on it. When it's revealed that Anica took the Rimfampin, the diagnosis of Munchausen's is confirmed but House isn't convinced.

Anica is discharged but House meets her outside for a leveling session. He knows the Munchausen's is true but he also knows that her anemia is real. He'll give her a cocktail of insulin and colchicine that will make her seize and get her readmitted. But, he cautions, if she's taking anything to cause the anemia, she'll die. We know how far she'll go for the attention; this is how far House will go to be right.

If House shows greater interest in Anica, it's largely due to their shared addictions. She craves fabricating problems; he lives to solve them. They both love racing. They both take drugs they don't need. Though Anica promised to get counseling for her Munchausen's, we last see her in a new emergency room with a new set of "problems." Like House, her addictions are bigger than she is. Meanwhile, Foreman meets with Cuddy, asking if she was serious about the offer. He's shocked when Cuddy points out that paper work getting done is one thing but his orders to discharge Anica would have caused her to die on the curb if House hadn't dosed her.

Highlight
House complains to Cuddy, "Chase killed that woman, and now Foreman's in charge?" And Cuddy replies, "Yeah, we have a pecking order here; if Cameron kills somebody, Chase takes over. There's a flow chart in the lobby."

Support Staff
- "Cripple coming through," House says at the racetrack as he's trying to make his bet in time.
- He threatens it up-yours style to Foreman because he's mad about the readjustment of power since "The Mistake."
- House stashes it on his motorcycle when he doubles Cameron against her better judgment.

Lies
- House botches the LP, not because he can't do one, but because he believes it will cause a reaction that will confirm his diagnosis.
- Munchausen's means the patient lies for medical attention. Anica lies about what she's done to herself to make herself seem sick.
- Cameron baits Anica with the medication she leaves in her room, trapping her in a lie.
- When he gives her the injection, House asks her to admit which of her symptoms are real and which self-induced —

or she'll die.

- House lies to the team about giving her the injection.

Exam Room

- Anica references Franklin Roosevelt's polio. The actress, Cynthia Nixon, played his wife Eleanor in the TV movie *Warm Springs* (2005).
- This is one of the few episodes where House takes a real interest in interacting with the patient. He may only be assigned to take the patient's history — a part of the procedure he usually avoids if possible, and yes, he is letting her fill out the forms herself — but they have common ground (betting), and a flirtation. One of the only other patients he has spent real time with is the schizophrenic mom who's not actually schizophrenic ("The Socratic Method"). Since this girl doesn't turn out to be what she seems either, maybe House just has a think for crazy girls? Then again, he has no interest in listening to her "issues," once she starts to rattle them off.
- In contrast, Foreman, in his new role as boss, is conveniently absent.
- The team's biases come out again on this one, as Foreman suddenly thinks it's alcoholism, and Chase thinks women at betting parlors must be prostitutes. Isn't Chase usually the one claiming the problem is alcohol? But that would mean Foreman would have to think the patient was faking — as he did in "Histories" — and oops, this patient *is* faking! So that won't work. The show bucks its own formula here. Cameron is willing to pursue true diseases, but is not willing to have her time wasted by someone who isn't telling the truth.
- This episode echoes the ones where House would call Cuddy for a consult to waste her time (to prove that the clinic was a waste of his time). With Foreman in charge, House now calls him to look in on the clinic patient who's been using strawberry jelly for birth control.
- Cameron asks House how he would describe her leadership skills. He says, "Nonexistent . . . otherwise, excellent." Later, as he gloats about his diagnosis, she ranks his leadership skills by saying, "There's more to being a leader than being a jerk."

Booboos
Off-track betting parlors aren't legal in New Jersey.

2.10 Failure to Communicate

First aired: January 10, 2006
Writer: Doris Egan
Director: Jace Alexander
Guest stars: Sela Ward (Stacy Warner), Michael Len (Eight-Year-Old Boy), Amy Margolis (Mother), Derek Anthony (Guard), Pat Caldwell (Mary Jean), Bruce French (Peter Foster), Mimi Kennedy (Greta Simms), Erica Gimpel (Elizabeth Stone), Michael O'Keefe (Fletcher Stone)

Episode Differential

As House, in absentia, treats a patient who is speaking like Gertrude Stein, "Failure to Communicate" also has House and Stacy communicating a little too well. The episode is vital not only because it shows his power over Stacy, but because it shows his power in the hospital — his staff, as competent as they are, can barely hold things together without him.

At a *New Yorker*–like magazine office, former gonzo reporter Fletcher Stone is toasting his editor, who's retiring. During a speech in which he dictates how far they've come, and how many addictions he's given up for his new wife, he collapses, hitting his head on a desk. Addictions are a running theme throughout *House*, and frequently the patients grapple with the problem, serving as parallels for House himself. This is the second episode in a row where the patient has deeply rooted addiction problems. But addictions aren't his only problem: when Fletcher comes to, he begins speaking in gibberish but doesn't realize it.

At the hospital, Cuddy brings the case to the still-in-charge Foreman. House is in Baltimore with Stacy justifying his Medicaid billings. Noticing she's not wearing her mother's crucifix, he suspects that Mark and her have had a blowout.

Back in New Jersey, the team has their own individual theories and subject Fletcher to a battery of tests that yield mixed results, except for an old scar that's in the wrong region of the brain to be causing the symptoms. When House calls in to check on the case, the team is somewhat relieved. He instructs them to get a more accurate history and to find out what drugs the patient has taken. As uncommunicative as he is, Fletcher is even less communicative when his wife is in the room. Fletcher obviously isn't as clean as his wife thinks he is.

At the airport, the message comes through that all flights are cancelled. Stacy, however, has a room booked already and tells House with his leg he wouldn't last the night on a cot. At the hotel room, things heat up with Stacy and House as she describes their attraction using the analogy of vindaloo curry. Nasty hot, and you crave it, but it would kill you if it were your everyday dinner. Nevertheless, Stacy goes for a bit of the House curry, and the two kiss until the team interrupts with a dire phone call.

House leaves his moment with Stacy and sets up an ersatz whiteboard in the airport, using Stacy's lipstick to write with. It's more dramatic than a paper and pen and it plays into his OCD personality. The team and House stay up all night wracking their brains around Fletcher's nonsense phrase, "couldn't tackle the bear." As dawn breaks and Stacy joins him at the airport, House starts to figure the phrase out. Put on speakerphone with Fletcher and the team, House starts diagnosing the patient based on the riddle. Fletcher is bi-polar (as in polar bear). While talking the team through the final tense moments, discovering Fletcher's previous experimental brain surgery, House battles an airport security guard who demands that he either get on his scheduled flight or be arrested. Stacy and House part ways with him on the no-fly list and their future together uncertain.

Highlight
Stacy attempting to sample the House curry.

Support Staff
- House fiddles nervously with it during the meeting with the Medicaid man.
- Tossed on the bed as House and Stacy hold each other up.
- Stacy handles it on the bed, while House is busy.

Lies
- Fletcher lies to his wife about his reformed high-low lifestyle.
- His editor also doesn't disclose it to his wife, though she does tell the truth to the team.
- The team waits for an MRI, to which House retorts, "I teach

you to lie and cheat and steal, and the second my back is turned you wait in line!"

- Fletcher hides the brain surgery from his wife.
- Stacy is honest about what she wants.
- Stacy is cheating on her husband.

Exam Room

- House implies that the Medicaid man, who is close to retirement, is also on erectile enhancer when he says, "Little blue pills improve blood flow, they're vasodilators. That's why you sometimes get the headaches."
- When House phones Wilson to check in on his team, he speaks to him couple-like.
- House steals the ball of the boy who's bothering him in the airport.
- Did you notice House's in-flight reading selection? *Lesbian Prison Stories*.
- Stacy's lipstick is "Crimson Desire," humorous considering hers comes to the forefront.
- Famous historical individuals who suffered from aphasia include: American poet Ralph Waldo Emerson, Confederate general Robert E. Lee, Swedish cinematographer Sven Vilhem Nykvist (known for his work with the late Ingmar Bergman), and French composer/pianist Maurice Ravel. Cartoonist Lynn Johnston depicted a grandfather with aphasia in her 2006 comic strip *For Better or Worse*.

Booboos

- Would House and Stacy really *fly* to Baltimore from Jersey?
- As we've seen before ("Honeymoon"), Sela Ward isn't so good at pretending her coffee cup is full with a hot beverage. She's better at heating up the screen.
- In the airport, the pen alternates between being in Stacy's mouth and behind her ear.
- Fletcher has breathing problems and has to be intubated, but the breathing problems vanish pretty quickly.

What's Up, Doc?

According to Politedissent.com, House's billings could have been handled through the usual communications routes — i.e. without this trip. And even more likely, they would have been handled in the state where House practices, New Jersey. Then again, that would have left the House vindaloo simmering instead of poured into elegant serving bowls.

2.11 Need to Know

First aired: February 7, 2006
Writer: Pamela Davis
Director: David Semel
Guest stars: Sela Ward (Stacy Warner), Edward Kerr (Ted Dalton), Julie Warner (Margo Dalton), Currie Graham (Mark Warner), Holly Daniels (Debbie), Elle Fanning (Stella Dalton)

Episode Differential

It's a fact that on *House*, when the private lives of the hospital staff are in overdrive we're often given a less than compelling case. Here, a sub-urban mom's self-destructive behavior takes a backseat even when she's driving into a garage. Suburban "super mom" and real estate agent Margo Dalton is fighting with clients on the phone, running the big-screen football party, dropping her daughter off to karate and a birthday party, and giving out her favorite recipes all at the same time. On her way out to an emergency meeting, her arm twitches. Once in the car and driving away, she begins to spasm, driving the car back through the garage door.

At the hospital, post-Baltimore, House is happy, on time, and sharply dressed, enough so that Wilson suspects something happened on the trip. While House begins to look at Margo's symptoms, Wilson confronts Stacy over the kiss, imploring her to think about how much it would destroy House if things didn't work out.

After ruling out pregnancy and Huntington's as possible causes for Super Mom's symptoms, House falls back on his favorite explanation: drug use — perhaps because of his own? And, count it, this is the third patient in a row to either use drugs or exhibit addictive behaviors.

House discovers that Margo has been using Ritalin to keep up with her hectic life. She's discharged with the cloud of a severe fight with her husband looming large. But a stroke in the hallway sends the team to square one again. They call House at home and in a perfect pan over shot, we see the sleepy House is in bed with an equally shagged-out Stacy.

Deceptive spouses are clearly the theme of the episode, though viewers won't realize it until the patient's final secret is revealed. Even then, the drama in this episode will overshadow any link between patient and doc-plot, with the House/Stacy roof scene and the House/Mark confrontation scene more memorable than Super Mom.

Margo's the symptoms don't make any sense until House considers the absurd. What if a woman on fertility meds didn't want to get pregnant so simultaneously took the birth control pill as well? The pill — and its interaction with her fertility treatment — would explain all Margo's bizarre symptoms. House confronts the patient but, unwilling to admit that she doesn't want to have a child with her husband, she insists on the biopsy that will remove the tumor (and half her liver).

In an unusual turn that left fans — and Wilson — disappointed, House confronts Stacy in her office. She's packed an overnight bag and she's prepared to tell Mark. In an about-face, and chastened by what Margo was willing to go through, House tells Stacy to go home to Mark. Both Margo and House are willing to be miserable for love.

Highlight

House's fake-out of "Cameron, I love you," which leaves her shocked and agape enough that House can swab her mouth for the HIV test.

Support Staff

- House uses it to depress the elevator button when he arrives at the hospital in the morning.
- House wakes Margo up by slamming it on her tray.
- House jumps the wall to get into Wilson's locked office the back way, but in order to jump the wall, he has to avoid putting weight on his bad leg when he comes down.

Lies

- House tells the patient's daughter, Stella, that the balloon shape is a dog.
- Margot lies about taking her daughter's Ritalin.
- House pretends to have a tox screen where the Ritalin shows up, but it's actually the cafeteria menu.

- House is deceptive when he attempts to steal a joint from Wilson.
- Stacy cheats on Mark.
- House dupes Cameron so he can swab her mouth.
- Margo has been lying to her husband and all her friends about wanting another child. She's also been lying to her fertility doctor, since she's counteracting treatments.
- Foreman doesn't lie to Margo's husband. But relying on patient confidentiality, he avoids telling the truth.
- House opens Cameron's confidential test results, and dupes her by handing her a different still-sealed envelope.

Exam Room

- House is six minutes early for his shift — a first according to Wilson and Cuddy.
- Chase uses lots of honey in his tea.
- As usual when the episode focuses on a patient's sexuality, it also zooms in on the sex lives of the staff. Margo is playing two fertility methods off one another while Stacy's playing two men.
- House plays his cards too early with Stacy, asking her after only one night when she'll tell her husband. Does he really think one night with him is all she needs to erase three years with someone else?
- Foreman and House argue over treatment, as per usual, but this time the power struggle is due to Foreman's continued reign. House mocks him and calls him a "wuss." At midnight when Foreman's four weeks are up, House lets him know to the minute. Foreman mocks House back when House says "hoo-hoo," by saying "He went to Hopkins," setting up their rivalry as one that goes back to alma maters.
- Three different diagnoses were required to get to the bottom of the patient's symptoms. The show is accustomed to dealing with zebras, but as Politedissent.com points out, this is about as far as the show's writers could get from "Occam's Razor" — a theme and even show title from season one, wherein the simplest solution is usually right.
- House pops his Vicodin after telling Stacy to stay with her husband, as if it physically pains him to say it.

- The title refers to Cameron needing to get her HIV test, but does it also refer to House's need to know whether Stacy would leave her husband for him? He gets his answer — and doesn't let her.

What's Up, Doc?

Rather casually, Chase plops the tumor down, examines it under a microscope, and declares it benign. About as scientific as the time House told the lying 15-year-old boy he could read his age from his X-ray ("The Socratic Method").

2.12 Distractions

First aired: February 14, 2006
Writer: Lawrence Kaplow
Director: Daniel Attias
Guest stars: Stephanie Venditto (Brenda the Nurse), Judy Louise Johnson (Surgeon), Michael Merton (Anesthesiologist), Kristen Pate (Paula), Dorothea Harahan (EMT), Dan Butler (Dr. Phillip Weber), James Immekus (Adam), Lisa Darr (Emily), Christopher Cousins (Doug)

Episode Differential

High-tech tests, magnetic scans, and lumbar punctures are the norm in the world of *House*, where Medicaid and insurance plans seem to cover everything, but a special case presents special problems to the team.

A father and his teenage son, Adam, are riding an all-terrain quad along a country road. The son convinces his dad to let him drive. Uh oh. Adam soon seizes, forcing his grip on the gas and throwing his father off while he, still seizing, dives into one of those convenient piles of pipes that help cars blow up in action shows. He's taken to Princeton-Plainsboro.

House is interested, though he has his own "distraction" cooking up — something Cuddy finds out about when she's asked to introduce a speaker at the hospital. A migraine specialist she's never heard of was booked by House, whom she finds hanging around the coma room, suspiciously inducing a migraine in the comatose man. Coma Guy and House himself will serve as patients in an episode largely based in humor surrounding what House will go through over a long-ago grudge.

Adam is in a drug-induced coma until the worst of his healing is over (like House was following the infarction in his leg). Since Adam has severe burns over most of his body, the team cannot do any of their standard tests — no EKG, no punctures, and no communication. House suggests a galvanometer — a turn-of-the-century device that will measure his waves. Up next is a Doppler-sounding device to check for bleeds in Adam's brain. Foreman finds evidence of the bleed and goes to find House.

He's sitting — in bad incognito — at the lecture of the migraine specialist, Dr. Weber, who's pitching the virtues of his new migraine cure. They are joined by Wilson, who soon figures out that the lecturer is the same doctor who once ratted on House to the Dean at Johns Hopkins for cheating on a test. House begins heckling Weber while a mortified Wilson growls under his breath, "Get a hooker. Anything." House claims that the studies behind the medicine are flawed and that when he tested it on a coma patient it didn't stop a migraine. Realizing that the heckler is House, Weber lashes out, saying House still doesn't do his homework, or else he would have realized that coma patients can't be tested because of their atrophied frontal cortexes.

House uses himself as the guinea pig this time. In agony from the migraine, he's also in ecstasy over proving that the medication does not work. In an oxygen chamber, also with confused feelings, is Adam. The pain/pleasure divide is the theme of the episode with House expressing his pain at losing Stacy through his college revenge plots, and Adam's poor wracked body which doesn't comprehend the difference. Adam begins to twitch, not in pain but in what appears to be an orgasm. Tiring of the limits of the case, House demands that the anesthesiologist wake the patient up. Coming to in extreme pain, Adam manages to tell House that he wet his pants while on the vehicle. After suffering through the severe migraine, House doses himself with a cocktail of LSD and antidepressants to clear his head.

Both Cuddy and Wilson confront House over his destructive post-Stacy behavior. As if to prove all the jokes and asides on the series correct, the final shot is House coldly receiving an attractive escort at home.

Highlight
Literally, a high: House sees music while tripping the light fantastic in the shower.

Support Staff

- House curls up with it under the diagnostic table.
- Wilson accuses House of using the pain as a way to get his mind off Stacy. "Next time, stick a needle in your eye," he says, and taking a subtle swipe at House's disability: "It's less annoying to the rest of us when you can still walk."
- He walks without it from the shower to the bench. It's hung on the towel hook.
- House goes into the clean room without his cane. He exits without it too and Foreman brings it to him as he's giving the parents the good news.

Lies

- The dad says he signed 15 pages of paper saying he wouldn't let his son drive, but he does let his son drive, breaking his promise.
- The son agrees he'll go slow, but he doesn't. This seems like a lie until House proves that he wasn't in control of his own actions.
- House sets up a lecturer without Cuddy's knowledge. He forges a memo from her. House admits to having done it though.
- House tells Wilson he has sudden chills and light sensitivity — hence his get-up in the lecture hall.
- For years, House has been calling Weber "Von Lieberman" when he tells the story about him.
- "At 16, they'll tell anyone anything," House tells Adam's parents.
- House tells his team he's going to take a leak when he's really trying to wake Adam up a second time.
- The son has been a smoker, and kept it from his parents.

Exam Room

- House can read Hindi.
- Stacy's been gone less than an episode and House is back to toying with Cameron. Then again, he toyed with her right after sleeping with Stacy, when he tricked her into opening her mouth for a swab.
- The cap House is wearing has a monster truck logo. He also

wore it in "Sports Medicine," while at the monster truck rally. Nice costuming consistency!

- Wilson tells House he needs more fulfilling hobbies than humiliating people. Yet House has a wide number of hobbies for a serious doctor — music, sports, foreign languages.

- We see exactly how long House will carry a grudge. He blames his obsession on Weber's shoddy science, but it goes deeper than that.

- Chase yells at Foreman for moving the contrast CT probe. Chase is often acidic in his retorts, but this is one of the few times we see him lose his temper. He yells at Foreman again when Foreman is doing the LP. Without House, tensions are up.

- The labels on the clinical trial migraine bottle and the nitro-glycerin that House injects are oversimplified for the television viewing audience.

- In a neat parallel, Cameron sees Adam experiencing what she thinks is pain (but is actually an orgasm), then walks in to tell House, only to see him actually experiencing pain from the migraine he induced. The parallel comes up again when House wakes Adam up in spite of the excruciating pain he knows he'll be in. And a third time when he tells Cuddy he took a cocktail of anti-depressants to cancel out the LSD. Anti-depressants are what Adam was taking (to quit smoking).

- Chase is the one who brings up the endorphin rush some people get from pain (such as from tattooing). He was also the team member who dated a pain fetishist.

- House references Dominic Larry, Napoleon's surgeon in chief, who used maggots for eating flesh and cleaning wounds.

- Cameron is the one to enter the shower room to retrieve House, who's wearing nothing but a towel. She reacts like a doctor whose patient is fighting for his life, not a woman who at one point quit because of her feelings for this half-naked man.

- "Way to go," House says, musing on Adam's age (16), when Adam's mom says he told them when he started having sex.

- We see one of the call-girls that House so frequently refer-ences. This one is named "Paula," and House admits he's called her because he's looking for a distraction.

Booboos
- Looks like they got a bit carried away with the special effects. The explosion looks like it would obliterate Adam — the 40 percent burn quotient is kind.
- Most teenagers haven't smoked long enough to really develop the kind of habit that would require anti-smoking meds.
- The pharmaceutical company would be highly unlikely to shut Dr. Weber down after investing in his trials, certainly not on the basis of one little (or not so little) e-mail from House.

What's Up, Doc?
- Foreman isn't actually doing an LP, though they call it one. The lumbar is farther down the spine. Since the area he's going into is at the top of the spine, he's doing a cervical puncture.
- House references a Belgian doc named Einthoven who invented the Galvanometer. The Galvanometer was invented by Willem Einthoven, but is named for Luigi Galvani, an Italian physician and physicist who conducted experiments on frogs' muscles using electricity. Einthoven was actually Dutch, not Belgian.
- Fun fact: the Galvanometer inspired portions of Mary Shelley's story of *Frankenstein*.

2.13 Skin Deep

First aired: February 20, 2006
Writers: David Shore, Garrett Lerner, Russel Friend
Director: James Hayman
Guest stars: Stephanie Venditto (Nurse Brenda), Cameron Richardson (Alex), Tom Verica (Martin), Jim Hoffmaster (Surgeon), John Burke (Austin), Donzaleigh Abernathy (Brady), Karis Campbell (Pregnant Woman), James DuMont (George)

Episode Differential
From Cameron to Cuddy to Stacy, it seems House has no idea how to talk

to women. A teenaged super model brought in tests House's ability to alienate everyone.

The episode opens on a hectic backstage of a runway fashion show. Alex, a 15-year-old girl, is given a Valium by her manager father before she goes on. Once onstage, Alex goes into a psychotic episode, stumbling, punching another model, and then passing out. On the surface, it may be normal super model behavior, but her case warrants the interest of House.

Sweating profusely in the hospital, a tox screen confirms everyone's suspicions that Alex is on drugs. She tests positive for heroin, but even withdrawal symptoms don't explain everything. House himself is going through suffering, as his leg nerves may be regenerating and he's experiencing intense leg pain. The team convinces Alex's father to let them put her through a rapid detox to clear away the withdrawal symptoms and figure out what is really wrong with her. During the night, while Alex is in an induced coma, she suffers a heart attack, flatlining for several minutes.

After a tense night, Alex wakes up, cognizant enough to flirt with Chase — although, unlike the nine-year-old cancer girl, he doesn't kiss her. He's amused until Alex begins to repeat sentences — short-term memory loss — and experience twitches. The team believes she may have been brain damaged from the lack of oxygen during her cardiac arrest, but House has another theory: post-traumatic stress disorder. Quoting an interview where Alex's father was strangely licentious about his daughter's "perfect apple-shaped ass," House suggests that her father molested her. As well, a lumbar puncture shows evidence of a viral infection, possibly an STD, according to House. The team thinks they've talked him out of such a reckless theory but while standing in a crowded hallway, and cranky from his own pain, House shouts, "By the way, did you do your daughter?" Absconding to a bathroom, House confronts the father privately, asking if he loves his daughter enough to admit that he slept with her. Daddy admits to it, once.

Wilson convinces House to undergo an MRI, to see if his leg nerves are regenerating and while in the machine Cuddy demands to know if House is sitting on information that his patient had been sexually abused. The authorities are notified but it goes no further: Alex denies everything. Later, admitting to Cameron that she seduced her father in order to gain more control, Alex tells Cameron that she's not that smart, but she is "that beautiful." Considering her puffy-eyed hospital state, she's a lot less beautiful than Cameron, just one of the episode's flaws.

There would be few fans to name this a favorite episode. But what makes it weaker than others? Is it that the House pain-drama overshadows the details of the case, that most viewers don't really want to think about a father and daughter sleeping together, or that the end diagnosis (keep reading) is touched on so briefly and negatively that the show may as well not have bothered?

After a brain biopsy shows no white matter disease, House begins to think it may be — altogether now everyone — paraneoplastic syndrome, a reaction to a cancerous tumor somewhere in her body. On a new scan, a tumor is revealed . . . on her testicles. Alex has pseudo-hermaprodism. As House notes, she's the perfect woman, without a shred of testosterone in her body. He delivers the news in a tone unusually harsh, even for House.

Desperate for pain relief, earlier in the episode, he had asked Cuddy to inject his spine with morphine. When he returns at episode's end for another shot she reveals the first shot was a placebo — a syringe full of saline solution.

Highlight

When Wilson suggests that House's pain might be a psychosomatic response to having lost Stacy, House whacks Wilson in the shin with his cane and says, "Aww, do you miss Stacy too?"

Support Staff

- House attempts to walk without it when he wakes up in the morning.
- House leaves his bike at home because his leg is hurting.
- House stumbles in the diagnostics room. "No really, I'm fine," he says when no one bothers to ask.
- He uses it to stop the father, who's angry about his daughter flatlining during the rapid detox.
- See Highlight.

Lies

- Alex hides her heroin use from her father.
- The team doesn't tell Alex about all of the risks associated with inducing a coma. It's her father's call and he opts to keep it from her.
- House tells the clinic patient that he's doing his wife and that

that's how he knows she's pregnant.

- The father initially lies, then tells the truth about having slept with his daughter.
- House says he doesn't want to report the father because he wants him there — in case they have any more secrets he needs to expose.
- Father and daughter both deny to the authorities that they've had any inappropriate relationship.
- Alex admits to Cameron that *she* seduced her father so she can get away with more.
- Alex's sex organs are lying to everyone. She's technically a boy.
- House's pain is lying to him. It is psychosomatic.
- Cuddy pretends to give House morphine when, in fact, it's a placebo.

Exam Room
- House's alarm is set for 9:19 — perhaps the extra minute is to accommodate his limp.
- We get the first hint to the gender-neutrally named Alex's condition when House says that his lackeys will be by to draw some blood, some urine, and "any other fluids you got." Like semen?
- The clinic patient provides an easy parallel as a man experiences sympathy pregnancy, including the onset of breasts, and also contractions.
- Cameron is grossed out by the way House sexualizes a 15-year-old, even if he argues that it's what society is geared toward when constructing notions of beauty.
- House is reading *Celeb Weekly*, which is where he finds Alex's father acting as her beauty agent, including inappropriate comments about her tush.
- "It's personal" is what the clinic patient tells Cuddy because he doesn't want to show her his breast growth; in the very next scene, it's what Foreman asks House. He thinks he's going through something, and as a result, attempting to speed the diagnosis.
- For once, the team oversees the brain biopsy rather than doing it themselves.
- The clinic patient exposes his breasts to Cuddy — and leaves his

shirt undone longer than necessary. Alex exposes herself to House when she feels that he's challenged her femininity — stripping her, essentially, of the one thing that makes her special.

- House and Wilson switch roles this episode with Wilson literally "playing God" while House is in the MRI. House plays along, saying he can't talk right now, and referring God to Cameron who keeps his calendar.
- Later, House bets that the model's breasts were crafted by God, to which Foreman replies, "I thought you didn't believe in God."

Booboos

- Cameron suggests Alex may not have menstruated because she hasn't reached sexual maturity. House says the rest of Alex's body begs to differ. But menstruation is not linked to breast size or other secondary sex characteristics.
- Child services would take this allegation very seriously, even if both father and daughter denied their sexual involvement. That would likely be expected, but the doctors' words would be given more weight than those of ordinary citizens.

2.14 Sex Kills

First aired: March 7, 2006
Writer: Matt Witten
Director: David Semel
Guest stars: Ron Perkins (Dr. Simpson), Bobbin Bergstrom (ER Doctor), Stephen DeCordova (Second Chief Surgeon), Greg Grunberg (Ronald Neuberger), Jean St. James (Cecile Arrington), Keri Lynn Pratt (Amy Arrington), Howard Hesseman (Henry Arrington), Yvette Nicole Brown (Stambler), Adam Busch (Tony), Noel Conlon (First Table East), Susan Grace (First Table North), Marcie Lynn Ross (Second Table West), Craig Patton (Second Table East)

Episode Differential

As House is fond of saying, there is no dignity in death, and, as if to prove that correct, House does everything in his power to cure a dead woman of an STD. Fans have pointed out the anti-sex theme running through the entire second season, but are these episodes — placed strategically around

House's own affair with a married woman — meant to show that sex is serious, and has consequences?

Henry Arrington (played by Howard Hesseman, best known for his roles as Dr. Johnny Fever on *WKRP in Cincinnati* and Charlie Moore on *Head of the Class*) is a divorced man in his mid-60s playing bridge with his daughter Amy in tow. While walking back to the bridge table, he has an absent seizure and Amy brings him to the hospital. After clearing STDs off the list, but finding out that Henry has started sleeping with his ex-wife, House quickly traces the illness to an infection — bruliosis, common in Europe from unpasteurized cheese. Though usually treatable, this is of course a complicated case — without a heart transplant, Henry will be dead in a matter of days. House tries to get him on the transplant list, but as a man in his 60s, there's little chance he'd get a heart even if one were available. Once again the show raises its favorite questions: who deserves treatment and who deserves to live?

After he tells his patient the harsh news, House begins searching for rejected hearts around the hospital. As House says, the hearts of the too-old or the overweight are rejected everyday. Soon, a car crash victim is brought into emergency. Within minutes, it seems she'll be announced dead. As House discovers from hacking into the hospital's donor system, her organs have already been deemed unsuitable because of her weight.

House dons a lab coat (not seen since the days of Vogler) and begins to ask the woman's soon-to-be-bereaved husband, Ronald, questions. Was she ill? How was she feeling lately? Inadvertently, the man thinks it means there some chance. Immediately, the hospital bereavement counselor comes up, and, mistaking House as the attending doctor, she assumes he's heard the news. His wife is brain dead. Ronald storms off, but House is persistent, using Amy as bait for the heart. Conflicted when confronted by this worried daughter, Ronald agrees, but only after sucker-punching House.

Now the team has to make sure the heart is free of infection, signs of which do show up on tests. Keeping Ronald's wife's body stable, they begin pumping it full of every antibiotic imaginable at deadly levels, which would destroy the kidneys and eyes — as some of the team point out. House's reply is that the "patient" is in little need of the kidneys or eyes. Throughout, House is about as sensitive about the weight of their "patient" as Chase is in season one's "Heavy."

They begin rebuilding the woman's life as if she were a living patient, investigating her home to try to find out what infection she may have had. Her secret is a dirty one, but they are able to do their transplant. Charged with telling the husband he must be tested and treated for gonorrhea, Cameron is cut off when Ronald admits that he picked up an STD himself some months before, was treated, and hoped he had never given it to his wife.

Continuing the episode's theme of husbands and wives, House also spends much of his Wilson-time exploring his idea that Wilson is having another affair and is headed toward yet another divorce. The final scene confirms this when Wilson shows up at House's place, bags in tow. The difference is that *she* was cheating on him.

Highlight
When House tells his team that they're going to cure the woman, Cameron asks, "We're going to cure death?" House comes back with a mad scientist cackle.

Support Staff
When House enters Henry's room to tell him the problem is in his heart, he uses it to part the curtain.

Lies
- Henry hides that he has slept with his ex-wife.
- House hides it from Henry's daughter too, telling her that Pop "met a woman in church." It's one of the few times House lies for a patient, not just to get a patient a procedure.
- Clinic patient lies about liking cows.
- "He told me he was 65. Liar. I'm outta here," House says to Cuddy when she says his transplant hopeful is 66. House is the one lying.
- Ronald's wife was lying about her affairs — or at least, her stash of photos of nude young men.
- Ronald cheated on his wife and never told her about his gonorrhea.
- Cameron doesn't tell Ronald about his wife's infidelities, figuring he doesn't need to know them right now.
- House instructs Wilson to admit nothing to his wife.
- Wilson is telling the truth when he says, "I'm not having an affair!"

- Wilson's wife is cheating.

Exam Room

- Joni Mitchell's song "Sex Kills" from her 1994 album *Turbulent Indigo* fills in as the episode's title.
- Everyone this episode is having sex and/or cheating — except House, and Wilson who's getting the boot. Oh, and a teenager from the clinic who's attracted to his mom. He pretends he's attracted to cows in the hope that House will give him something to debilitate his erections.
- After Henry confesses that his right testicle is twice the size of his left one, Foreman tells the team. As Sarah M on the website *Television Without Pity* points out, "House listens to this while playing with his giant tennis ball, which is twice the size of a normal tennis ball."
- Foreman and House have a conversation where Foreman says most people can control their impulses, so they don't always have sex and aren't inappropriate in the workplace. This doesn't apply to House. At the same time, it may not apply to Foreman either — he had a work-related affair in season one.
- House and Wilson play foosball this episode.
- Chase is almost always the one who defibrillates the patient, and this episode is no exception.
- House is definitely at his most insensitive this episode as he compares Ronald's wife Laura to "a fridge with no power" and also calls her "meat." Some people believe that how you treat and speak of the dead reflects how you feel about the living . . . however, we do know that House doesn't believe in the afterlife, so perhaps his actions fit his character. Still, this isn't his best working method for getting Ronald's cooperation in his transplant mission.

Booboos

Wilson stands in the hallway outside House's door. But in "Hunting" he and Wilson exited the apartment directly onto the porch. And when Cameron came to see him in "Role Model," she also stood on the porch directly looking in. Ditto for the episode where call-girl Paula arrives ("Distractions"), and in upcoming episodes.

What's Up, Doc?

A scrotal ultrasound is safer than a biopsy when diagnosing testicular cancer.

2.15 Clueless

First aired: March 28, 2006
Writer: Thomas L. Moran
Director: Deran Sarafian
Guest stars: Yareli Arizmendi (Maid), Peter Birkenhead (Vincent Lambert), Eddie Mills (Bob), Stephanie Erb (Charlotte Lambert), Samantha Mathis (Maria)

Episode Differential

While the creators of *House* modeled some of his characteristics on Sherlock Holmes (and a little bit of Scooby Doo), House never came closer to actually saying, "Elementary, my dear Wilson," than in this tale of a seemingly perfect marriage.

The camera prowls a bathroom as a woman, Maria, showers. It soon turns into a terrifying scene that suggests a sexual assault is about to occur as a stocking-wearing man drags her from the shower to the bedroom. While they're struggling on the bed, the would-be attacker begins to hyperventilate. Maria is suddenly concerned, asking if he's okay. The man is her husband, Bob, and it was just a role-playing game but Bob is really turning blue.

After the theme, in a variation to formula, the action is still set outside of the hospital. At 221 Baker Street (or 221 Wherever Street), a groggy House awakes to the sound of toenail clipping and Wilson grooming himself with a blow dryer. House is shocked and annoyed enough that he tells Wilson it isn't working out. After chiding House for sleeping in, he announces he's looking at apartments anyway. Hence, two relationships have been established in the first two scenes.

At the hospital, several doctors who don't know why Bob's throat is seizing have referred his case to House. Making a note that most people have no knowledge of anatomy, House suggests his team start looking at his lungs. For House, it appears to be classic heavy metal poisoning. But of course, which one is it and how has the patient been exposed to it? When the test for the common culprits comes back negative and the treatment for lead poisoning isn't having any effect, Cameron votes for allergies while Foreman suspects perennial favorite lupus. House begins to suspect the wife. But as the team has interviewed them, all they can report back is that they seem like a perfect couple with an adventurous sex life. To House the cynic, it's all over-compensation. She's poisoning him and he's going to find out how.

As sometimes happens, a clinic patient accidentally provides the missing element to House's puzzle. After diagnosing a "happily married man" with herpes, the man and his nonplussed wife demand a meeting with Cuddy and House. Neither the man nor his wife will admit to an affair. House tricks the husband into an admission and the wife tosses her wedding band. Picking it up, House gets his "Aha!" moment from the gold band. Racing back to the hospital after retrieving a vial from his apartment, House catches up to Maria in the bathroom. Grasping her hands as she exits the stall, he explains that he was an air force brat, that his father was stationed in Egypt and that House, as an 11-year-old, searched a lot for mummies. He didn't find any but he did find out that Egyptians used stannous chloride to harden ruby glass and to turn gold bright purple. House looks down and Maria's fingers have turned purple. She's been poisoning Bob with her gold-based arthritis medication.

A montage shows Maria arrested and a nearly destroyed Bob being told. Back in the land of the Odd Couple, House erases a phone message from Wilson's prospective landlord. We don't know why exactly he wants Wilson to stay, but apparently, some relationships do work out.

Highlight
Trying to buy an easy out of the marital breakdown he started with the herpes couple, House offers, "Have you ever used a public toilet seat?" House figures the guilty party will grab the ready excuse. Before a repulsed Cuddy can correct the fake fact, the husband deadpans, "I just never knew."

Support Staff
- It's the first thing House sees when he awakes to the clipping of Wilson's toenails.
- Cane is in its favorite spot — hung up over the white board in the first diagnostic session.

Lies

- The intro is a lie to us, since the couple would be aware that they're play-acting. We believe that we're witnessing an actual attack (or at least those of us who are naive do).
- The clinic patient lies to both House and his wife, since he knows he is the one who went outside the marriage.
- House lies about ways to get herpes.
- Maria lies about wanting her husband to get better, though she does have a hard time saying "I love you," when he requests it.
- House hides the apartment offer from Wilson because he wants him to stay.

Exam Room

- House tries a new "caffeine delivery system": something called "5 Gear Energy Drink."
- Much to the shock of her teammates, Cameron shows she's not against couple experimentation, including their threesome with the wife's college roomie.
- When House arrives agitatedly in the bathroom where Wilson is already primping, Hugh Laurie makes as if he is urinating — but there's no sound. The camera doesn't show why he's turned to the side, but it seems to be the implication. His gesture doesn't quite last long enough for morning though.
- House's celebrity magazine habit pays off (again) when he's able to ask Foreman if the ant he saw at Maria's house was "Halle Berry brown or Beyoncé brown?" The ultra-white Cameron doesn't know the difference.
- When Wilson is looking at the schedule of shows on House's TiVo, and trying to choose one, *Blackadder* is among those listed. It was one of Hugh Laurie's first shows. The scene becomes more hilarious when House steals the remote and shows Wilson how to "watch something," because it's not *Adder* that he chooses.
- The other shows House has include: three episodes of *The OC*, three of *SpongeBob Squarepants*, *Monster Truck Jam*, and eight episodes of *The New Yankee Workshop*.
- We see Wilson wearing a McGill shirt for the first time — a reference to the Canadian university in Montreal. We glimpse

it when he's sleeping on the couch. He'll sport the same logo in "House vs. God" when he attends the poker game.

- Wilson references the Parker Bros. board game *Clue*, getting the conservatory's name wrong. It's logical that House would correct him on this point, because that's what House does to Wilson, and also because of his love of the piano.
- Wilson points out that House eats nothing but soup and peanut butter.
- At the end of the episode, House's answering machine intones, "One new message," though the counter on it reads "02." Is House saving a message?

Booboos

- Fans on TV.com have posited that when House finds the bottle he is looking for, the close-up on his fingers are clearly not those of Hugh Laurie — that they are too short for our piano-playing hero, and without wrinkles.
- Wouldn't Wilson have given the potential landlord his cell phone number, since, as a doctor that would be on at all times? He might give his landline at the hospital, but it does seem unlikely he'd use House's phone number.

What's Up, Doc?

The herpes husband-wife situation hits its mark, since doctors are frequently the bearers of such bad news, diagnosing people in "monogamous" relationships with STDs.

2.16 Safe

First aired: April 4, 2006
Writer: Peter Blake
Director: Felix Enriquez Alcala
Guest stars: Michelle Trachtenberg (Melinda), Mel Harris (Barbara), Lance Guest (Lewis), Jake McDorman (Dan)

Episode Differential

If there's a motif to the midseason of *House* it must be the title of one of the episodes — sex kills. In "Safe" however, the culprit isn't a virus or a vengeful spouse. It's so odd it "ticks" House off to no end. There's also a bit of a youth theme. Kids will be kids, and likewise, House and Wilson will act like bratty college boys.

Melinda is a teenage girl who not only suffers from severe allergies, but the previous year after sneaking out, she had a seizure and crashed a car; the steering wheel crushed her chest, leaving her with a transplanted heart. In the opening scene, Melinda's overprotective mother sees Melinda's boyfriend, Dan, up to her daughter's clean room, only after making him scrub and put on a mask. Once alone, the teenagers begin making out, only to have Melinda go into anaphylactic shock.

House is intrigued: why has the girl had an allergic reaction in a clean room? House and the team battle the parents, who preside over every aspect of Melinda's life — and battle to save Melinda's heart as she continues to exhibit allergic reactions. During a test with Chase, and proving that young women just can't resist confiding in the golden-haired doctor, Melinda admits that she's worried that she'll never experience life before her heart gives out. (Transplant patients generally live over 10 years after a transplant.) The youth theme continues when Melinda's mom tells Foreman he should lie to her daughter because she's a teenager.

This episode we view the Holmes-Watson/House-Wilson relationship up close. Their roommate dynamic, like so many other elements of the show, plays into fantasy: gee, wouldn't it be great if my best friend weren't married and we could spend all our time together, goofing around and watching late movies? When House erased the message from Wilson's landlord in "Clueless," we may have believed that House genuinely cared about his friend and didn't want him to be alone during his divorce. But House is simply using Wilson to alleviate his boredom (and laziness). Theirs has moved from a husband-wife dynamic to that of frat-boy buddies, with House hiding dirty dishes so he won't have to do them, and foolishly placing the snoring Wilson's hand in a bowl of water in an effort to make him pee himself. Something the brilliant doctor won't take into account is that it's his very expensive leather couch that will be the real victim. But House as a character does sometimes lack foresight. . . .

As Melinda worsens, the team begins to look to boyfriend Dan. House easily decimates the teen boy's defenses and discovers that, well intentioned as he may have been, Dan stupidly loaded up on penicillin (another thing Melinda is allergic to) in hopes that it would help them make it through a tryst. They think they've found the perfect solution until the boy's sperm comes back showing traces of non-penicillin antibiotics. There are some funny lines revolving around Dan having to give them a sperm sample, and the mocking (and again righteous) Cameron calls their two-year relationship "practically a lifetime." It's more than a bit of a contradiction, since we already know that Cameron's own longest relationship was her marriage — six months. But these more abrasive Cameron moments pave the way for the Cameron of Contradictions who emerges in season three.

In rebuilding the boy's midnight visit to Melinda, House theorizes that a tick may have come in with him, and latched onto Melinda. Still attached to her, it would continue to pump out greater and greater amounts of toxins. On the way to ICU, Wilson helps fake a diversion and Foreman and House take the patient into an elevator. To the shock of Foreman, House stops the elevator to search for the tick. As always Foreman and House disagree, and struggle physically before House gains control and continues his tick-quest — between her legs. *Voila!*

After Melinda recovers, her parents realize that it was their smothering that caused Melinda to sneak around, and they decide to let her attend school again, and let kids be kids.

Highlight
House has been playing schoolboy pranks on his new roommate. Wilson, in a rare show of strength, saws halfway through House's cane, leading to House collapsing in the hospital hallway.

Support Staff
- In the morning, House walks around his kitchen without it.
- House taps it against the white board.
- House uses it to block Cuddy from getting on the elevator with them.
- Foreman and House physically fight over the cane.
- See Highlight.

Lies
- Dan tells Melinda's mom that he hasn't seen her for a week.
- House tells Wilson he did the dishes.
- "These are your big ideas? Somebody's lying?" Cuddy asks. "Hasn't let me down yet," House responds.
- "She is 16 years old. Lie to her," the mother tells Foreman

after he tells her daughter there's no medical reason she can't go to school after she's better.

- The teenagers withhold the information that they had sex the night before Melinda's attack.
- "Lying to your parents is usually the right thing to do, but there is the impending-death exception," House says.

Exam Room

- House wears his usual PJ pants and T-shirt to bed. His character seems like he'd be more of an underwear man, but he's nothing if not unpredictable.
- House references 1976 TV movie *The Boy in the Plastic Bubble*, when he says, "Mommy builds her little angel a John-Travolta quality bubble." In that role, Travolta played an immune-compromised boy. House would be about the right age to remember such a film, since his character would have been 17 when it aired.
- House uses sugar in his coffee this episode.
- House's address in this episode is missing the B — it's just 221.
- When Cameron and Chase send Dan into the bathroom to give them a semen sample, Chase taunts, "No thinking about Dr. Cameron. We'll know." She waits until Dan has been in for a few seconds, then taunts back, "Too bad it's not you giving the sample, we'd be done by now." She is taunting back, but it's a low blow. In "Hunting," when Chase said that their tryst "didn't suck," Cameron looked happy. She didn't look like she thought it sucked either. Has regret changed her mind? Or just the day-in/day-out of working with Chase?
- "Just be a minute, honey," House says to Foreman when Foreman demands that he turn the elevator back on. House and Foreman, House and Wilson, House and Cuddy — he'll verbally partner with anyone except the young co-eds Cameron and Chase.
- Obviously, Wilson is an expert when it comes to partway-sawing, since House uses the cane all day before it snaps. He even engages in physical combat with Foreman, wrestling with the cane between them without breaking it. Perhaps their tussle is the straw that broke the camel's back, since it gives out

only a few moments later, leaving House on his ass.

- We see Wilson watching TV, and hear its audio. It's Hitchcock's *Vertigo* — appropriate since Wilson has a *Vertigo* poster in his office.
- Otis Redding's "Pain in My Heart," is used in this episode where the patient's heart is their primary concern.

Booboos

Whether Chase is wearing one or two gloves changes in the scene where he attempts to intubate Melinda.

What's Up, Doc?

Foreman explains how the centrifuge works, and tells Melinda's parents that white blood cells are the heaviest. Red blood cells are.

2.17 All In

First aired: April 11, 2006
Writer: David Foster
Director: Fred Gerber
Guest stars: Laura Allen (Sarah), Daylon Reese (Child/Michael), Purva Bedi (Teacher), Michelle Harrison (Nicole), Al Espinosa (Dr. Wells), Carter Page (Ian), MacKenzie Astin (Alan)

Episode Differential

While much of the drama on *House* is spread over a matter of days, many medical crises happen suddenly, with staff up all night fighting to keep patients alive. Here, a charity casino at the hospital becomes the background for House to do battle with an old foe. And the structure is set up as an "It all happened one night . . ."

At a science center school trip, a pregnant teacher and her class of six-year-olds walk through a giant heart, ironically, the organ where the episode's climax will take place. When the teacher begins to experience contractions, she asks Ian, one of her students to get help, until she sees that blood is seeping down his pants. It's another absolute psych-out like the one we saw in "Humpty Dumpty," although it lacks the humor.

At the hospital, the staff is dressed to the nines for an oncology benefit casino. Yes, even House! Chase is mocking nurses. Cameron reveals her feminine side with a luscious red dress that makes even House drop jaw, and Cuddy, Wilson, and House are locked into poker combat. An intern comes to inform Cuddy that Ian, her patient, is dehydrated. She orders fluids as she continues to consume hers. House is intrigued and begins to ask questions. "Bloody diarrhea" has him throwing a flush hand so he can sneak off. As we'll eventually learn, House's foe is Erdheim-Chester disease. Years ago he lost a patient, Esther, to it and was never able to properly diagnose it (the family refused an autopsy). House predicts Ian's disease will send kidneys and liver into failure, then the heart, then death. House's seriousness is revealed when he actually visits the patient right away and discovers neurological involvement — another symptom. He gathers the team for their best-dressed differential session yet.

Chase reveals that several years ago House, so obsessed with solving his old case, put a trucker who came in complaining of bloody stool through a battery of dangerous and painful tests with nothing but a diagnosis of a bad cheese sandwich to show for it. This episode is yet another in a string meant to show us how hard our hero will work, not for the benefit of his patient but to solve his puzzle. We also, for the first time, get to see how House reacts when the chips are stacked against him and he's bested by the disease. Temper, temper.

After the parents go searching for Cuddy, upset that their son has gone from ill to near death after a heart biopsy, Cuddy returns and indeed throws House off the case. He's near defeat and lashes out at not only the concession counter's metal gate in his attempt to get a late night cup of coffee. He also lashes out at his whiteboard, which he knocks over — somewhat like Chuck Norris realizing that for this fight, he has to go this one alone.

House goes to visit the comatose boy. Near dawn the team regathers. They have small piece of the heart from the biopsy. Enough for three tests. They pick two most likely diseases that Cuddy is least likely to test herself. Spurred on by Wilson's story of his poker win with "pocket aces," House demands they retest for Erdheim-Chester. He says it may have been too early to test before. The team is aghast that he would waste one of their precious tests, but — as we know by now, House can never really be wrong — it comes back positive and they begin treatment as the sun comes up and House and Wilson have a morning game of poker. That case of House's old patient Esther is finally solved with Ian's.

Highlight

To permanently destroy a flirting session Chase is having with a woman at the benefit, House walks up and loudly asks about his anal fissures.

Support Staff

- House holds it up for Ian to grab, but Ian can't figure out where to reach.
- He uses it to break into the coffee counter.
- He uses it to tip over his white board.

Lies

- The disease lied, by not showing up on the first test. It lied in both Ian's case and Esther's.
- If bluffing counts as a lie, Cuddy lies.
- Chase lies about swimming with sharks without a cage ("Those are for tourists").
- House lies when he fabricates a story about Chase in the stairway with a woman who has an Adam's apple.
- House initially tells his team that Cuddy assigned him to the case.
- House lies to Wilson when he gives him card advice — to help Cuddy keep winning.
- Foreman tells the truth when the mother asks him if Esther suffered when she died. He tells her he doesn't know.

Exam Room

- House repeatedly loses his cool this episode, and while they often argue with him, this time his team doesn't trust his judgment, feeling his obsession with Esther is leading them astray. In a role reversal, Foreman at first has faith in House where Chase stands up to him, telling him he screwed up with Esther, sorry, but that this kid's not her. The team comes around quickly though, as Ian's condition worsens.
- Esther's file reads: "Doyle, Ester" and has an admission date of "February 2, 1994," which is even before House worked for Cuddy.
- Chase says that the way some people see the Virgin Mary in danishes, House sees Esther in paint peeling. "Paint peeling"

was also referenced in the previous episode where House yelled at Foreman in the elevator about which House problem to deal with first — the paint peeling, the water boiling, or the house being on fire.

- Wilson apparently wears toenail polish. House threatens to tell others unless Wilson goes "all in." Wilson obliges, so presumably this is true and serves to balance out his obsessive hair-drying.
- *Moby-Dick* by Herman Melville is referenced by Wilson. Erdheim-Chester is House's great white whale.
- Ian flatlines for eight minutes. Chase asks House how much longer he'll continue to try to get him back, even though when Chase had a baby die in season one, he refused to stop shocking. House does get the boy back though.
- "You're not God, House," Cuddy tells our hero. "Sometimes you lose."
- "Ian" is the name of Hugh Laurie's character in *Flight of the Phoenix*, which he was filming when he auditioned for *House*.

Booboos

- Fans have claimed that House is smoking a cigar, which disappears when he gets up from the poker table — but this is untrue. The booboo belongs to the fans. Hugh Laurie simply moves it from his mouth to below camera level. It's back in the next shot as he exits the frame.
- The name on the file folder is *Ester*; House writes it as *Esther* on the white board. Impossible to know which is correct.
- House bungles his pop culture. "While you were all wearing your Frankie Says Relax T-shirts . . ." House begins. But no one was wearing Frankie T-shirts in 1994. Maybe he should have gone with "While you were all getting sun-burned at Lollapalooza . . ."
- During the respiratory distress scene, we see Foreman pull Ian's pillow away. In the next shot, Ian's pillow reappears.

What's Up, Doc?

An absolute effective treatment for Erdheim-Chester has yet to be discovered though we're left with the feeling that now the puzzle has been solved, young Ian will be just fine.

2.18 Sleeping Dogs Lie

First aired: April 18, 2006
Writer: Sara Hess
Director: Greg Yaitanes
Guest stars: Jayma Mays (Hannah), Dahlia Salem (Max), Julia Ling (Anne), Alice Lo (Mrs. Ling), KT Thangavelu (Surgeon), Kendall Clement (Anesthesiologist)

Episode Differential

In this episode about conflict resolution, the team is torn apart because of House's questionable leadership skills. In his defense, he does apparently know much about the dynamics of lesbian relationships.

Two women, Max and Hannah, are in bed at home. Hannah hasn't slept in days. As the night wears along background sounds — drips, radiators — become amplified. Max wakes in the morning to find Hannah crouched in the kitchen. She's taken an entire bottle of sleeping pills but still hasn't slept.

Cuddy finds House sawing logs in an exam room, a journal covering his eyes. He claims that he's a night owl and Wilson an early bird. The theme for the episode is obviously sleep. House initially dismisses Hannah's case as a psych issue. He changes his tune when he's told that the patient took an entire bottle of sleeping pills and still no shut-eye. In the diagnostics room, Cameron has learned that Foreman has published an article on the same case she's written an article on. The difference? Her article has been sitting on House's desk for months waiting for his signature. Foreman bugged House to sign his three weeks previous, which House did, without even reading it. Now it's been published (rather quickly it should be noted) and Cameron is livid. While Foreman and Cameron bicker, House focuses on the case.

The team catches Hannah in a lie. She and Max recently bought a dog that had to be returned after Hannah said she was allergic. House declares that Hannah is going to break up with Max. But their love life is the last thing that matters when tests reveal that Hannah's liver is flat out dead. She won't make it without an immediate transplant — which will be unlikely with an undiagnosed disease. Max, who's a blood match for Hannah, volunteers a piece of her liver. The ever-ethical Cameron doesn't believe it is right for Max to risk her life for Hannah's at this point. Confronted about their relationship, Hannah reveals to Cameron that she was indeed going to leave Max. Cameron thinks Max should be able to make an informed decision about her liver donation, but House intervenes all that he can, keeping the two separate and keeping Cameron away from them both.

Talking to Max afterward, Cameron learns that she knew Hannah was going to leave her but now that they share a liver, she knows Hannah can never leave her. This episode echoes the format of "Sex Kills," in that Cameron believes herself to be the bearer of a terrible secret only to discover the other party has an angle too. Things aren't nearly so amicable when Cameron tries to clear the air with Foreman who announces that they're not friends. They're colleagues and he's done nothing he has to be sorry for. Cameron really ought to have seen this coming, since it's consistent with what he's said and done throughout the episode. Early on, when she's examining Hannah, he comes in and asks if she needs help. She snaps at him, and he reiterates calmly, "I wasn't asking for forgiveness. I was asking if you needed help." Their dispute will be the next through plot line, replacing the House-Stacy drama that we've been missing.

Highlights
Cameron talks back to House. When House says Foreman was just being human, doing what worked out best for him, Cameron remarks, "That's not the definition of being human. That's the definition of being an ass." Another great point is when the team enters House's office to announce a new symptom in the patient. Cameron exclaims, "We've got rectal bleeding." And House replies, "What, all of you?"

Support Staff
- House hooks it over the chair when he takes apart the three-dimensional brain.
- He hooks it over the counter while making coffee.
- He hands it to Cameron as he quickly puts Hannah under before she can confess to Max.

Lies
- In *House*, no one gets to be noble — lesbians lie to each other too. Hannah lies to Max about being allergic to the dog.
- Hannah has been stringing Max along.
- Max lies in that she knew Hannah wanted to leave her, but

continued to pretend nothing was wrong.

- House doesn't tell Cameron or Foreman about their respective papers.
- The clinic patient's daughter is trying to score pills for herself — she's lying to both her mother and House.

Exam Room

- The book that covers House's face at the beginning of the episode is *Medical Journal of Experimental Medicine*. Considering "medicine" is already in the title, is the first "medical" really necessary?
- The publication with Foreman's article is *Midwest Journal of Experimental Medicine* in a remarkably similar font.
- Three weeks for a journal is not enough lead-time to select an article, edit it, incorporate into layout, send to print, and get it out to subscribers by mail. Even if the journal solicited specifically from Foreman, and slipped him in at the last minute, the journal would not wind up in Cameron's hands only three weeks after he finished the article.
- Chase defends Cameron's honor over the article. He tells her that he told Foreman with the number of weird cases they work on in a year, he could have written up any one of them.
- This is one of the few episodes where House goes to Cuddy for help, asking her to be what he's always saying she's not — a real doctor. In this instance, he needs her to counsel Max about her surgery so he can avoid the conflict of ethics.
- As if to show that not all women in medicine are as emotional as Cameron, Cuddy pep talks her during the surgery, telling her to "write another article," if she wants to get ahead in what is largely a man's industry. In her opinion, success is the best revenge.
- House's knowledge of world languages now includes Mandarin (not unexpected, as House was a military brat shipped around the world). His response of *"Gong xi ni, ni kuai zuo zhu mu le"* to the mother of the girl trying to score birth control pills does translate as "Congratulations, you're about to become a grandmother," according to fans' translations.

What's Up, Doc?

The surgical teams in the episode must love playing with fate as they operate on a patient with an unknown illness without facemasks. Perhaps they didn't "read" well on screen.

2.19 House Versus God

First aired: April 25, 2006
Writer: Doris Egan
Director: John F. Showalter
Guest stars: Thomas Dekker (Boyd), William Katt (Walter), Tamara Braun (Grace), Sandra Marshall (Agnes)

Episode Differential

Liston versus Clay, Alien versus Predator, House versus God. Sooner or later, House had to meet his only competition.

At a storefront church, Boyd, a guest preacher who's a teen sensation on the healing circuit, is leading the congregation through "you are healed" sessions. Like House, God is nothing if not ironic. Just after delivering a sermon about the ills of man's medicine, Boyd is struck down with nerve shocks and pain.

At the hospital, Wilson ambushes House in the hallway, asking why he hasn't been invited to House's weekly poker game. It seems like a trivial question, but as we know in this show almost all of the light banter eventually has impact on the plot. Foreman and Chase, meanwhile, attend to Boyd in emergency. While asking him about his last few days, Boyd announces that God talks to him. As House summarizes later, "You talk to God, you're religious. God talks to you, you're psychotic." House talks to Boyd, giving the excuse of actually speaking to a patient as "God talks to him. It would be arrogant of me to assume that I'm better than God." As they test the boy, trying to see if his visions are also part of an illness, the young preacher wanders the hospital, offering his visions and advice. To Foreman, Boyd says that Cameron is harboring vengeful thoughts. When Boyd runs into Grace, a terminal patient of Wilson's, he says God willed him to heal her cancer.

Wilson is more upset than he should be when he tells House that this kind of experience could undo Grace's acceptance of death. Grace and

Boyd take to meeting and praying with each other. And worse, Grace's tumor is shown to have shrunk legitimately. Boyd enters House's office, and House asks Boyd for proof of his conversations with God. He is genuinely shocked when Boyd says, "God wants you to invite Dr. Wilson to your poker game." Ever the smart odds player, House does what God says, for the time being, and comically gives a point to God on the whiteboard where he's keeping score.

While Wilson is at the poker night (featuring a stellar array of House's accountant, his dry cleaner, and "Guy from the Bus Stop" — apparently House *does* have other friends, they just don't have names), House has Chase search Grace's home. Chase phones to report that men's clothing occupies the closet. House stares down Wilson from across the table and tells Chase to relax, boyfriend won't be showing up. Jilted for a girl, House lashes out on a rant about ethics in front of everyone at the game. Wilson's dating his terminal patient, and it's one of the reasons he's no longer living at House's.

After Boyd spikes a fever, House recalls that some viruses temporarily shrink tumors. A lumbar puncture would reveal the virus but Boyd is refusing "man's medicine." Thinking back to Boyd wanting to purify himself by drinking too much water at the beginning of the episode and putting that with the fact that Boyd is probably like any other teenage boy, House looks for a herpes rash and finds one. He may be close to God, but it doesn't mean he's not a sinner.

In the end, it's a draw between House and God. At the very least Wilson's patient (who calls off the romance so she can travel) has been given a few extra months because of the virus. Wilson pontificates on the chances of her coming into contact with exactly the right strain of virus to produce this reaction and concludes that God really might be the winner.

Highlight
When Foreman tells House that Boyd told him that Cameron is harboring vengeful thoughts, House replies, "Yeah. I can tell that from the Berlin Wall of body language between you two. I'm shocked that he picked up on it."

Support Staff
House uses it to rap on the outside glass door of Wilson's office when he interrupts him with Grace.

Lies

- Boyd lies to House, his father . . . and God.
- House lies to Wilson about the poker game.
- Wilson lies about his relationship with one of his cancer patients (thereby turning him into a temporary Cameron).

Exam Room

- The church where Boyd is performing his miracles is called Church of the Shining Light. It's right next to Lights Out Mini Mart.
- Before he ever meets House, Boyd preaches, "Asa was diseased in his feet until the disease was exceedingly great. Yet he didn't seek help from the Lord, but from the physicians." The show frequently references leg and foot pain to keep House's predicament at its core even in scenes where he's not present.
- The urine sample bottle of Boyd's gives his last name as Stanley and his birth date as April 24, 1990, making him exactly 16 and a day on the airdate.
- Boyd's name needs only two letters reversed to spell "body," a clue that what is wrong with Boyd is not in his brain.
- House plays with his yo-yo this episode.
- Chase defends Boyd's belief system and the fact that God talks to him.
- Boyd wears a white hospital gown; House wears a white T-shirt, open white collared shirt and off-white jacket, giving the two of them a sense of glow as they talk. They are parallel characters. Both call themselves healers. Boyd does what House does: he notices little things about people and passes it off as knowledge. The difference is that Boyd attributes his to a higher power.
- "Trust has to be earned; you can't trust someone who's hiding in a closet," House says to Boyd. It's a foreshadowing of what House will discover about Wilson. House says he trusts no one, but he does seem a bit perturbed when he discovers Wilson's secret.
- When you re-watch the consult between Grace and Wilson in his office knowing they have a relationship, there are double meanings to their words. She says, "You've done your best, and I have been a good soldier. It's time we

accept it's over." She means her life, her treatment, but she could also mean their relationship. He says that they'll find the right combination to fight her pain, and "Don't give up on us." Does he mean the medical system? Or him and her? Both, it would seem.

- House is sleeping with a book over his head. The book? *Gray's Anatomy*. Either he's brushing up or giving a sly nod to the show's competition.
- Another Canadianism: Wilson wears a McGill sweatshirt to the poker game, a nod to the university located in Montreal.
- The film *Mean Girls* is referenced. House tells Dr. Wilson that he will return his DVD player because "After all, how many times can you hit pause at the part where Lindsay Lohan wins the spelling bee? What is it about girls who can spell?" Wilson corrects him, saying, "It's a math contest." House then retorts, "What it is about girls who can count?"

What's Up, Doc?
- Household radiation has no effect on tumors.
- The show isn't as edgy as it thinks it is. A herpes rash generally presents in a place much more revealing than the back.

2.20/2.21 Euphoria, Parts 1 and 2

First aired: May 2, 2006 and May 3, 2006
Writer: Matthew V. Lewis
Director: Deran Sarafian
Guest stars: Scott Michael Campbell (Joe Luria), Charles S. Dutton (Rodney Foreman), Loreni Delgado (Haines), Chioke Dmachi (Babyshoes), Chil Kong (Morgue Tech)

Episode Differential
We know right away that we're in for an action-packed episode when "Euphoria" starts with a quick-cut sequence that's closer in style to a cop show than a medical drama. "Euphoria" may be deemed a somewhat dismissively "a very special episode" because of the emotions manipulated in having a regular character become ill and near death. To the show's

credit, it manages to keep the drama high even when veering into that territory. After all, very special episodes of *Growing Pains* never had Alan Thicke shooting a corpse in the head.

In a Jersey slum, a huffing and puffing patrol officer, Joe Luria, is chasing down a suspect, Babyshoes. When he corners him, Babyshoes gives up peacefully. But while reading the Miranda rights, the cop starts to act strangely, laughing uncontrollably and waving his gun around. Fearing for his life, Babyshoes shoots the officer in the shoulder and flees. Joe the cop lies on the ground, still unable to stop laughing.

The ER crew treats the wound but the fact that Joe can't stop laughing has House interested. While Foreman has distinct distaste for treating a crooked-seeming cop — as he states, he knew cops like that when he was growing up — he's the one who goes to Joe's utterly filthy apartment and is doused by the sprinklers before he leaves with samples. House visits the police station to investigate; he notices an ancient air conditioning unit by Joe's desk. Several other cops are coughing near by. House comes back triumphant that he found the cause — Legionnaires disease.

With a positive test, they begin treating the cop for Legionnaires, but Joe only gets worse. House wants to do an MRI but doesn't know whether the bullet fragments in the cop's skull will be ripped out. So House takes a revolver down to the morgue and shoots a John Doe corpse in the head, which causes Foreman to "grin foolishly." They then take the corpse into the MRI room and ruin the incredibly expensive machine when the bullet fragments fly out of the corpse.

When the cop gets worse, crying out in pain, Foreman begins laughing at him too and House realizes that whatever Joe is suffering from, Foreman also has. They are placed in isolation together, so that Foreman's foe is now his cellmate.

While being examined by Cameron, Foreman demands that someone go back to the apartment for another search. Cameron, in spite of her grudge against Foreman for stealing her article, has suggested this same thing to House only to be shot down and forbidden from doing so. When she tells Foreman the apartment is too dangerous to go near, he impulsively stabs her with a used needle, giving her the excuse she wanted to continue the search to save her colleague. Like House, Cameron — in spite of her grudges and righteousness — believes to the end in doing the right thing. We see here that even though he is a good and caring doctor, Foreman does always protect himself at all costs.

With part two, we know we'll get a more intimate glimpse into Foreman's life as his fate hangs in the balance, and family members need to be called in. The show opens with Foreman getting worse and House trying to figure out the reason he's deteriorating so fast. Cuddy makes the safe decision to impound the now-dead cop's body until the CDC arrives — a decision that pits the whole team against her. In the past, Cuddy has not been against bending rules for House or looking in the other direction, but her concern is that the rest of the team — and the hospital at large — will be put at risk otherwise. It's obvious the decision hurts her, but she is a boss and stands her ground (something House should be familiar with since he himself seldom compromises once his mind is made up).

Without a Joe autopsy, there's little House can go on except that the cop had Legionnaires and Foreman, now blind, doesn't. What if the Legionnaires could slow down the illness? House wonders. Against everyone's wishes, he tosses a bottle of Legionella into Foreman's room, guaranteeing he'll come down with the infection. While Foreman improves enough to buy the team time, his father arrives for a tense reunion and we learn that Foreman's mother has descended into Alzheimer's, which is why she's not there. Foreman's father is a man of faith, and the theme from "House Versus God" is resurrected as he urges his son to look to God.

But Foreman's faith lies elsewhere, in a most unlikely place: his co-worker. It is her forgiveness, not God's, that he begs. In a moment of understanding between the two combative co-workers, Foreman makes Cameron his medical proxy. Going against the supposition that blood is thicker than water, Foreman chooses her because she knows the medicine and because she is his friend. If he has to be put in a coma, Cameron, not his father, has to make his decisions for him. He also states that he wants them to do a gray matter biopsy — deep in the brain — to find out what the agent is, even though it could cause permanent, drooling brain damage.

In this episode, we see House pull a reverse Cuddy, proving, perhaps for the first time, that he is not above human bias. When she cares too much (as we saw in "Humpty Dumpty" and will see again), she rushes head first into complex treatments. Because House cares too much, he's unable to take the risks he normally would. He retreats from Foreman's case until Cuddy forces him back into action. The third trip to Joe's apartment is House's. He realizes the cop stole everything: dinners, cable, and, it turns out, water from a rank rooftop reservoir. Examining a sample of the water House finds the amoeba Naegleria. He phones the hospital only to learn that Cameron has also found the cause — she went ahead with the brain biopsy. When Foreman wakes up, cured, he seems in control of his faculties, until it comes to a left/right test. Foreman is suffering from aphasia, but, as we'll learn next week, the cliffhanger is little more than a quick deke to make us all tune in again.

Highlight
An African-American character on primetime television *wasn't* killed off. Finally, Omar Epps gets an episode — two, actually — focused entirely on Foreman.

Support Staff
- House lays it on the diagnostics table as he brings in the case of Joe Luria.
- He swings it against the vent at the police station when he's checking things out.

Lies
- Joe tells the truth when Babyshoes asks if he's high.
- "I keep a pretty clean home," Joe says, tallest tale of the year.
- House admits it's his fault when he ruins the MRI, "My bad."
- Cameron and Chase both consult with Foreman on the case behind House's back.
- Joe lies about stealing cable, water, and, um, pigeon crap.
- Cameron hides the fact that Foreman stabbed her with a needle.
- House lies to Foreman's father about Cuddy's power over the situation.
- Cameron doesn't come clean about being Foreman's medical proxy until he is out, so if Foreman's dad has problems with it, he will have to take them up with her, not Foreman.

Exam Room
- The episode begins with the issue of faith and the rift between Foreman and his father, as Chase chuckles about the religious quote Foreman's father has written in the margin of a clipping from Foreman's article. Foreman says, "Everything I do right is God's work. Everything I do wrong is my own damn fault." Right away we have a clue that Foreman's father will play a

key role in the episode (or at least part two).

- House tries to pass off his speeding tickets as part of his disability.
- "Why don't we agree to disagree?" House says to Foreman as they argue over whether Joe's symptoms stem from Legionnaires or drug-related toxins. The phrase seems like it ought to have been said a long time ago, as it's been the crux of their relationship since day one, season one.
- House calls a cop "Officer Krupke," a reference to *West Side Story*.
- Promotional plug? House mocks Cuddy's procedural seriousness by saying, "Better call Jack Bauer."
- House invents several new euphemisms for masturbation in the clinic when a mom with an active young girl comes in thinking her daughter has epilepsy: "Finding Nemo," "Ya Yaing the Sisterhood," and "Marching the Penguin."
- Should we read into Joe's name — Joe, as in Joe Average, Luria as in Lure, a character who is little more than a lure into danger for one of our heroes?
- We see how far Cameron will go to save the life of her colleague. She claims she's trying to save her own life, but, as House points out, her reason for returning to the dangerous apartment isn't because Foreman injected her. If she thought she was already infected, she wouldn't have felt she needed to don a safe suit.
- We learn more about Foreman's background, including — like Chase — his break from faith. Unlike Chase, Foreman and his father haven't drifted from one another in spite of their differences.

Booboos

- Babyshoes pulls his revolver and shoots the officer. When he pulls his gun and points it, he holds it with both hands. When the shot changes to a slow motion shot of the bullet flying, his facial expression has changed, and he's suddenly holding the gun with only one hand.
- When the patient, Joe Luria, has a tachycardia episode and an ocular bleed, the blood disappears and reappears between shots.

What's Up, Doc?

- According to Politedissent.com, Cameron can't attend and be a legal proxy at the same time. "She could refuse a test in Foreman's name, but not order one. Later, it seems as if she is acting as the lead physician, which is a clear conflict of interest. She can't be both lead physician and proxy at the same time."
- Naegleria is a common amoeba but infection is rare: only 24 cases in the United States, thus making a double infection doubly doubtful. As well, Foreman is unusually lucky. Should infection actually occur, the CDC cautions, "Several drugs are effective against Naegleria in the laboratory. However, although a variety of treatments have been used to treat infected persons, their effectiveness is unclear since most infections have still been fatal."

2.22 Forever

First broadcast: May 9, 2006
Writer: Liz Friedman
Director: Daniel Sackheim
Guest stars: Hillary Tuck (Kara), Kip Pardue (Brent), Toni Lewis (NICU nurse), Kevin Moon (EMT)

Episode Differential

With Foreman back from the brink of death but forever changed and Chase hiding in NICU (Natal Intensive Care Unit), the team is barely holding together when a mother and her near dead son come through emergency.

In a grim and poor apartment, Brent, a young father feels sick on the way out to work. He says goodbye to his wife Kara and their newborn that she goes off to bathe. Once outside he vomits and walks back in, telling his wife he's decided to call in sick. Another fake-out: when he makes it to the bathroom Kara is in the tub, seizing, and their son is motionless under water.

At the hospital, both husband and wife are run through the emergency room with Chase attending to the baby. Though Chase is trying to distance himself from the department, he seeks out House's help when, after the baby stabilizes, his lungs collapse. Chase thinks chemicals from the bath got into the lungs. House votes for bacteria. Examining the mother, a still shaky Foreman thinks her seizing was psychological in nature. As well, it's learned that Brent and Kara met in AA. A diagnosis of DTs is temporarily given to her while House confronts Brent about their drinking. On antibiotics the child gets better, and Chase returns him to his mother. House enters Kara's room only to find Kara smothering the child who, even after he is liberated from her, eventually dies.

The team is divided on treatment of Kara. Can they find an underlying cause for the psychotic episodes? Foreman, who's still cruising on a gift-of-life trip, infuriates House with his positive attitude even in the face of a mother killing her child. House thinks back to the child's lungs and wonders if mother and child may have had the same condition, especially after Kara is induced to have another seizure and vomits blood. When Chase autopsies the child, a moment that tries his willpower and faith, he discovers celiac disease — a condition where any gluten product that enters the body damages the stomach and intestines. Kara very likely has stomach cancer and it's possible the cancer has triggered the psychosis. When Wilson fails to convince her to receive treatment — she believes she deserves to die — House drafts the distraught husband to help her.

In a parallel cancer subplot, and a subtle baby theme, House discovers through Wilson that Cuddy is hoping to have a child. Having invited Wilson out to dinner, House thinks Cuddy wants an oncology consult, not a date. It's enough to make Wilson steal her dinner spoon and run tests on her DNA looking for a cancer marker. It comes back clean but House notices high estrogen levels. She's shopping for a donor — a plot that sets up season three.

Highlight

House challenges Wilson, who's doing a PCR test, saying, "You're doing it yourself. In the middle of the night. On a spoon. Cuddy's spoon." Wilson responds, "I'm checking her saliva for cancer markers." House's quick comeback: "Yeah — I do that after all my dates too. People think you're the nice one."

Support Staff

- House hooks it over the counter while getting his coffee, as he frequently does.

- He uses it to point at Foreman as they argue over Foreman's recent tendency to agree and compliantly do as House instructs him.

Lies

- Chase lies when he says that Cuddy says he's stuck working with the kids.
- Cuddy's a bad liar when House confronts her about Chase's choice to go to NICU.
- Chase says he left diagnostics because he was tired of patients lying. "Nothing more honest than a dead baby," House retorts cruelly.
- House breaks into Cuddy's office, and goes through her trash to try to get to the bottom of the case of the Cuddy-Wilson dinner.
- Brent lies about his drinking.
- Kara lies about her drinking.
- Wilson steals a sample of Cuddy's DNA during their date and tests it without her knowledge.

Exam Room

- Lesbian expert Dr. House confides that he watches *The L Word* with the sound turned down.
- "I'm recently single; she's single," Wilson says of his date with Cuddy. Their instant friendship, and House's befuddlement at it, sets up the date-like subplot of season three.
- House makes further Aussie references this episode about Chase's polo pony when he learns Chase has abandoned diagnostics.
- Foreman's so high on life, he hugs Cameron as vigorously as a lover; he's even willing to stomach House's racial comments. "I take mine black," House says of his coffee, "the way I take my brain-damaged neurologists."
- House opens the coffee packet with his teeth.
- "You don't need me for this," Chase says when House tries to include him in the diagnostic session. "Of course I need you," House says, admitting for the first time that he needs his staff — and Chase, whom he's always disliked in particular. "We're a team." It's partly true, and partly antagonistic since House,

with his narcissist-like behavior, thinks of what they do as more important than all other medical pursuits or cases. It's why he can engage in antics — such as ruining the MRI — without considering how it will affect all the other patients at Princeton-Plainsboro. Only a second later, he's calling Chase a moron.

- Chase pulls out the "physical contact helps the healing process" stuff in NICU with the dad and his infant son. Chase learned this soft approach from Cameron in season one's "Maternity."
- The Cuddy-Wilson dinner is particularly funny on re-watch as she asks about his divorce and mentions kids twice. It's not the consult he thinks it is, and she's not husband-shopping — she's daddy-shopping.
- During dinner, Cuddy is drinking water from a wine glass — a caution in case she's already pregnant? Wilson's glass is full of red wine.
- We get two close-ups on an eye opening as its owner wakes. One is Brent's, one is Kayla's. Both precede major accidents with Baby Mikey.

What's Up, Doc?
- Chase gets a new specialty overnight? He's an intensivist, not a neonatologist.
- Foreman heals far too quickly given the severity of his illness.

2.23 Who's Your Daddy?

First aired: May 16, 2006
Writers: Lawrence Kaplow, John Mankiewicz
Director: Martha Mitchell
Guest stars: D.B. Sweeney (Dylan Crandall), Aasha Davis (Leona), Christopher Carley (John Linehan), Owen Pearce (Max)

Episode Differential
House has a friend other than Wilson? Yes, and this, the weakest episode of the season, can be as confusing as figuring out patrimony.

Unfortunately, we'll learn little about House and his idea of friendship that we don't already know. This episode also launches us into a plot we'll see plenty of in season three: Cuddy auditioning men for the job of being her baby-daddy.

On a plane out of New Orleans, a 16-year-old black girl named Leona sits beside middle-aged white music writer Dylan Crandall. Orphaned by Hurricane Katrina, and surviving the aftermath alone in the ruins, Leona has just recently told Crandall they're daughter and father. Leona begins to hallucinate filthy water flooding the airplane and she goes into what seems to be cardiac arrest.

At the hospital, Crandall stops House with the shout of "G-man!" At first House plays dumb, pretending not to recognize him, but then they half-embrace. Crandall was House's college best friend and he's brought Leona to him for diagnosis. When House finds out Leona is the granddaughter of his favorite jazz pianist, Jesse Baker (who Crandall wrote an unfavorable book about), he's hooked into the case. As we saw before in "Sports Medicine," House is no stranger to celebrity cases, and, as in "DNR," particularly loves those involving musicians. It follows then that even if Crandall weren't asking him to take the case, he might be tempted. Crandall, who's not too bright, doesn't seem House's type. When quizzed about their friendship by the seemingly jealous Wilson, House confesses, "We were 20 years old. He had a car. If he'd been a woman, I would have married him." Sounds like the same old House.

House doubts his friend's role in Leona's procreation. Whether or not a paternity test is done is a running debate during the show. The team is stumped until House listens to a recording of Leona's grandfather near the end of his life. Baker says the piano is out of tune, but to House's own musician ear, it's not. Adding this genetic component, House is able to diagnose hemochromatosis, a buildup of iron. As they treat Leona, the suddenly free iron combines with an unknown crisis in her lungs, cutting them to shreds. When taken off the ventilator, Leona confesses she wasn't staying at a shelter in New Orleans. She was staying in her grandfather's flood-ravaged studio. The team is able to finally diagnose the lung infection and complete Leona's treatment.

While there are good scenes, as a whole, the episode doesn't gel. The medicine is considered the sloppiest of the season — something as radical as a bone marrow transplant is not the first choice of treatment for an autoimmune disorder. It's not even third. However, House's counseling of Cuddy through the ins and outs of sperm donors is humorous and after Cuddy seems intrigued enough by House to ask him to help inject her fertility meds in a revealing place, a possible plot for the next season is apparent. We get the distinct impression that she might be interested in House himself for the job. Or maybe House just wants to think so.

Highlight
Men take note from House's swabbing of Cuddy's butt cheek — *slow* and *romantic* circles.

Support Staff
He uses it to retrieve his jacket with his pills in the pocket.

Lies
- House pretends he doesn't know Crandall.
- "Pulled a hamstring playing Twister, just gonna walk it off," House says about his leg when Crandall mentions it.
- Crandall says Leona's mom lied for 16 years about who the father was.
- House lies to Crandall about the procedure: "Test is perfectly safe. We do it every day."
- Leona lies to everyone about where she stayed during Katrina.
- Leona lies to Crandall about their relationship.
- House lies to Crandall by secretly running the paternity test.
- House lies to Leona when he tells her she told a bad lie: Crandall is her dad.
- House brings Cuddy's possible donor into the hospital under false pretenses. He's not being considered for a position; he's being paraded for humiliation.

Exam Room
- Crandall is also the surname of the show's costume designer, Cathy Crandall.
- House's Vicodin intake is up, again setting up themes for season three, and we see his secret stash for the first time as he climbs a stool to get to the morphine-filled box at the top of his bookshelf.
- We hear House's message machine for the first time, also a joke, "You've reached a number that has been disconnected and is no longer in service . . ."

- Toxins and mould are the first suggestions from Cameron and Chase when they learn Leona is a survivor of Katrina.
- Even this late in the season, House is still taunting Cameron about her feelings for him. "Hold me," he says when they're play-acting her plan to get Crandall to sign procedural release forms. She continues without batting an eyelash.
- House references Bill Nye the Science Guy.
- When picking donors, Cuddy reveals "I'm leaning towards 613" and House responds, "Oh sure, go with the Jewish number." He is referring to the 613 commandments in the Torah. The first is "be fruitful and multiply."

What's Up, Doc?
Chase and House confuse the functions of the liver and kidneys. They really are just actors after all.

2.24 No Reason

First aired: May 24, 2006
Writer: David Shore
Director: David Shore
Guest stars: Elias Koteas (Moriarty), Chris Tallman (Vince), Michelle Clunie (Judy), Obie Sims (Cuddy's Patient)

Episode Differential
Bobby Ewing didn't really die. The cast of *Dynasty* wasn't really shot by terrorists at a European wedding. TV-land likes to torture its viewers with "it was just a dream" logic, but the season finale of *House* plays with the clichés of television enough to make even the clichés seem interesting again. Letting the viewers in on the joke as soon as possible, as *House* does, is always a plus. Though similar in structure to "Three Stories" and "The Mistake," this episode didn't garner any extra award nominations for the show.

Consulting with his team during the morning, House is regaling them about a patient with a grotesquely swollen tongue. Cruelly, House put him through "verbal tests" just to hear him try to pronounce words. The meeting is broken up when a man walks into the office, takes out a gun, and shoots House to the ground.

After the credits, House is in ICU. He wakes up and by his beard growth figures he was out for two days. Cameron is by his side. And over to his other side is the man who shot him, handcuffed to his gurney — he was shot by security while trying to flee. It's the first element of this post-surgery world that doesn't seem quite right. As he converses with his shooter, House learns that the man was a patient of his (one we never saw on-screen), one whose wife he informed of his affair. She later killed herself.

While House defends his innocence, his team is still consulting with him. The man with the swollen tongue is only getting worse, with a seemingly endless array of bizarre symptoms that don't add up. House, feeling that his leg has somehow improved, steals his surgical report and notices that he was given ketamine, an unusual anesthetic that causes disassociative comas. House thinks it might explain his leg and his odd mental state, which seems like he's lucid dreaming through the day. Soon he's wandering around the hospital in his gown, working on the case of the swollen tongue patient, which becomes more and more grotesque. Our sense of reality begins to be tested when the team meets — with House still in hospital gown — at a burrito joint. Back in his room, the shooter informs House it's all a hallucination. Is it? Is the swollen tongue man the stand-in for all the patients House has mistreated? A representation of his self-loathing?

House goes to Cuddy and demands to know why he was given ketamine. She reveals that studies in Germany have shown that patients with chronic pain have been cured with ketamine comas. House is walking around without his cane, but what's real? The swollen tongue patient is literally exploding, his eyes and testicles popping out of his body. The team needs to operate, but it could kill the patient. House suggests using a new robotic surgical device that makes micro incisions with little bleeding. This is the ultimate tip-off as to the fantastical nature of this episode as the device is an evil science-fiction confabulation, complete with CGI arms. As the patient is prepped, House decides to prove to himself (and the horrified team) that this is all a hallucination and eviscerates the patient. For a moment, the scene is quiet and shocking enough to make the viewer wonder if House was wrong. Instead, House does indeed wake up. He has been shot and is being wheeled into emergency. His last words as the season ends are: "Tell Cuddy, I want ketamine."

Highlight
Possibly House's robo-surgeon seduction of Cameron. Or that the show's creators didn't wait until next season to tell us it was all a hallucination.

Support Staff
We're led to believe House won't be needing it anymore. He walks unaided, as he always does in his fantasies or dreams, for much of the episode.

Exam Room
- The feel-good Foreman may be gone and the Foreman who can stand up to House truly returned. "And why do we care?" Foreman says after House details the tongue patient's temperature is 103 degrees. In a rare and taunting role reversal, House replies, "Because we're human beings. It's what we do."
- The shooter says he was a patient of House's, yet he doesn't know what House looks like. He does know what Cameron looks like though, so presumably this is one of those cases where House managed to get away with never meeting the patient.
- "Moriarity," the name of House's would-be assassin (revealed only on closed captioning) is also the name of Sherlock Holmes' arch nemesis.
- The DOB on House's patient wristband is Hugh Laurie's actual birthday: June 11, 1959. (See "The Socratic Method" for fan debate regarding House's birthday.) His armband also details that Cuddy is his doctor, and gives his admittance date as April 5, a fair amount of time before the show's airdate.
- "I got shot. Diagnostically boring," House says about himself. The line explains much about House and justifies all his antics — he's bored by everything. Even himself. Boredom, like lies, is a theme that runs throughout the series. We see it specifically in "Spin" when House is setting up domino-style objects on his desk, "Distractions" when he resorts to razzing Weber to avoid his own life, and in "Forever" where Foreman returns, positive, compliant, "boring." The very word is repeated throughout those episodes. It's also the excuse House uses every time he wants to avoid taking a case.

Lies
Um, the entire episode.

What's Up, Doc?

Ketamine rebooting the brain? The journal *Neurology Today* reports, "Two approaches to using ketamine to treat the complex regional pain syndrome (CRPS) — one employing anesthetic doses, the other subanesthetic — both show promise despite the risks associated with prolonged administration of the drug, researchers say. Neither technique has yet been validated in a randomized, or even an open prospective trial; indeed, the more extreme of the two approaches, using ketamine to induce a coma, has not been published in a peer-reviewed journal."

SEASON THREE

3.1 Meaning

First aired: September 5, 2006
Writers: Lawrence Kaplow, David Shore
Director: Deran Sarafian
Guest stars: Kathleen Quinlan (Arlene), Edward Edwards (Richard), Carter Jenkins (Mark), Clare Kramer (Caren), Terry Rhoads (Artie)

Episode Differential

What's more shocking: Cameron's new bangs or the fact that House is walking? Not just walking, but running. House returns to the hospital after surviving multiple gunshot wounds. His hallucinatory state, for the time being, is relieved, and he no longer requires the use of the cane. In fact, he feels so confident upon his return to work that he decides to take on two patients at once on his first shift back. This is, of course, unheard of.

Richard, who was paralyzed after brain cancer surgery eight years previous, landed himself in House's care when he drove himself and his wheelchair into a swimming pool, head first. The second patient is Caren, a young woman who has been paralyzed from the neck down after a yoga session. House continues to be frustrated with the lack of progress with Richard, and is somehow convinced that Richard, like House, will walk again. Why shouldn't he be right? Look what happened in "DNR." House does not, however, have any solid evidence with which to back his claims, and the rest of the medical team are suspicious that he's just bored.

Acting a little more like himself with his other patient, House suspects Caren is faking her paralysis. He tests this theory by burning her foot, to which she appropriately reacts with movement of her limbs. House then notices an irregularity in her breathing, and inspects her chest instead, only to find there is blood build-up around her heart. House orders the patient to undergo surgery to remove the tumor that he now believes to be there, but just before, discovers that there is discolouration in her toenails. He diagnoses her with scurvy, curing her instead with orange juice. Having cured Caren, House admits defeat with his other patient, even though his final guess of Addison's (something that could be cured with cortisol) hasn't been tested.

Is it Cuddy's faith in House or simply curiosity that guides her next action? As she sees Richard and his family out of the hospital, she decides to test House's hypothesis and injects the patient with Cortisone. Richard stands up out of his chair. Cuddy and Wilson decide not to let House know that he was right. A little humility, they assume, will help him be less reckless. How they reach this conclusion, however, when he's only been back at the hospital for one case is a bit puzzling. Perhaps they're basing their assessment on the notion that a newly walking House is likely to be changed for a couple of months while he is on a feel-good upswing, then go back to his cynical and nasty, nasty ways (the same way that Foreman's brush with death turned him only temporarily benevolent). They've known House longer than we have, yet somehow we know it's all going to end badly.

The episode closes on House forging a prescription on Wilson's pad, perhaps signaling that the pain is returning.

Highlight
House says to Caren, "I'm not going to stab you. I'm going to *burn* you."

Lies

- Wilson and Cuddy conspire against House — for his own good.
- Caren lies about her extreme Atkins diet that gives her a third-world disease. She is faking her paralysis.
- House lies by using someone else's prescription pad.

Exam Room

- Guest star Kathleen Quinlan was in Oliver Stone's *The Doors* — which was Lisa Edelstein's film debut, in the breakout role of "Makeup artist with cigarette."
- Both patients have forms of fake paralysis. The difference lies in how fake. Richard can't walk, but he can under the right circumstances. Both cases play off House's new ability to walk, forming a triple parallel. His ability to walk isn't fake, but it is about to give out. . . .
- Cuddy and Wilson have both known House for more than a decade. Cuddy crossed paths with him at University of Michigan, which, based on their birthdates, would have been in the '80s. She graduated at the age of 25, and became Chief of Medicine at the age of 32 (as she revealed in "Humpty Dumpty"), which would have been in the mid '90s if we assume that the 10 years she hasn't been a practicing doctor puts her age at 42. She was also House's doctor around that time (as we saw in "Three Stories") and is familiar with Stacy, which means she's seen House through several different periods in his life. Wilson is also friends with Stacy, so we can assume his friendship with House also dates back to the same period. Duration of familiarity, however, doesn't equal insight.

Booboos

On the whiteboard, someone has spelled diarrhea as "diarea." A New Jersey variation?

What's Up, Doc?

- Patients who don't use their legs for eight years do not stand, even if given sudden power to use them again. Even Tarantino knew to turn that fact to comedy in *Kill Bill* when Uma Thurman's character psychically willed her big toe to move after years in a coma.
- According to Politedissent.com: "At the end of episode, House sneaks into Wilson's office and writes himself a prescription for Vicodin, forging Wilson's signature. . . . It shows that House has written a prescription for 'Vicodin ES 5-500.' Now the standard dose of Vicodin is 5mg Hydrocodone + 500mg Acetaminophen, but Vicodin ES is 7.5/750, so there is no 'Vicodin ES 5-500.'"

3.2 Cane and Able

First aired: September 12, 2006
Writers: Russel Friend, Garrett Lerne
Director: Daniel Sackheim
Guest stars: Edward Edwards (Richard), Skyler Gisondo (Clancy), Sheryl Lee (Stephanie), Johnny Sneed (Todd)

Episode Differential

Even if House is playing God a little less, thanks to Cuddy and Wilson's ruse, he still has to confront whether there's life beyond Earth after encountering a young patient. House's mental stress over — as far as he knows — not having cured Richard causes him to be in physcial pain again, and though this is apparent in his symptoms, he continues to deny that there's a problem.

His new case is a seven-year-old boy who has rectal bleeding and is constantly telling the staff that he was the victim of an alien abduction and torture. He also tells the medical team, after conflicting tests and examinations are done, that he has a tracking device in his neck. Chase, showing signs of his lingering faith, believes there's something to the young boy's story. When the medical team discovers that Clancy has cells of a different type of DNA in his body, they decide to investigate his claims of "alien abduction" a little further. They conclude that brain surgery is best to determine which part of his brain is causing the hallucinations. The surgery includes enducing the hallucinations by way of electrical shocks. The results are disturbing, and House concludes that these are nightmares brought on by a bleeding disorder.

In other news, Cameron discovers what Cuddy and Wilson have been keeping from House and is taken aback. Cuddy, however, convinces her not to tell House. At least, not just yet.

Several tests are run on Clancy, and in spite of conflicting opinions between Foreman and Cameron, the team concludes that the boy has chimerism, a condition that's the result of two fertilized eggs fusing in the uterus. The metal found in his neck is thought to be the remains of a surgical pin that migrated via his circulatory system. This particular episode is like a bad day on the *X-Files*, which means that the boy's duality, or twin-like condition, doesn't wind up being addressed in relation to House's. We could read the boy as a mirror for his doctor — House's Gemini birthdate, his up and down personality, the walking House versus the non-walking House, the House who flaunts his drug use versus the one who hides it — but the show never really steers us in that direction, opting instead for straight sci-fi.

An odd episode, it only seems to serve as an ending to the plot line of Cuddy and Wilson's attempt to reign House in.

Highlight

Upon House's return, Nurse Brenda says to Cameron in the clinic: "Don't blame you for spending extra time down here. Heard the artist formerly known as Gimp is back upstairs."

Support Staff

- The episode's title references the Bible story, but it's also a wink at our old wooden friend.
- The final shot is House contemplating, and then taking his cane out of the closet.

Lies

- Cameron is now in on Cuddy and Wilson's lie that House didn't cure Richard of his paralysis.
- When Cuddy confesses that House did cure his last patient, he doesn't believe her. He speaks directly to her abdomen, as if talking to her future child, "Oh, your Mommy's in such trouble. She's such a liar!"
- Clancy isn't lying — he hasn't been abducted by aliens or implanted, but something is definitely askew.
- When they remove the pin from Clancy, House jokes that the metal is not found on Earth. The gullible Chase momentarily believes him.

Exam Room

- Cameron says that they will need "a cunning plan" to solve the case. This was Baldrick's catchphrase in all four seasons of *Blackadder*.
- This episode, which reads like an *X-Files* case, nods in that direction when House directly references it.
- House also references popular '70s flicks *Jaws* and *Star Wars:* "We're gonna need a bigger boat," and "Foreman, you take Alpha Centauri, Chase can check Tatooine, and Cameron can

setup an Intergalactic Checkpoint." Comparing Chase to Luke Skywalker and Cameron to Princess Leia is doubly funny since the actors share some resemblance.

- This is the first episode where House denies his godlike status. When Wilson says, "I was afraid you'd think you were God . . . and that your wings would melt," House replies candidly, "God doesn't have a limp."

Booboos

On a monitor the misspelled phrase, "DNA Specimin" appears twice.

What's Up, Doc?

This episode features the absolute worst surgery scene ever in the series with House conducting open brain surgery that doesn't exist. While chimerism is very real and common, there is no "cure" for it. Human DNA codes over 25,000 different genes, and Cameron cannot sort out which are which over-night, nor can House excise chimerical matter from a brain.

3.3 Informed Consent

Originally aired: September 19, 2006
Writer: David Foster
Director: Laura Innes
Guest stars: Joel Grey (Ezra), Stephanie Venditto (Nurse Brenda), Leighton Meester (Ali), William Charlton (Mark)

Episode Differential

House's new patient is Ezra Powell, a renowned researcher and medical pioneer who collapsed in his lab while studying rats. They promptly enact revenge on the comotose researcher's face with substantial gnawing — calling to mind Orwell's *Nineteen Eighty-Four*.

With the ketamine treatment wearing off, House is already back to using his cane, which he doesn't want to discuss with the rest of the staff. His frustration increases throughout the episode as he puts Ezra through his usual: a rigorous line of diagnoses, only to determine nothing but death itself at the end of all the testing.

Ezra's health is rapidly deteriorating and he demands that the team stop the testing and let him die in peace — "peace" meaning that they give him a large injection of morphine. "Every doctor's done it," Chase says, agreeing with the patient. House says he will, but bargains with Ezra to let him do one more day of tests before giving up. The moral conundrum strikes the team in very different ways as they consider the repercussions of assisted suicide and the potential knowledge gained by continued testing. With the medical team divided, the episode continues with notable tension. When there is no conclusion within the agreed-upon day, House pulls a House, and decides to put Ezra into a coma instead of killing him. During a colonoscopy, however, Ezra's lung gives out and House is forced to bring him out of his coma, which means that Ezra is well aware of House's broken promise.

Meanwhile, an attractive and very teenage daughter of one of House's clinic patients starts to nurture an obsessive crush on him, much to his conflicted torment. It seems to set up season three's sub-theme of House turning from escort-buying lecher to irresistible leading man.

During the end scenes, Ezra is seen crying in his hospital bed after being told he is indeed dying. The following morning, Cuddy comes into House's office to let him know that Ezra passed away at 2:30 a.m., although he was declared stable at 2:00. House denies any knowledge of it and asks Cuddy if she would want to know even if he did. House then goes to Cameron, who is seen dressed in black, crying at the hospital chapel, suggesting that it was she who aided in Ezra's passing. Is this a new character development for Cameron — that sometimes one has to do wrong to do right?

Highlight
Revenge of the lab rats!

Support Staff
House references his limp: "I'm a cripple, remember? Accommodations must be made."

Lies
- The whole episode is about what constitutes a lie on the part of a doctor to a patient and what the boundaries are of informed consent.

- House acts as if he is giving Ezra a lethal injection, but in fact puts him into a coma.
- We're given the impression that Cameron gave Ezra a lethal injection, but if she did, she's not saying anything.

Exam Room

- Early in season three, fans debated whether Cameron was full of more contradictions. She is, at the same time as she isn't. She has always been the good girl, but incur her wrath by violating her sense of justice and she always had the power to become vehement. Ezra says he doesn't regret what he did, "informed consent — patient rights — holds back research." Cameron cuts him, slicing a skin sample from his arm. "Informed consent is holding back our diagnosis," she retorts. This scene echoes one from "Spin," in which Cameron revealed that she had removed a sample from the cheating cyclist's leg, the most painful place, according to Chase.
- However you interpret Jennifer Morrison's portrayal of Cameron this episode, it should be noted that she believed this was a shining moment in the series. She and actor Joel Grey submitted this episode for consideration in the 59th Emmy Awards for "Outstanding Supporting Actress in a Drama Series," and "Outstanding Guest Actor in a Drama Series." Unfortunately, neither one picked up the Emmy.
- House references the film *The Wizard of Oz* when testing Ezra's sensations.
- If we think about how the episode's title "Informed Consent" applies to House himself, the theme does hearken back to his original infarction surgery, especially when we consider the power he had in his more recent treatment.

Booboos

- When House is about to inject "morphine" into Ezra's body, the amount of morphine in the syringe changes between shots.
- Ezra's left leg reacts, but House says, "No sensation in the left leg, abdomen, right arm," when he's detailing to the team.

What's Up, Doc?

- There are several very common chemical stress tests that can be used to stress the heart, without the use of treadmills or even ephedrine, especially when the patient is ill and elderly.

3.4 Lines in the Sand

First aired: September 26, 2006
Writer: David Hoselton
Director: Newton Thomas Sigel
Guest stars: Braeden Lemasters (Adam), Geoffrey Blake (Dominic), Heather Kafka (Sarah), Leighton Meester (Ali)

Episode Differential

This is an episode where many of the characters are drawing lines in the sand: House about his carpet, Cuddy about inappropriate behavior, and Foreman about what being a doctor means to him.

House finds himself in the middle of drama on all sides. He's still being pursued by Ali, the 17-year-old girl whose infatuation began in the last episode and is getting to a more serious level with frequent calls and hospital visits. House doesn't seem to mind as much as the medical team thinks he should. In addition, his new patient, a severely autistic 10-year-old named Adam, prompts more misdiagnoses. The team is dumbfounded by Adam's illness, and House, himself obsessed and withdrawn, develops a rapport with the boy.

Foreman loses his patience during a series of medical tests, and even goes so far as to ask Wilson to perform tests for cancer, in a portent of Foreman's coming schism with House. Foreman also searches the family's backyard and finds Jimson Weed, which could be a cause for the case. Despite the ethical breach, the team discovers that the austistic child has roundworms that he picked up from raccoon feces in the backyard sandbox.

On Cuddy's suggestion, House also confronts Ali about her infatuation. He explains that she will regret being with him, even if it is legal. When she starts to cry, he looks into her eyes and sees that her tears are milky. He concludes that an earthquake in California, where she recently vacationed, may have caused her to pick up the same spores that were released into the air that the rest of her family did. House also informs her that there is a chance that symptoms of the illness include a lack of mental clarity, which would in turn explain her infatuation with him. The situation is resolved, despite his intense disapointment. House, however, receives satisfaction in other ways. He successfully lobbies for the return of the sentimental carpet from his office, which became stained with blood when he was shot in "No Reason."

Highlight
Foreman — who, as usual, disagrees with House — makes his point about testing their screaming patient by saying, "I had a date last night. She screamed! Should we spend $100,000 testing her?" House's comeback: "Course not . . . this isn't a veterinary hospital. ZING!"

Lies
- Cuddy lies to House to keep him away from Ali.
- It's never confirmed but one gets the suspicion House may be lying to Ali about her illness to get her to give up her crush on him. Everyone lies, after all.

Exam Room
- The clue for the final diagnosis is right in the title. We ought to know from the get-go that the answer will have to do with sand.
- When the old carpet is being re-installed in House's office, the carpet is shown to be slightly too big for the room.
- The age of consent law in New Jersey is 16, not 18 as discussed in this episode, making Ali on the side of legal but not on the side of good taste for a middle-aged doctor.
- House references the film *Dog Day Afternoon* when he's chanting "Attica" in Cuddy's office, trying to convince her to return the carpet. He also relies heavily on *Casablanca* quotes when ditching Ali. He references Mel's Diner from the 1974 film *Alice Doesn't Live Here Anymore* and later the TV series *Alice*. And going for two episodes in a row, he summons up *The Wizard of Oz* again when he invokes Margaret Hamilton's "Hello my pretties . . ."
- Foreman makes a play on the Beatles' LSD-referencing song "Lucy in the Sky with Diamonds," when he says, "Our kid's been tripping on 'Lucy in the Sky with Cubic Zirconium.'"

What's Up, Doc?

- It's a tradition on the show, apparently, to confuse "pleural effusion" with "pleural edema."
- Coccidioides immitis, what House diagnoses Ali's love sickness as being caused by, does present with personality disorders but only in conjunction with deadly meningitis, which the alive and walking Ali doesn't seem to have.

3.5 Fools for Love

First aired: October 31, 2006
Writer: Peter Blake
Director: David Pratt
Guest stars: David Morse (Michael Tritter), Jurnee Smollett (Tracy), Raviv Ullman (Jeremy)

Episode Differential

A young interracial couple, Jeremy and Tracy, are victims of a diner robbery. Her husband attacks the two robbers, and we think one of the bad guys may wind up being the patient — when Tracy's airways suddenly close.

There are no signs of allergic reaction when she's taken to the hospital, although it can be characterized as anaphylaxis. After a series of tests and bloodwork, Tracy reveals that she and her husband had been smoking marijuana previous to the diner incident. Suspecting salmonella poisoning, and with nothing else to go on, House orders the treatment. For an instant theme, House and Foreman toss around a few words about interracial dating, and dating in general, then place a bet on whether Wilson is seeing the fair and blonde Nurse Wendy. (Knowing the series' tricks with audience expectation, you just know how this is going to turn out.)

Michael Tritter, another patient under House's clinic watch, has a rash on his genitals that he wants swabbed. When House tries to explain that it's probably due to dehydration brought on by his use of nicotine gum, an argument ensues. Tritter ends up tripping House with his own cane. House performs the swab, but not without requesting on his exit that Tritter bend over so that he can take his temperature with a rectal thermometer. He leaves the room with Tritter still bent over. While this is seemingly classic House behavior, it will have dire consequences for House and those close to him.

As House gets distracted by Wilson's potential relationship with Nurse Wendy, the mystery of Tracy's illness deepens. STD tests come out clean, but Tracy's abdominal pain continues to worsen and she experiences intense hallucinations about Jeremy's father. She lapses into a coma.

House has been summoned to Cuddy's office where his former patient, Tritter, is waiting for him. Tritter demands an apology for the thermometer incident. House flat-out refuses and leaves the room. After a series of disappointing test results, Jeremy's symptoms — which mimic his wife's — intensify. It is concluded that the couple must share hereditary angioedema, which prevents the body from producing a vital protein. They are half-siblings, Tracy the result of an affair that her mother had with Jeremy's father — the real reason for his rage over their relationship, not his bias. The couple is devastated to discover they're related. Foreman the Sensitive steps in, but can't convince the couple that they'll be able to work it out.

The shift over, House speeds away from work on his motorcycle, only to be caught down the road by a police officer. The officer turns out to be his patient, Tritter. Tritter accuses House of driving in an altered state. Conducting a search, he finds House's Vicodin, after which he arrests him for narcotics. This episode in which the past comes back to haunt a young couple in love also sets up how House's own recent past will come back to haunt him in the form of Tritter.

Highlight
When House asks why Nurse Wendy is hanging around diagnostics, Cameron casually replies that she's been "hitting that." Her delivery is so dry it makes you double-take . . . "Did she just say —?" Yes, yes she did.

Support Staff
- "Ask him about the time he sabotaged my cane," House tells the woman he thinks is Wilson's new love interest, Wendy the nurse. It's a reference to "Safe," where he and Wilson play dorm-style pranks on each other.
- The clinic patient, who turns out to be Detective Tritter, accuses House of getting away with treating people like idiots because of his cane. He also kicks the cane out from under House.

Lies

- House accuses Wilson of lying to him about dating Wendy: "You're lying to me. That's interesting." Wilson evades by saying, "As long as it's interesting . . ." He's telling the truth.
- Cameron jokes that she's doing Wendy. She clearly isn't.
- House breaks into Wendy's locker. Doesn't lie about it though.
- When Cuddy asks House to apologize to the clinic patient, House tells the man that what they are both going to do is lie — that he gets to tell his friends how he humiliated the doctor, and House will tell Cuddy he actually apologized. Neither of these lies occur.
- Foreman doesn't come clean until the end that he's the one dating Wendy. He makes a bet, knowing what its outcome will be when he makes it.
- Wendy has lied about loving jazz. She just wants to make beautiful music with the neurologist.
- Cuddy wasn't lying to House when she said, "Baby's in your mind." She's not pregnant.

Exam Room

- Michael Tritter is introduced as House's new nemesis. One of actor David Morse's early roles was on the original doc-drama *St. Elsewhere*. He played Dr. Jack "Boomer" Morrison.
- Season three is turning out to be as bet-heavy as the previous seasons. House and Foreman bet $100 on whether the treadmill will trigger an allergy in the young wife. The bills ride again on Nurse Wendy. House also barters with Cuddy, striking the bargain of an apology (for clinic patient, Tritter) in exchange for a brain biopsy (for the young couple).
- This isn't the first time we've seen an interracial couple on the show. "Maternity" featured a two-mommy couple of different backgrounds. In neither episode does the show make it a big issue. It's discussed here, but only in passing.
- When House is talking about taking the young husband off morphine to influence his decision about a biopsy for his wife, the team is not about to be pressured. Chase puts it all on the table, saying, "Cameron and Foreman are too ethical and I'm too scared of being sued." It's the truth, but is it really what he would say? It seems like a line written specifically to bring

this season's new viewing audience up to speed with the rest of us on the character dynamics.

- Foreman seems perplexed by his own attempt to convince the half-brother and half-sister to stay together. He makes a face that seems to say, "What am I doing here? I don't buy what I'm saying either."

3.6 Que Será Será

First aired: November 7, 2006
Writer: Thomas L. Moran
Director: Deran Sarafian
Guest stars: David Morse (Tritter), Pruitt Taylor Vince (George), Stephanie Venditto (Nurse Brenda), Kadeem Hardison (Howard), Mary Elizabeth Ellis (Sophie), Cooper Thornton (John), Damien Dante Wayans (Haller)

Episode Differential

George Hagel, a 600-pound man is found presumably dead in his apartment. That is, until he releases a bout of flatulence while being moved that indicates he is, in fact, in a coma.

When House is asked his opinion concerning the patient, he advises checking the apartment, since George has no health problems typical of men his size. Cameron discovers, through speaking with neighbors, that George has prostitutes frequently visit. Syphilis is thrown into the basket of possibilities while the medical team has substantial troubles running tests on George, including when he wakes up in the middle of an MRI scan, struggling and demanding to leave. He is unconvinced that this current medical drama has anything to do with his weight and insists that he feels fine.

House, having spent the night in jail after being arrested by his former patient, Officer Michael Tritter, is investigated further following his release. He is up against several charges, including resisting arrest. The staff are each questioned, in an echo of Vogler's divide and conquer tactics in the first season, about their knowledge of House's Vicodin abuse. House's apartment is also searched later that day with Tritter telling him that he has a large enough quantity of the drug to land him on suspicion of trafficking. House returns to the hospital and discharges George. But as

George attempts to leave, he becomes disoriented and falls through a glass window taking Cameron down with him. Later, that good girl Cameron admits that it was her fault — she didn't want George discharged and did what she had to to keep him in hospital. This behavior is consistent with the more risk-taking Cameron we've been seeing this season.

George, still conscious, refuses any treatment that has to do with his weight. House concludes, in the end, with an X-ray of his hands, which are clubbed, that George has terminal lung cancer. George's what-will-be-will-be attitude isn't going to do him any good this time, and we get the distinct impression he wishes they'd listened to him and given up their search.

The outlook is not good for Wilson or House either — Wilson has discovered via Tritter that House stole his pad for forging his prescriptions. As he tries to come up with a plausible cover story without incriminating House further, Tritter informs Wilson that if he was the one who wrote those prescriptions, he is now considered an accomplice. Wilson claims that the prescriptions bear his signature yet we suspect that even the ever-charitable Wilson has his limits.

Highlight
House makes one of his most ludicrous and hilarious suggestions to date: that he remove a man's arm because it hurts from being slept on.

Support Staff
After being sprung from the joint, House walks around briefly without his cane when getting himself a change of clothes and joining in a diagnostic rap session at the same time.

Lies
- House pretends to Foreman that Cuddy's not looking for a sperm donor.
- House doesn't lie — he's telling the truth to Cuddy about having forbidden his team to do an MRI on the overweight patient. Cameron jumps in, admitting she went against his order.
- Cameron has drugged George to make him off-balance so he'll agree to stay in hospital. Her lie results in the 600-pound man falling through a window and taking her with him.
- Wilson lies about House's prescriptions. They aren't all his signature.

Exam Room

- When House is in jail, his cellmate is singing the old '70s hit
  "(You're) Having My Baby." It's a very subtle irony, since at
  that moment, House has no idea if Cuddy is pregnant yet.
- Chase is very specific about the way he peppers his tomato
  and cream cheese bagel. It's one of the few times we see him
  eat, and quickly afterward he's making disparaging remarks
  about the patient's obesity. This is the second time Chase has
  shown a big, fat fat-bias. Foreman calls him on it, asking if a
  gang of fat kids surrounded him and beat him up when he
  was a child.
- When Cameron goes to George's place, she discovers their
  patient is a lot like House. His apartment is decorated in dark
  tasteful shades; he owns a saxophone; he's a loner and his
  only visitors are call girls. He's also stubborn, but the parallel
  isn't really pulled all the way through the show. It pretty much
  ends there.
- When Tritter comes sniffing around the hospital, House
  doesn't hesitate. He pops a Vicodin right in front of him. Is it
  his cockiness — does he really think nothing bad can happen
  to *the* Dr. House — or, like George, is it just his *que será será*
  outlook?
- We see Wilson eating beets in his salad, which House comments on, stealing one. Later we see beet-boy at the chip
  dispenser, which is not entirely out of character for Wilson
  since House was stealing his Lays back in season two . . .
  although Wilson may just be there to get an instant coffee.
- The guitar House owns is a Gibson Les Paul.
- Tritter calls House on his intimidation factor, saying he's been
  working with nurses too long. Later, we see House snatch a file
  from a nurse. Is the gesture to nudge us toward believing the cop
  is right? A nurse is also the one to rush to the patient's assistance
  when she sees House attempting to force him to drink. George
  has called for her help as if he knows that the doctors and nurses
  at Princeton-Plainsboro play for opposite teams.
- House is close when he says he's buying a $400 butt plug; the
  lawyer's hourly rate is $450.
- Clubbed fingers have been mentioned before. In "DNR,"
  House speculated wildly; this time we see it for real.

Booboos

- Is it out of character that Cameron would put the patient at risk by putting him on a table that may — and does — collapse under his weight? She stresses that he deserves the same level of care as anyone else, meaning the MRI, but Cameron normally exhibits more forethought. Even though we know her to be determined, she wouldn't make such an obvious error in judgment.
- The patient goes blind during the brain biopsy, and though he plays his blindness with more believability than some on the show, he does tussle and knock away the juice the doctors want him to drink with a certain amount of accuracy.
- Fans have pointed out that the level of liquid in the juice bottle changes between Cameron's attempt to make George drink and House's attempt.

3.7 Son of Coma Guy

First aired: November 14, 2006
Writer: Dors Eans
Director: Dan Attics
Guest stars: David Morse (Michael Tritter), John Larroquette (Gabe), Zeb Newman (Kyle)

Episode Differential

As Tritter continues to apply pressure to everyone in House's life, a quid pro quo between House and a patient lets us discover new information about House's history.

The episode begins with Wilson, who walks in and confronts House over the fact that House stole a prescription pad. He tells House he's been questioned by Tritter. While they're arguing, the son of a comatose patient, Kyle, passes by them. House realizes from the boy's previous reactions that he may be unable to see some moving objects, making him a possible candidate for seizures. House attempts to provoke one. Sure enough, as soon as House is verbalizing this, the boy collapses and is admitted.

After a number of theories are thrown around, including liver failure (due to the large amount of empty wine bottles found in Kyle's backpack), House still maintains that his condition is genetic. Kyle's only living relative is his comatose father, making it impossible for the team to conclude anything from family history. With the rest of the medical team there to disagree, House decides to wake up Gabe, the father, by giving him a large dose of a cocktail mixed with amphetamines — something Cuddy opposes even as House shoots him with the cocktail. The test is a success, and Gabe is once again conscious. He requests discharge when he's told he has one day until he lapses back into his coma. He wants to drive back to Atlantic City to get a hoagie. House agrees, and goes along with him in Wilson's car, with Wilson sitting in the back seat the whole way. House questions Gabe concerning his family history, and they play a back-and-forth version of 20 questions where House must answer a personal one for every medical answer Gabe provides.

Back at the hospital, Cameron is questioned by Tritter about House's Vicodin usage. After answering with a gross underestimation, she asks the rest of team that they stick to the same numbers whenever questioned. Cameron may have hard edges this season but she still has a soft spot for House.

During their drive, House finds out many interesting points about Gabe's family, including that his son may have had mercury poisoning and that a great majority of his wife's family died during accidents and during the night. Suspecting MERRF syndrome, House calls the hospital, at which point he learns that Kyle has a fatal cardiomyopathy. Upon hearing the news, Gabe decides to donate his heart to his son. House asks Wilson to leave the room and then proceeds to inform Gabe of the ways he can kill himself without damaging his heart.

At the end of the episode, Wilson is given a nasty surprise by Tritter when he finds his bank account has been frozen as part of the ongoing investigation into House's drug use.

Highlight
We find out why House became a doctor.

Support Staff
Wilson steals the cane in order to provide an alibi for House.

Lies
- House reveals Wilson's lie to the cops to his patient.

- We think that House is lying when he says that the woman he loved shot him, but he goes on to elaborate that it was paintball.
- Cameron lies to Tritter, or more likely, tells the truth but through her tendency to see House — and his drug use — through rose-colored glasses.
- Foreman lies to House, says that Chase is in the lab when he's actually being interrogated by Tritter.
- We don't know whether Chase lies to the cop or not.
- House lies to the son. He gives him his own final words, not the father's.

Exam Room
- "Only in your world would that be simple," Wilson says in response to House's theory that Gabe doesn't like his son. House is right, of course. And the theme of father-son clashes continues. Previous daddy-issue episodes include: "Cursed," "Daddy's Boy," "Hunting," "The Mistake," and (even though we didn't see the father) "Fools for Love."
- House makes a reference to Woody Allen's film *Sleeper* and the Orgasmatron.
- Wilson lends his car to House after bailing him out *and* covering his ass about the prescriptions? Can we say "doormat"?
- Gabe is not happy to find out M&M's have been changing the colors of their candies in the 10 years since he last had some. The brand name isn't given or shown though.
- Foreman's scene with Tritter is brief; we don't get to find out if he still hates cops the way he did before being roomies with one in "Euphoria."
- Instead of clinic patients, the basic structure for this episode is set up around the back and forth House has with Gabe. At the same time they're playing 20 Questions, Tritter is playing a more hardball version with House's staff.
- Similarly, power is a mini-theme. Tritter tells Chase that medicine attracts people who are attracted to power. Gabe tells House that his questions are a matter of retaining power. House wants answers; Gabe wants something in exchange for those answers.
- House holds up his hand, as if counting "five" as he pops a Vicodin in front of Wilson.

Booboos
- Why would the son ask Chase to pass him his backpack unless he wants to get caught with the open bottles that are inside it? Alcoholics aren't stupid. Occasionally they misjudge, but most know how to get — and keep — what they want. If he wants to keep his stash, he wouldn't ask Chase to pass it to him.
- Both Gabe and his son wake up witty and talkative, almost as if they were actors rather than actors-playing-patients.
- Let's throw the show a bone and assume that House knows both the father's and the son's blood types, and that they're compatible before he lets the father sacrifice his life for his son.

What's Up, Doc?
- Anyone who's had a leg cast will know that walking again isn't easy after your muscles have been given a good long rest, like, six or eight weeks. Gabriel comes out of a 10-year rest and all his muscles are hunky dory. He's raring to get up and walk out of the hospital to go get that hoagie.
- "Genetic tests take forever," Chase says when House attempts to order one. It's one of the criticisms put forth by Andrew Holtz in his book, *The Medical Science of House, MD*. The show gives it the old-college try: answering those nagging questions in the same manner that produced a strong essay back in university — by addressing the concerns of one's critics before they can attack. In this episode, the answer is in the genetics, and House doesn't need the test results to prove it.
- Chase doesn't say "Clear," when he uses the paddles on the patient.

3.8 Whac-A-Mole

First aired: November 21, 2006
Director: Daniel Sackheim
Writers: David Shore, Pam Davis
Guest stars: Bobbin Bergstrom (Nurse), Marco Pelaez (Pharmacist), Deborah Lacey (Lorraine), Alan Rosenberg (Bruce Steinerman), Mandy June Turpin (Beth), Dustin Seavey (Rodent), Tanner Blaze (Will Walters), Patrick Birkett (Old Man), Patrick Fugit (Jack Walters), Cassius Willis (Officer), Cassi Thomson (Kama Walters), Dorothea Harahan (EMT)

Episode Differential

Like the game of the episode's title, the team will find one symptom only to see three others up. In the same way, Tritter's investigation continues to have a ripple-effect through the hospital — though he's one mole who doesn't show up.

House's newest patient is Jack, an 18-year-old orphan who collapses while working at a restaurant/arcade popular with youngsters. Tests done by team reveal multiple infections, the cause of which are unknown. Jack has two siblings in his care: a brother and a sister. The medical team quickly diagnoses him with chronic granulomatous disease and deduces that he needs a bone marrow transplant. His eight-year-old brother is a match. But Jack refuses the treatment — he will not put his brother through the risks of donor surgery. Without the surgery, he won't be well enough to work to support the kids, and they'll be taken into foster care.

Foreman advises Jack against this to no avail. Jack prefers the disease to the burden of taking care of them. Foreman seems to be acting more like Cameron this season in terms of his empathy for patients' personal lives. In "Fools for Love," he tried to convince the related couple they could stay together; in this episode he counsels Jack on what he should do, more or less telling him he believes in him. To be sure, Omar Epps deserves the screen time, but these scenes don't fit with the character he's been playing for two years. In contrast, Cameron is adopting some of House's behaviors this episode. Spurred on by House before they had their diagnosis, she stooped to putting stress on Jack to trigger an attack. Her switch into aggression was so quick it was almost comical, not very believable either, given her usual sensitivity and over-whelming guilt.

We're seeing very different outcomes this season — less neat-and-tidy happy endings. The team is no longer in control of their own lives, or of their patients. The patients are refusing treatment, breaking up, and, as we see in this episode, breaking up as a family, in spite of any words of wisdom the team tries to impart. They're curing the illnesses — or at least proposing solutions — but life solutions remain out of grasp.

Meanwhile, the ongoing battle with Tritter continues, though we do not see him visit the hospital in this episode. Since he froze Wilson's bank account, he has also had him barred from writing prescriptions. Wilson and House's arguments escalate and Wilson is forced to shut down his practice as result of being barred from giving his patients adequate care. Wilson has, for two and a half seasons, gone on about how much House's friendship means to him and what he's willing to do for it. But the title of the episode ought to clue us in to an upcoming turn . . .

Highlight

Patrick Fugit, best known for his roles in *Almost Famous* and *Saved!*, takes the cake this episode when he vomits on it at the arcade birthday party. Or maybe when he becomes the exploding boy, spurting blood from his IV puncture, his ear, and his nose.

Support Staff

- House totters across the room without it during the first diagnostic session.
- His masseuse asks if he's ever thought about using his cane on the proper side. She also says he needs the "proper equipment."
- "Nice cane," Cameron says mock-sexually of the granny stand House had been forced to use.
- House steals another man's cane.

Lies

- Wilson is warned by his divorce lawyer that if he keeps on lying to protect House, he'll be the one in jail.
- House says kids lie because they have something to hide, not because they have trust issues. At the same time, the only lie we see from the "kids" this episode comes from Jack, the 18-year-old orphan/guardian. The actual children do not lie.

- Cameron and Wilson evade his patient's question about why she is sitting in.
- House lies to Jack about there being another donor.
- Jack has pretended he's refusing treatment in order to protect his little brother. The truth is he doesn't want to get well. Getting well means having to take responsibility for his siblings forever.

Exam Room
- The theme of games is clear in the episode's title. We see games in the opening scene, which is an arcade; the "Itchy Foot Game" House plays with his team; his suggestion that there is a foot race between illnesses; and his reference to "game over" for the patient. It should be noted that Sherlock Holmes used the phrase "The game is afoot." When House predicts the outcomes of his team's diagnoses, he writes on the envelope, "The game is a itchy foot." The grammatical error makes the phrase more similar to Holmes'.
- House references the TV show *Party of Five*, calling it "the OC of its day." This episode is a mirror, since that show also featured a brother raising his siblings after the death of their parents.
- Given the similarity between their names, one might expect Cameron and the little girl, Kama, to have more scenes/dynamic.
- House is in the locker room with Cameron, who gives him her PMS pills with a snarky comment. Frequently we see Cameron enter the men's room or the shower to find House or to continue a consult at his invitation. This is the first time we've seen him intrude on her private space. Normally, hospital locker rooms are gendered — so House really has intruded in this scene.
- House asks Foreman about Wendy, but we don't see her this episode. It's a painless one-liner to continue the previous show's plot — in case the writers need the dynamic again later in the season.
- Detective Tritter has Wilson's car towed and impounded. Tritter features in the plot, but never makes an appearance.
- The underlings are changing their tunes. Though they remain

faithful, we see them saying no in back-to-back scenes. Chase first tells House no when House tells — not asks — him to write his prescription. In the very next scene, Cameron says no to Wilson, refusing to write prescriptions for patients she doesn't know.

- There's an intimate moment where Cameron helps House put his sling on. Though the love has never really faded from her side, we begin to see a re-blossoming of it here.
- There are no clinic patients this episode. Instead we begin to see Wilson's patients, a trend that will continue in the next episode. Since he can no longer provide prescriptions for them, Cameron sits in.

Booboos
Omar Epps flubs the word "misanthropy," putting the stress on the first syllable when it belongs on the second.

3.9 Finding Judas

First aired: November 28, 2006
Writer: Sara Hess
Director: Deran Sarafian
Guest stars: Alyssa Shafer (Alice), Christopher Gartin (Rob), Paula Cale (Edie), David Morse (Michael Tritter)

Episode Differential
The title of this episode is so blatant, it's playing to the back of the room. Unfortunately, House doesn't have 12 disciples, so this one abandonment will mean that much more.

Six-year-old Alice is at an amusement park with her father when she goes on a ride and starts screaming uncontrollably — the second screamer this season. When brought to the hospital, House's team suspects pancreatitis. Her parents, meanwhile, are locked in a bitter divorce and custody battle. They're also in the habit of arguing, in the hospital and in front of Alice, so much so that the hospital — Cuddy specifically — will be put in charge of her care and decisions.

Tritter is back in the hospital, researching hospital records and taunting every member of the medical team about House's faults or their own. He also deceptively has their accounts frozen, only to re-open them later — Chase's in particular — to promote distrust and frustration among them. Tritter's end game strategy reveals the chinks in every staff's armor, making them all wonder which has turned or will turn first. Under stress and without his precious meds, House is particularly out of control this episode.

With Alice's skin reacting to everything as though through an allergy, House suggests that it may be an infection. The symptoms worsen when the team decides to play it safe and just administer one antibiotic instead of many. Alice now suffers from muscle rigidity and liver failure, and reacts poorly to surgery after a clot is found in her arm. House can only conclude that Alice has necrotizing fasciitis — her affected limbs will have to be removed. The team objects to such a drastic measure, but have no other theories to counter his proposal. Chase then has an epiphany and realizes that it's a possible case of erythropoietic protoporphyria, which includes being allergic to light. After a violent altercation, one that's obviously been building for years, House decks Chase but agrees and the surgery is halted. This is perhaps the first time someone other than House has found the complete and final answer to a case.

After another outburst by House at Cuddy, including criticizing her abilities to take care of Alice, Wilson finally seems to have had it with all of the drama and incrimination. At the end of the episode, he's seen speaking to Tritter. "I'm going to need 30 pieces of silver," Wilson says, aware that he is the disciple who is selling out his leader to the Romans. House plays a death figure, and a god figure throughout the show's run. Here, Wilson places him in the role of Jesus.

Highlight

And the prize goes to . . . Lisa Edelstein. Cuddy breaks down for the first time, revealing to everyone's confidant, Wilson, that she's had two fertilized eggs implanted that didn't take, and another that she lost.

A close second might be Omar Epps' performance, since he has good lines this episode. Cool as a cucumber Foreman is back; empathetic Foreman has been put away for the time being. "I really hope no one dies while I'm sitting here not-talking to you," he tells Detective Tritter.

Also, when House is jonesing for his meds: "I say we draw straws. Loser drives down to Trenton and scores him an 8-ball."

Support Staff

This episode is so packed with drama and revealed secrets that there's no time for leaning.

Lies

In a come-clean episode, the only deception is the unfreezing of their bank accounts by Tritter in an attempt to make Chase look like a rat.

Exam Room

- "It's never lupus," House says as to why he hides his stash in a book on the disease. He speaks the truth. In spite of the number of times the team has suggested it might be lupus, it's never actually been lupus. (For a montage of *House* lupus clips, visit itsnotlup.us.)
- Chase reveals, a very long time after the fact, that his father cut him out of the will. While their relationship was strained, we had no indication that there was ill will on his father's side.
- We also get more of Foreman's backstory when Tritter reveals that Foreman's brother, Mark, is in jail for drugs. This finally explains his bias in the season two kick-off "Acceptance."
- Is everyone talking like House now? Alice's mother says pointedly, "You're the doctor. I'm the mother. I outrank you."
- Cameron being Cameron, she thanks the woman she speaks to on the phone who informs her that her bank accounts have been frozen. "It's not her fault," she tells her bemused co-workers.
- House references the 1996 film *The English Patient* based on (Canadianism alert) Michael Ondaatje's novel of the same name: "A simple procedure turns a little girl into *The English Patient*. What gives?"
- Wilson makes a play on Samuel Beckett's *Waiting for Godot* (1952): "Beckett was going to call his play *Waiting for House's Approval* but thought it was too grim." This is Wilson's second *Godot* reference; in season one's "Poison," he suggests waiting for "Godot would be faster" than the CDC.
- Regarding the case, Foreman says, "Doing nothing is not a plan, it's specifically a lack of a plan!" This is an echo but exact reversal from something he said in "Euphoria," when

he asked if doing nothing was an option. Of course, he was
high then!

- When Alice goes missing, Chase is wearing jeans and sneakers
  — very un-Chase. Is it possible that only the sneaker-wearing
  doc gets to make the diagnosis?
- Chase is *finally* the hero when he puts two and two together
  at the last minute, and rushes to find House and stop the little
  girl's amputation. Too bad about the fist he runs into.

Booboos

- Throughout the Tritter plotline, his character behaves as if he
  is a district attorney, rather than a cop. Like the medical team,
  Tritter gets to do it all because it makes for more dramatic television viewing.
- Why would Chase agree to meet at a public lunch with Tritter
  in the first place? Chase is good at playing angles, so he
  should realize when others are about to.

3.10 Merry Little Christmas

First aired: December 12, 2006
Writers: David Shore, Liz Friedman
Director: Tony To
Guest stars: David Morse (Detective Michael Tritter), Kacie Borrowman
(Abigail), Meredith Eaton-Gilden (Maddy), Michael Medico (Clinic Doctor),
Teddy Vincent (Mrs. Zebalusky), Shyann McClure (Little Girl), Marco Pelaez
(Pharmacist), Cole Evan Weiss (Teenage Boy), Bobbin Bergstrom (Nurse)

Episode Differential

A small patient teaches House that he's not as big as he thinks, but unfortunately, by the time he realizes it, it's too little too late.

Wilson tries to strike a deal with House and Tritter, but, thanks to
House's bull head, he is unsuccessful. Wilson finally convinces Cuddy to
take House off Vicodin altogether, forcing him to go through withdrawal as opposed to rehab. House is then removed from his newest case
involving a 15-year-old dwarf named Abigail, who's suffering from a
collapsed lung and anemia.

The patient is also suffering from various ailments that include carti-
lage-hair hypoplasia, liver cancer, and diabetic ketoacidosis, as well as —
it turns out — a granuloma pressing against her pituitary gland, creating
growth hormone complications. In spite of her dwarf mother, this dwarf
is not a dwarf after all.

House offers the girl treatment, only to have her refuse. Her explanation? She doesn't want to be normal, "boring." House and the mom
converse in the hall, and House puts away his sarcasm stick, and barbs
about talking "Tolkien," long enough to talk about his own freakdom.
It's a rare admission by House and a sign that Tritter's war may be getting to him after all. House wants the mom to convince her daughter
that being small is not the best way to go through the world. Her mother,
egged on by House, is able to convince her that she'll still be special if
tall, and she's eventually treated. Abigail's full condition is understood as
an extreme case of Langerhan's cell histiocytosis.

Finally, House finds his humility but it's the morning past the Tritter-
Wilson deal expiration. And Tritter tells him so.

Highlights

When House asks about the particulars of the patient's conception, her
dwarf mother sassily replies that the father lay flat while she spun. A
beat or two later, House hits on her using a pun: "Care to go for a
spin?"

Another high moment this episode belongs to Wilson when House
has barged into his consultation with a grieving widow. Wilson's quick
on his feet, realizing House is not just there to berate him, but to pocket
pills from his deceased patient.

Support Staff

- "You're afraid of pain," Wilson accuses House. House holds
  the cane up threateningly: "And you're not?"
- House tries to measure the dwarf with his cane.

Lies

- Cameron arrives on House's doorstep to check in on him,
  bandage his self-inflicted wounds (as in "Detox," he's been
  hurting himself for the high), and pump him for a diagnosis.
  She claims she wasn't sent to House by Cuddy — that Cuddy
  wouldn't trust her not to bring House pills. We see her in the

next scene, reporting to Cuddy about House's condition.

- House lies to the pharmacist to get the dead man's prescription.
- House tells the mother to lie to her daughter so she won't spend her life on the short side.

Exam Room

- This is the first time an episode goes all the way through to the theme music without setting up who the patient will be. We see Wilson and Tritter in the clinic, revealing Wilson's betrayal of House head-on. Given the usual formula, we expect one of them will become the patient, but the patient isn't introduced until after "Teardrop" sounds. House interrupts Cuddy in the clinic and steals her patient.
- Foreman is always the first to voice his opinions and this episode is no exception. He's the first of the team to tell House he should take the District Attorney's deal. Cameron also tells him to take the deal.
- We see Foreman doing an on-premises B&E when he picks the lock on Cuddy's desk drawer at House's request. It's not the first time he's interfered in Cuddy-House bets regarding House's drug use. Foreman focuses on short-term solutions: a medicated House is better for him.
- The hospital House visits in an attempt to score his pain meds is called St. Sebastian's. St. Sebastian's appears also in "Deception." Sebastian was a martyr in the third century, shot with arrows by Christians under the Roman emperor.
- No meds make House a hungry man. He has a plate with four hotdogs and an order of fries he at first refuses to share with a six-year-old.
- When he finally gets his pills, he downs them with booze. Maker's Mark, to be specific. This is the second time we've seen him drink this brand, the first time being in "Three Stories." He leaves a phone message for his mother that sounds more like a cry for help than well wishes.

Booboos

- The hospital might have a manger in their chapel at Christmastime, but not in their front lobby.

- Cameron shows extreme insensitivity when she offers to boost the 15-year-old dwarf onto the examining table as if she were a five-year-old child. Cameron is seldom insensitive, and she would know better. This is a definite character inconsistency.
- Chase holds back the patient's hair while she vomits blood. This is a friend thing to do, but as a doctor, wouldn't he have more pressing concerns for his patient than keeping her golden locks golden?
- When House phones his mom, he enters seven digits. His parents aren't local — we know this from the "Daddy's Boy" episode — but even if they were, he'd need to dial ten.
- Would House really be able to walk into Tritter's office on Christmas day? Even if he were there, it would be unlikely that the door would be wide open.

What's Up, Doc?
Some fans claim Hugh Laurie flubs "thallium scan" as "gallium scan" the second time he says it.

3.11 Words and Deeds

First aired: January 9, 2007
Writer: Leonard Dick
Director: Daniel Sackheim
Guest stars: Bobbin Bergstrom (Nurse), Jason George (Brock Hoyt), Hira Ambrosino (Anethesiologist), Aulani Rhea (Nurse), Terryn Westbrook (Sarah), Tory Kittles (Derek Hoyt), Martin Mullen (Ennis), Brian Leckner (Ivan), David Morse (Michael Tritter), Meagan Good (Amy), Helen Carey (Judge Helen Davis), Kadeem Hardison (Howard), Donald Sage MacKay (Neil), Vyto Ruginis (Assistant District Attorney Velez)

Episode Differential
At the beginning of the episode, Derek, a firefighter, has just exited a burning building when he suddenly has trouble breathing and becomes delirious. He attempts to re-enter the building before being stopped by a fellow firefighter, Amy. He complains that he's freezing. The team's first diagnosis is MRSA but then Derek tells the team he's also seeing blue. They

theorize that it may be male menopause, and House orders a hormone panel. Derek's condition becomes more perplexing when he exhibits disturbing behavior and attempts to choke Cameron.

House's attempt to apologize to Tritter is unsuccessful. House's next step is to reveal that he is voluntarily checking himself into rehab. It's a brilliant move, considering Tritter was looking for a guilty plea from House in exchange for two months in rehab from the judge. House has simply side-stepped the "guilty" part and gone straight to jail of his own volition, taking all the power away from Tritter.

Back at the hospital, the team is still running various tests on Derek, who is consequently having another heart attack. The heart attack is theorized to be brought on by stress related to Amy, whom Derek says is engaged to his brother. In love with her, Derek is literally killing himself with the effort of being around her. To test this, the team brings Amy in. Their suspicions end up proving true. Rather than tell Amy anything, Derek agrees to an unorthodox procedure that involves electrocuting his brain, in an attempt to erase the memory of loving her, along with everything else. Treatment is successful but when Cameron congratulates Amy on her upcoming wedding, Amy says there isn't one. The team quickly realizes that Derek fabricated the memory.

There's a pain parallel running through the episode. Derek was hiding his pain at work; House is the opposite, doing nothing but wallow in how much pain he is in — in front of his staff and superior. "I'm fine by the way, thanks for asking," Cameron snipes at House after she's been strangled. Going through withdrawal, he later parrots her phrase. The episode also delves into non-physical pain — heartbreak — made physical. "Love kills," House says of the patient, but he directs the comment at Cameron.

In the middle of his hearing with Tritter, House is notified of his patient's situation and — what else would we expect of House — runs out of the courtroom to get back to the hospital, followed by the threats by the presiding judge that he will be held in contempt. Cuddy is then questioned concerning the medication of Wilson's dead patient that House "picked up" for him from the pharmacy. She testifies that the pills were replaced with ones from a placebo group, and the case is thrown out, with Tritter ordered to halt his investigation. While spending the night in jail for contempt, House reveals to Wilson that he bribed the rehab supervisor into giving him Vicodin — we've been duped by our own favorite doctor even as we were rooting for him. Although Cuddy reveals that she fabricated the evidence to the court and has assured House that she now controls him, we know nothing will really change.

Highlight

The face Jennifer Morrison makes when her character is being strangled by the patient: priceless. Romantics might favor her hugging of House though. Is it really the closest they've ever gotten?

Support Staff

No special moments this episode for House's trusty sidekick.

Lies

- Echoing the episode's title, Tritter says, "People like you, even your actions lie," about House and all addicts.
- What the patient believes to be true — that Amy is engaged to his brother — is actually a lie. They aren't even dating.
- Under oath Cuddy says that she switched the medication in the pharmacy. Later, she has a conversation with House that reveals she has perjured herself and she's not happy about it.
- House has been taking the Vicodin, slipped to him by the rehab worker, who House points out works for minimum wage. House has never been above paying for his pleasures.

Exam Room

- This is the second time this season the show has featured fire-fighters as an opening. The first was in "Que Será Será" when they thought they needed to remove the fat man from his apartment. Anyone smell a deal on the costumes and the truck?
- Cameron is adamant that House do his job well even when his mind is on his trial. This seems like Cameron, who doesn't believe in putting oneself ahead of one's patients. At the same time, she says to the rest of the team that House "did this to himself." Previously, she hasn't held that he has a problem. She may have changed her mind since seeing his condition at Christmas. At the same time, she was fairly sympathetic to him then.
- House chooses Andre the Giant's ghost as his Higher Power while going through the twelve steps. It ought to be a clue to

us about how serious he really is about kicking his habit.

- We see House drink a glass of milk in rehab. Normally he favors cola or coffee. Has rehab really changed him or do they refuse to stock the drug caffeine?
- House smokes cigarettes in rehab while speaking of "idealized despair." We've seen him with cigars, but never cigarettes.
- House makes his first apology to Wilson.

Booboos

- Though an emotive actor, the woman playing Amy is not nearly big enough or buff enough to carry anyone out of a burning building — good thing she only has to wear the hat.
- If Derek the firefighter is willing to hide his physical pain to protect his job, why would he suddenly allow himself to be given a treatment that would make him "forget" everything, including his job training?
- The judge questions why Cuddy is only bringing forth her admission now, but the defense is under no obligation to provide their evidence beforehand.
- We discover House has been taking Vicodin throughout his time in rehab. Why the puking then?

What's Up, Doc?

- Electro-shock therapy really doesn't work this way. After five rounds of treatment, Derek might be a little fuzzy, but he wouldn't lose recollection of his brother, friend, and even the state in which he resides.
- Well, if the diagnosticians are going to draw all their own blood work, process all their own tests, look at all of the imaging instead of leaving it to a radiologist, perform nearly every surgery, why shouldn't they have the pleasure of dressing up and playing electro-shock docs too?

3.12 One Day, One Room

First aired: January 30, 2006
Writer: David Shore
Director: Juan J. Campanella
Guest stars: Bobbin Bergstrom (Nurse), Sean Christopher Davis (Father), Todd Sandler (Ear Patient), Roger Ainslie (Nose Patient), George Williams (Doctor), Michelle Gardner (Dr. Stone), Randy Evans (Patient #1), Ray Chavez (Sick Patient), Michael Rivkin (Patient #4), Nick Slatkin (Hiccuping Patient), Jason Gallloway (Patient #5), Joel David Moore (College Student), Hope Shapiro (Patient #6), Marco Pelaez (Pharmacist), Bryna Weiss (Patient #3), Kristen Glass (Beautiful Woman), Geoffrey Lewis (Older Man), Katheryn Winnick (Eve), Drew Matthews (Kid)

Episode Differential

One day, one exam room, and one more little detail about House's past — this episode really does lurch into "very special" territory where others have only skimmed the edges of that state. However, we do see the man behind the monster as House realizes his doctoring must also include bedside manner. This is also the first episode in which House has bonded with a clinic patient.

Given extra mandatory clinic duty by Cuddy, House examines three patients who suspect they have STDs. After an unsuccessful attempt at getting out of this talk-and-swab circus, Cuddy takes House aside and challenges him. She recognizes he is bored in the clinic. She tries to make it more interesting for him by betting. She'll pay him $10 for every patient he can diagnose without touching; he has to pay her $10 for every one he can't. It's going well until House has to diagnose an attractive young woman in a low-cut dress. . . .

One of the original three patients is the psychologically unstable Eve, who has been diagnosed with chlamydia. Upon hearing the news, she breaks into sobs. When House explains that the disease is entirely curable she suddenly shouts for him not to touch her. House realizes that she is a victim of rape. Eve insists that House treat her from then on. She doesn't want to talk about the rape though. She is looking for normalcy and wants to discuss anything else. House insists on talking to her about the rape. She requests that he tell her something terrible that happened to him. Convinced he must confide in her to gain her trust, he does. But she thinks he's lying.

In another hospital room, Cameron deals with a terminally ill cancer patient. Homeless and alone, he wants to die in suffering so that someone will remember him. If it sounds familiar, it is. We've seen this dynamic before with Cameron but how will this instance end?

Back in Eve's room, both she and House end up breaking down, and in a rare display of emotion, the viewers are given a sad revelation about House's childhood. In an effort to empathize with the patient, he eventually tells her that he was abused by his disiplinarian father, bringing the dynamics we saw in "Daddy's Boy" into a new light.

Highlight
Hands down — pardon the pun — the bet between Cuddy and House.

Support Staff
House uses it to trip the delirious clinic patient, then tosses it to Cuddy while stabbing him with a paralytic.

Lies

- House lies to Cuddy about his caseload, claiming he has three.
- Cameron tells Cuddy the truth — that House was lying about having a case.
- Cuddy discovers House's lie about rehab when he pops a Vicodin right in front of her.
- In an attempt to dissuade the patient from wanting him as her doctor, House tells her that he'll lie to her. (At least he's honest about that.)
- House is lying when he says her case doesn't interest him. It may not interest him, but he does care. Is there a difference?
- "Tell her the truth," Wilson says about the patient wanting to know about House's bad experiences.
- House reveals that he often lived with a grandmother who believed in discipline — a bath in ice, sleeping in the yard. He says he never told his parents. The patient accuses him of fabricating the story. "It's true for someone," he says. Later, he reveals it to be a true story, except for the grandmother part — it was his dad.

Exam Room

- The opening is a fake-out. The delirious man is not actually the patient this episode. House tries to convince the team to run tests on him that he doesn't need so House can lay low. The real patient emerges from a routine clinic exam.

- This episode shows what people frequently use walk-in clinics for: issues they don't feel comfortable having their personal doctors knowing about.
- House resents clinic so much this episode, he's paying patients off if they'll go home (trying to sort the real maladies from the not-so-pressing ones). An elderly man who has coughed up blood on his handkerchief has the initials D.S. monogrammed on it — David Shore.
- The clinic gets a bit stale this episode, repeating the man who can't stop hiccupping ("The Socratic Method"), but this time as a drug-seeker rather than a man with a true malady.
- It's been some time since we've seen House on his Gameboy, but he's making use of it while waiting for the rape patient's sedative to wear off.
- Cameron and Foreman disagree about the best way for a rape victim to recover. True to their characters, Cameron thinks House should tell her that his life is good, and Foreman thinks House should tell her something awful about himself so she'll realize that people can be survivors of unfortunate events. Easy-way-out Chase thinks House should just keep her medicated and let her sleep.
- Cameron has her own patient this episode, but the technique falls flat since it explores a concept the show has already dealt with once ("Acceptance"): that somebody should be affected by a death. Previously, she chose to befriend a dying cancer patient. This time it's forced upon her.
- When House and Wilson are playing foosball, House takes advantage of Wilson's empathy to score, which pretty much sums up their relationship.

Booboos

- The old man Cameron is treating knows about her husband, having heard it from the nurse. There's no reason that the nurse should know the story, and even if the nurse did, no reason she would share it with a patient.
- When House and Wilson play foosball, House's hickey-like

bullet wound is missing during the close-up.

What's Up, Doc?

- It is standard to test for pregnancy along with sexually trans-mitted diseases in rape cases. House may have been surprised or shaken up, but even the inveterate rule-breaker would know how to follow procedure in this case.
- House says chlamydia is one of the lesser STDs, a luckier one to get as far as sexual infections go. He's right in that it is eas-ily treated once identified. But his statement is only true if the disease has been caught quickly. Frequently, chlamydia does not exhibit any symptoms in women. Left to its own devices, the disease will severely damage a woman's fallopian tubes and ovaries.
- Similarly, this patient arrives at the clinic because she knows she has been raped, and therefore possibly exposed. She would not be exhibiting symptoms of chlamydia after only one week of exposure.

3.13 Needle in a Haystack

First aired: February 6, 2007
Writer: David Foster
Director: Peter O'Fallon
Guest stars: Jake Richardson (Stevie), Rob Brownstein (Franklin), Arabella Field (Judy), Jessy Schram (Leah), Wendy Makkena (Dr. Julie Whitner), Ron Perkins (Dr. Simpson)

Episode Differential

After the conclusion of the Tritter arc, this episode seems to be coasting like House on a slow clinic day. As well, a literal interpretation of this episode title pretty much reveals the medical mystery from the get-go. The team should, literally, be searching for a needle-shaped object. If you're interested in solving the mysteries before the team does, bear the title trick in mind every time for upcoming episodes. And with the introduction of yet another female character it seems this season could be dubbed "Dr. H and the Women."

House arrives at the hospital one morning to find that his parking space is occupied by a wheelchair-accessible van. He soon finds out that the space belongs to a new researcher, Julie Whitner, who is paralyzed from the waist down. After she and House have words, he is determined to get his space back, even if it means using a wheelchair himself to get it back. Bearing the bumper sticker, "I'd rather be walking," House starts traveling around the hospital tire-style in an attempt to win a bet with Cuddy.

Meanwhile, he's in a clash over 16-year-old Stevie's treatment with the boy's gypsy parents. He believes Stevie's condition has to do with Wegener's granulomatosis, but in the end, the symptoms are simply related to a digested toothpick. As in season two, we see some sex negativity again on *House*, since it was a make-out scene that opened the segment and led to Stevie's hospitalization (the toothpick penetrated his intestines, just as he was thinking of doing some penetrating as well). During treatment, Foreman sees a bright kid kept back by his family and risks his license for him. It's the first time Foreman has done such a thing. Normally he cares about his patients but never loses sight of the divide between him and them.

House approaches Cuddy at the end of the episode and asks her if she told Whitner about the bet. She more or less admits that she had, and that she never intended to give him back the space, which in turn explains why Whitner was so confident around him. In an attempt to make Cuddy feel guilty, House says to her, "Don't make promises you won't even bother to keep." He walks without his cane, showing off his limp to full effect. Cuddy feels guilty in misleading House, but in typical fashion, House expected her reaction and had planned on causing her to feel that way. Due to his crafty emotional manipulation, he gets the parking space back and ditches the wheelchair.

Highlight
House takes the stairs in a wheelchair to get into the surgery where he insists on handling the boy's intestines.

Support Staff
- House doesn't have it out immediately as he exits his car. He whips it out straight; this one's collapsible.
- When House takes on Whitner, the doctor in the electric wheelchair, it seems like he's met his fast-talking match. He

dons driving gloves and plays chicken with her. His cane has been temporarily traded in for the chair.

Lies

- Stevie and his girlfriend lie to the cop when they tell him they'll leave. They keep making out in the parked car.
- The patient lies about his home address and his parents' cell phone numbers. When the doctors expose his lie, Stevie says he'll tell them anything, but he continues to fib. It's his girlfriend who dishes.
- Foreman tells the family he needs to bandage their son's penis. He really wants to talk about experimental treatment, which he knows the parents won't allow. He asks the patient to take it, and lie to his parents.

Exam Room

- In contrast to House's dietary habits, we see Cameron drinking orange juice in this episode.
- The clinic patient parallels House in that he's faking his sore throat. He doesn't need to see the doctor; House doesn't need the wheelchair.
- Surprisingly, when they go to the house they think is their patient's, they see a really messy kitty litter, and actually show the clumps even though the whole thing turns out to be a ruse.
- Also, considering how many things their patients find to lie about, it's surprising that this is the first time a patient has lied about his or her address.
- Foreman waffles between cool-as-a-cucumber and overly caring; in this episode it's the latter — so much so that it feels as if he's selling life insurance.
- House doesn't meet the patient at all this episode, except to feel his intestines.
- When House says, "Because we need to take the center square to block," he's referencing the game show *The Hollywood Squares*. An enormous grid with celebrities in each spot, it engaged its contestants in a game of trivia tic-tac-toe.
- Because of the wheelchair, Wilson compares House to Ironside, who was played by Raymond Burr in the late '60s and early to mid '70s in the detective TV show of the same name.

What's Up Doc?

Thankfully, human intestines are a little more attached to the body than House's cavalier handling of them might suggest.

3.14 Insensitive

First aired: February 13, 2007
Writer: Mathew V. Lewis
Director: Deran Sarafian
Guest stars: Mika Boorem (Hannah), Jenny Robertson (Abby), Kimberly Quinn (Nurse Wendy), Josh Stamberg (Bobby Herrick)

Episode Differential

The episode begins with the teenaged Hannah who has the rare ability to not feel any pain when injured. She is brought to the attention of the medical team when she gets into a car accident with her mother. An object has gone through her leg, which she does not feel, and her mother is unconscious. Her introduction sets up the man of constant sorrow versus the girl who can't feel pain. This episode sparks when House hits the insensitivity ceiling (attempting to steal some of the girl's spine for his own research/benefit), and continuously interrupts Cuddy's Valentine's plans.

When Hannah is being examined, House notices that she has CIPA — in spite of her attempts to hide it — and orders a battery of tests on her, including a spinal nerve biopsy. The medical team disagrees, telling him that the biopsy could kill her. Since she feels nothing and her mother is still in the OR, there are also problems with trying to sedate her. Her current medication has made her paranoid, and only through a fight, she eventually reveals where she can be sedated. House eventually gets permission from Cuddy by confronting her in the middle of a date.

Although permission has been granted, the team is still hesitant, believing that if they could cause her to feel pain, they would know where the problem is. Continuing in her manipulative nature toward the staff, Hannah ends up faking pain so that they will remove the restraints during a procedure. Indicating further paranoia, Hannah then threatens to jump off the railing from one floor to the clinic below.

House makes a personal visit to Cuddy's house to ask her medical opinion, which she sees right through considering he could have asked the resident specialists. Her comments about him possibly being jealous of her date fluster him, and he leaves, as does her date who's had enough of the third wheel winning Cuddy's attention. Is this the set-up we've all been waiting for, and since the butt swab-that-launched-a-thousand-ships been teased with?

House returns to the hospital only to find Hannah's condition worsening. He realizes that it isn't just a vitamin B12 deficiency, which his team has already tried to treat, but a combination of that as well as something else. House dramatically removes a 25-foot tapeworm from her body that has been causing the problem all along.

Meanwhile, the staff drama continues with the shocker of Cameron asking Chase for non-commital sex. Is this in keeping with her new sometimes wrong-is-right persona? Chase, who's just been assured she doesn't want love, looks plenty happy to be used. When it comes to the love game, Foreman, who's usually very direct in his methods, shows himself to be as evasive as Chase usually is. Instead of being upfront with Nurse Wendy, he hides behind a mask of goodness, saying he has a gift for her. He has helped her secure a foot-in at another hospital. The truth is that he wants her out of range. With Tritter gone, will the staff be their own worst threat in terms of creating workplace instability?

Highlights

This episode is packed with highlights. First, House and his 16-year-old CIPA patient face off, playing "Your Mama" with pain. His pains are the experience of pain, while Hannah's involve its absence. She attempts to trump him by showing him her butt, which she burned on the stove at age three, only to get injected by a fast-and-ready House who has a sedative in hand.

Then, after House interrupts her date twice, Cuddy asks point blank if he likes her.

When House unveils Hannah's struggling tapeworm, one of the OR staff snaps a picture of it on a cell-phone camera.

As a final kicker, Cameron offers Chase sex — on an ongoing basis.

Support Staff

House uses it as "reason six" for how he knows the patient can't feel pain: he hits her with it during her exam.

Lies

- The patient lies about feeling pain. She pretends she can feel it.
- The staff lies about her mother's surgery going well. The mother will recover, but there are hints that the surgery is complicated.
- House wants to contribute to a CIPA study which would require him taking tissue from Hannah's spine; Wilson talks him into going about it the honest way.
- Foreman chooses a backhanded way of breaking up with Nurse Wendy.

Exam Room

- The love-commitment theme is just in time for Valentine's Day. Cuddy goes on a date; Foreman tells Cameron she may have been married but has no idea what a commitment really means; Chase submissively follows Cameron after her offer of continued coitus; Wilson and House gossip about their soap — the lawyer is dating a tranny nurse; even the hospital's own Nurse Wendy returns long enough for Foreman to indicate he wants his space.
- The team discusses who says no to House; they decide, rightly, that no one does.
- Wilson actually calls himself House's conscience in this episode — something we've seen a lot of but never had verbalized.
- This is the second character we've had named Hannah. The first appeared in "Sleeping Dogs Lie." Similarly, there have been two characters named Max — the girlfriend from that same episode, and Baby Maxine ("Maternity.")
- House and Cuddy frequently fire sex shots back and forth, but this is the first time she discusses her desire directly. "I like him and I like sex," she says, "Do I need to stitch a letter onto my top?" She's referencing Nathaniel G. Hawthorne's *The Scarlet Letter*.
- This is the second tapeworm we've seen (the first was in the pilot episode). Apparently, the world record for longest extracted tapeworm is 37 feet — a worm found in Sally Mae Wallace in Great Grits, Mississippi, September 5, 1991.

Booboos

- The mother seems to know about the girl's CIPA status, so why is it a secret the girl tries to keep from the doctors?
- Fans have pointed out that the amount of snow on Chase's hat changes.

What's Up, Doc?

- How does House know exactly where the tapeworm is?
- Would the cell-phone camera be allowed in the operating room?

3.15 Half Wit

First aired: March 6, 2007
Writer: Lawrence Kaplow
Director: Katie Jacobs
Guest stars: Dave Matthews (Patrick Obyedkov), Kurtwood Smith (Dr. Obyedkov), Dru Mouser (Arlene)

Episode Differential

This episode gives House another musical patient and plenty of chances to show off his own ivory ticklers.

Patrick Obyedkov, a 35-year-old pianist, is in the middle of a concert when there is a painful and involuntary muscle spasm in his left hand. He begins missing notes — something his father says has never happened before. He is admitted to Princeton-Plainsboro Hospital with a rare movement disorder and his case attracts the attention of House. Patrick had been brain damaged since he was 10 years old due to a bus accident that killed his mother. Intrigued by Patrick's musical ability, apparently inherited in the wake of his accident, House wants to study his brain.

As always, House has a fascination for how disabilties inform people's identities. Would House be House without his own pain? Between his ketamine treatment and his detox, this has been the primary question put forth this season, and we see it mirrored now in someone more innocent.

Patrick has a bout of seizures, leading House to present a very difficult option to Patrick's father — a neurological procedure that would allow Patrick to live normally without spasms. Unfortunately, he would no longer be able to play the piano.

After opening his mail, and then breaking into his apartment, Cameron finds out that House is going for brain cancer analysis at another hospital — setting up a brain subplot to the brain main plot and making this episode tighter and more dramatic than others this season. In an interesting turn of events, the team is emotionally centered on House's problem instead of the patient's. They go through a series of their own theories, including testing House without his knowledge — something that requires the staff members to try to get close to the uncuddly doctor in their own ways.

Finally, the team concludes that House doesn't have cancer after all. Confronting him, he admits to sending another patient's file with his name in order to trick Boston General into thinking that he was the one with the disease. His desire for drugs runs this deep — an "instant pleasure center" he calls it — and the entire medical team is disappointed in him, believing he has stooped too low, even for House. Wilson advises House to start with the smaller pleasures, such as eating pizza with him. The episode ends with House outside the restaurant where Cameron, Chase, and Foreman are having dinner, about to go in.

Highlight

Cameron moves in for a kiss. House hesitates, then responds, opening up for the real thing. But the real thing is a deception. Cameron has a needle in her pocket. Mid-kiss, House stills her hand before she can use it. "If you need a sperm sample, come back without the needle," he tells her. It's a Tabasco-hot scene, and the comedy amps up the drama.

Support Staff

- At their 5 a.m. meeting, House uses his cane to retrieve the bagel bag from the end of the table.
- House twirls it like a drum major while Cuddy and Wilson are privately discussing the possibility of his being ill.
- House lays it atop the piano twice.
- When his team shows up on his doorstep, House walks to the door without his cane, but uses it to form a barrier and stop them from coming in.
- When the patient begins to button his shirt on his own, House uses the cane to stop the father from going to help him.

Lies

- House keeps his Boston treatment from everyone.
- Cameron and Chase both lie when House asks, "Did you two shower together?" They've shown up for the morning meeting with hair of the same wetness. "No!" they declare together, leaving House (and us) to deduce that they did.
- Cameron writes her own letter of recommendation, but does ask House to sign it, thanking him when he does since it keeps her from having to fake his signature (again).
- Cameron's kiss — what a delicious lie.
- Chase's hug — he steals a hair for testing.
- House has been faking out Boston General, and now the whole staff of Princeton-Plainsboro.

Exam Room

- This is the only episode without the regular theme/credit sequence. "House MD" flashes simply with a piano note, and the names follow *sans* "Teardrop."
- Kurtwood Smith, perhaps best known in TV-land for his role on *That '70s Show*, has played opposite Robert Sean Leonard before — in *Dead Poets Society* (1989) where Smith played stern father to a teenage Leonard.
- Hugh Laurie played the piano in all of the scenes in this episode while musician Dave Matthews (Patrick) had a hand double.
- The note attached to the bagel bag in the diagnostic room reads: Good Morning Read Now xoxo.
- House chomps a plain bagel, uncut, untoasted.
- The first song House plays with Patrick is "I Don't Like Mondays," by the Boomtown Rats.
- In another scene, House reveals to Wilson that what he played to the patient was his own composition. He played it, the patient echoed it, then completed it — with better notes than House says he had ever managed to find.
- House is partial to the red lollipop again; this is not the first time we've seen him suck one.
- In a twist, House has become the patient. Cameron and Chase break into his home. "Come with . . ." Chase says to Cameron as he leads the way toward the bedroom, implying

they have been involved, even though Cameron says she's not going to "do it" with him in House's bed.

- House hits on Cuddy with an ass-grab of eighth-grader caliber. She walks away from the situation easily. She's not about to dish out any sympathy sex.
- House was going to have something put into his brain; his patient had half of his taken out.
- Even though House makes wisecracks while Chase is hugging him, as he leaves the room, House does thank him in a seemingly genuine manner. Given the final scene, where House debates joining his staff for dinner, after Wilson's suggestion that maybe House should try the simpler pleasures, are we to deduce that this elaborate deception of House's is a cry for attention — that he really is lonely?

Booboos

The patient bent his fingers backwards during the fundraising concert. They looked broken. In the scene after admittance, he is already playing piano with House — nothing is amiss with the man's ivory ticklers.

3.16 Top Secret

First aired: March 27, 2007
Writer: Thomas L. Moran
Director: Deran Sarafian
Guest stars: Marc Blucas (John Kelley), Annie Quinn (Gina), Hira Ambrosino (Anesthesiologist), Keisha Alfred (Technician), Bert Belasco (PFC Garcia), Marco Morales (Cpl. Foley), Bobbin Bergstrom (Nurse)

Episode Differential

House's newest charge is a U.S. Marine, John, the nephew of a major hospital donor. John's complaints and symptoms are consistent with Gulf War syndrome. House has also just had a dream in his office chair — before Cuddy's entrance with the file — that included the Marine. This causes House to spend much of his time trying to figure out how he could have possibly met this man before, if at all. Curious as always, House instructs his team to investigate the patient's identity as much as his medical history. Is this the start of House's new career as a psychic or will the laws of the physical universe win out, as they usually do?

Meanwhile, House isn't the only character whose dreams are a concern. John will need monitoring at night. While they're supposed to be monitoring the Marine, Cameron convinces Chase they should have sex in an empty room in the sleep lab. When their patient wakes up unexpectedly, Foreman storms in to discover the patient alone. When he asks Cameron why, she confesses that she and Chase were having sex — and he thinks she's joking, which is obviously the reaction she expected though the handsome Australian is flummoxed.

House's strange dreams are interrupted by the fact that he is having difficulty urinating — limiting his ability to sleep and in turn to perform on the job. He catheterizes himself to relieve himself so he can rest. House suddenly awakens from a dream in which he urinates all over the floor but diagnoses his patient. His catheter has come loose, but he has the answer to his case.

At the hospital, House discovers how he remembers the patient. As the nephew of a hospital donor, John and Cuddy had hooked up as dates a couple years back at a hospital event. When House confronts her, she claims he remembers because he was jealous. Giving us confirmation that she and House had a thing back in Michigan, she tells him to get over her. And similarily, Chase doubts that Cameron is over House. The episode ends with Chase and Cameron being caught in a storage closet by House, who walks away with a grin of satisfaction on his face.

Highlights

When Cameron tells Foreman the truth about the sleep lab. Chase protests Foreman's skepticism, "She had sex with me once." Foreman laughs, "She was stoned." Foreman says that House would sleep with Wilson before Cameron would sleep with Chase again.

Another hilarious moment is when John experiences lower limb paralysis. House yells, "First we're going to need to know one thing: Have you ever appeared in any pornos?"

Support Staff

- House hangs it over the urinal wall while Wilson pees and House pretends to pee.

- When he's in the bath, he uses it to pull the stool with his cell phone over.
- He walks without it to his bed after putting in the catheter.

Lies

- Both dreams are lies to the viewing audience.
- When questioned by Foreman, Cameron tells the truth.
- Cameron and Chase both believe the patient is telling the truth.
- Cuddy dated the patient, something she withholds.

Exam Room

- House and Wilson reference the Village People.
- Wilson believes House's dream was his subconscious and had to do with House's father since he was in the air force.
- Foreman points out that Chase is willing to believe Cameron but not him about the patient's Gulf War syndrome. Foreman and Chase are both excellent doctors, but they've seldom been on the same side, regardless of any shift in the energy between Cameron and Chase.
- If Chase had his shirt off fast in "Hunting," it's now Cameron's turn. She doesn't wait for the sleep lab camera to be blacked out.
- We've seen House urinate a lot throughout the show as he tried out his new caffeine delivery systems. This is the first time we've seen him not-pee. He goes three days, to Wilson's amazement and concern.
- Foreman frequently disagrees with House, but this time he defies him, treating for the uranium in the patient's urine.
- Someone in the casting department must be a fan of *Buffy the Vampire Slayer*: Marc Blucas (John) is the third *Buffy* cast member to appear on *House*. (Tom Lenk, "Spin," and Michelle Trachtenberg, "Safe," are the others.)
- John's urine, House's urine. Need more be said?

3.17 Fetal Position

First aired: April 3, 2007
Writers: Russell Friend and Garret Lerner
Director: Matt Shakeman
Guest stars: Anne Ramsay (Emma Sloan), Tyson Ritter (himself), Jeff Sugarman (Fetal Surgeon), Bobbin Bergstrom (Nurse)

Episode Differential

The pee theme continues this week as House discovers a fetus with urinary problems, and Cuddy loses sight of the big ultrasound — er, picture.

Rock photographer Emma Sloan, who is pregnant, passes out at a photo-shoot after slurring her speech. Because her baby's biological father is a neurologist, she knows the mnemonic CAST, and diagnoses her stroke as it occurs. She is admitted to the hospital and it is found that her kidneys have shut down. Though the reason for her stroke is still unknown, it's suspected that she has a clot in her heart.

Cuddy, finding out Cameron and Chase's arrangement, assumes that Cameron will be the one to get hurt by the pairing. Foreman assumes the same thing, except he's cautioning Chase not to hurt her, but his reasons aren't chivalrous. He just doesn't want her to be any more unbearable, which makes it three for three in terms of the way Foreman feels about his co-workers.

After House suspects mirror syndrome — the mother mirroring symptoms affecting the fetus — the case is taken on by Cuddy due to her interest. But the case must be transferred back to House when she realizes she has too much empathy for her patient, seeing as they have both striven to be mothers at a late age by way of artificial insemination. Now close to the end of the season, is this a sign that Cuddy will conceive yet? Is "mirror syndrome" a clue?

Through further investigation, House concludes that there are issues with the fetus' lungs. Cuddy is able to proceed with the surgery to let both the son and the mother live by insisting on applying the paddles to Emma, even though she might have lived with House's suggestion of simply by removing the baby altogether. Emma is able to carry the baby to term, as is suggested by a flash-forward shot of her caring for her son four months later.

Highlight

Cuddy has the paddles. She's trying to save Emma; House is trying to cut the umbilical cord to save Emma. Cuddy tells House to step away or he'll be electrocuted.

Support Staff

- House hangs it from Emma's IV while he's doing the ultrasound.
- He hangs it from the door frame when he enters his apartment at the end of the episode.

Lies

- "Even fetuses lie," House says when there's more wrong than the urinary tract.
- Chase says, "I always glow," rather than telling Cameron that he was looking at a picture of her when Emma snapped his own mug.

Exam Room

- The banner in the rock photo shoot is for "the all-American rejects." The Replacement's song "Bastards of Young" is playing as Emma shoots. Ironic choice since Emma's baby will be a bastard, though she isn't young.
- Chase and Cameron discuss whether it's weird that House caught them having sex. Chase thinks House doesn't give a crap. Cameron thinks otherwise.
- Two more Canadianisms emerge as House makes vacation plans: House lists creator David Shore's hometown — London, Ontario — as a place he doesn't want a layover. Later, Cuddy books him a flight to Vancouver Island. "Who doesn't like Canadians?"
- The patient predicts how Chase feels about Cameron, and later snaps his picture when he is looking at hers.
- "Somebody's gotta be Cuddy's Cuddy," Foreman says in one of Epps' best lines to date. Wilson is sent.
- House says, "Sorry. Just realized I forgot to TiVo *Alien*," referencing the 1979 film where a creature pops out of John Hurt's chest.
- At the end of the episode, House tears up his ticket, pops a

Vicodin, and watches the Discovery channel. Are we to conclude he'll be going on a bender for his vacation?

3.18 Airborne

First aired: April 10, 2007
Writer: David Hoselton
Director: Elodie Keene
Guest stars: Jenny O'Hara (Fran), Meta Golding (Robin), Tess Lina (Keo), Jamison Yang (Peng), Krista Kalmus (Joy), Melissa Kite (Sour Faced Girl), Pej Vahdat (Indian man), Connor Webb (12-year-old Boy), Gayla Goehl (Businesswoman), Ben Carroll (Businessman), Karla Droege (Mother), Savannah Argenti (Crying Child), Victor Buno (Passenger #1), Donna Silverberg (Passenger #2), Bobbin Bergstrom (Nurse)

Episode Differential

Possibly the funniest episode in season three, "Airborne" is similar in structure to "Failure to Communicate," since the team must again try to get by without House — and, in this case, without Cuddy either. The humor is raised to 10,000 feet above sea level, and the high moment will belong to once again to diagnostician Chase.

House and Cuddy have been at a pandemics symposium. While on their flight back from Singapore, a passenger begins vomiting. His symptoms are consistent with a highly contagious disease, and Cuddy is convinced that he has one. House isn't, and convinces the flight crew not to turn the plane around. After another passenger vomits, House convenes a mock diagnostic team, similar in physical appearance to his own at Princeton-Plainsboro, and concludes that the sudden illness must be a symptom of ciguatera poisoning. In a gesture that seems to imitate the comedy classic *Airplane*, he then instructs everyone who ate seafood to go to the bathroom and vomit. Although contradicted by Cuddy, who is exhibiting the same symptoms and never had the seafood, House continues with his experiments. He tests a theory of mass hysteria by lying to the passengers. He tells them that one of the symptoms of the "illness" is a shaking left hand, which many of them suddenly exhibit.

Peng, the first man to vomit, however, plunges into worse shape, and may very well die. Suspecting he's a drug mule with cocaine in his system, House prepares the most rudimentary of operations. The nine-year-old whom House has trained to speak in an Australian accent and agree with everything he says fulfills the role of Chase in House's makeshift diagnostic airplane team. When this lad leans forward to secure Peng's limbs before House can cut into him, House realizes that Peng simply has joint pain. A search of Peng's wallet reveals that he went scuba-diving previous to boarding the plane. He is diagnosed with the Bends and the crew is told to descend the plane to stabilize his condition.

Running in a parallel plot, at the hospital, a 58-year-old woman named Fran has been admitted with seizures and vision loss. Her "friend" is actually a call girl, though it takes some time for Wilson to clue in. Cameron and Chase investigate her apartment to find that the place next to hers was fumigated, and some of the toxins leaked in through one of her electrical outlets, poisoning her. As the airplane surgery is halted, so too is Fran's. Like Chase's breakthrough diagnosis in "Finding Judas" the show is cutting Chase some slack and showing he can sleuth as well as House.

Unfortunately, Chase may be a great diagnostician, but he's done playing doctor with Cameron. She breaks things off immediately after he asks her for a more serious relationship. We also see Wilson pulling a House move for the first time since he sawed into his cane — the final scene shows the oncologist calling up his patient's "friend" for a play date.

Highlight
"Heart's fine, breasts are fine," House tells Cuddy, as he examines her on the plane. Likewise, when he discovers her rash has spread, he tries to undo her pants to examine her and she tells him to imagine. When she finds out it's all in her head, she must be glad she made that call.

Support Staff
House regretfully mentions that his $900 cane has been confiscated as a weapon when he and Cuddy board the plane.

Lies
- Patient says she went to Duluth to see her sister but confesses almost immediately to having been in Mexico, snorting coke off "a homosexual man's stomach."

- The call girl says she's Fran's friend, but eventually comes clean to Wilson.
- Cuddy *believes* she's sick, but her sickness is a lie. Nonetheless, she exhibits all its symptoms.

Exam Room

- House makes Cuddy sit in coach while he orders a rib eye, medium-rare.
- Like the movie *Airplane*, House predicts the problem is the sea bass. He also says he was "Kinda lookin' forward to landing this puppy myself."
- House acknowledges the formulaic nature of the show when he assigns passengers: one to agree with everything he says (Chase), one to disagree with everything he says (Foreman).
- When the flight attendant tries to communicate with Peng, she says, "*Nilalagnat ka ba?*" Fan translation: "Are you suffering from a fever?"
- House is nothing if not a man of habit. He adopts a white board technique while on the plane. "Extensor pasturing" is shown, but the Chase-like little boy doesn't know that word, so goes for "extension pasturing."
- The cases couldn't be more different, but the team does do a lumbar puncture on their patient while House attempts one on the plane. Similarly, two surgeries are about to begin — one for bends, the other for fumigation. Since both conditions are inoperable, both are cancelled in time.
- This is the second episode in a row where Cuddy has lost her control.

Booboos

- When Cuddy is sitting in the economy section on the plane, a man leans on her, sawing logs. House eventually switches seats with her, but when he's in coach the seat next to him is conveniently empty.
- Of all his languages, House doesn't speak Korean?

What's Up, Doc?

Most planes carry a fairly extensive first aid kit, so would House really need to pass the hat in order to get antibiotics?

3.19 Act Your Age

First aired: April 17, 2007
Writer: Sara Hess
Director: Daniel Sackheim
Guest stars: Erich Anderson (Deran), Bailee Madison (Lucy), Slade Pearce (Jasper), Carla Gallo (Janie)

Episode Differential

"Act Your Age" starts with a boy whose nose is bleeding severely from a fight he got into while at after-school daycare. While his father and teacher discuss his aggressive behavior, his little sister Lucy has a heart attack.

The medical team is baffled by what transpires, as it is increasingly evident that Lucy's ailments typically belong to those of older bodies. It seems she has already begun to menstruate. Seemingly at their wit's end, the team has a breakthrough when Lucy's eight-year-old brother develops a crush on Cameron, the kind of intense crush that might be expected at the age of 12 or 14. The boy brings her flowers he stole from someone else's hospital room, and he goes into a fit of rage when he sees Chase act affectionately toward her. With the boy exhibiting symptoms of early puberty also, the team can narrow their search to genetics and environment.

House and Cameron have difficulty agreeing on how to treat the girl. The tension between them is palpable and in many ways brings up the old wounds of Cameron's previous infatuation with House. In another odd criss-cross, House interferes with Wilson and Cuddy's dating, which may or may not be "dating," and likely is not. House suggests to Wilson that Cuddy's motivations for dating him are not purely friendship. Opposite their patients this week, the staff seem to regress in age and maturity with House and Wilson acting like school boys, Cameron playing coy with Chase, and Chase actually seeming to get upset that she is acknowledging the crush of an eight year old.

After a search and questions posed to their father, it turns out that both children have been exposed to their father's sexual enhancement cream, which he keeps in the house. It is concluded that the increased levels of testosterone in their respective systems are causing them to go through puberty several years early, causing very different, but equally adverse reactions.

Highlights

"You did not just play the dead husband card," House says when Cameron convinces the patient's parent to agree to her treatment right underneath House's nose. She wants consent to remove Lucy's pituitary.

Also, at the episode's end, Wilson makes a convincing case when he confides that he's going to march right down the hall and kiss Cuddy, even if it gets him fired. It's his ultimate psych-out of House. Score one for James 007 Wilson.

Support Staff

House uses it to point at Foreman. "You went home? Good for you. Way to delegate."

Lies

- Foreman tells the father that he would lie if he were abusing his daughter.
- Wilson says he slept with Cuddy twice. House believes his lie.
- Foreman proposes to Chase that Cameron is lying about not wanting him to share his feelings.
- House sends Wilson flowers signed by Cuddy. He signs them with X's.
- House asks Wilson if he wants to kiss Cuddy, and Wilson admits he does. "Really?" House inquires. "No," Wilson replies, having completely played House for a fool.
- The dad lies about dating the woman who runs the daycare.

Exam Room

- Due to their arguing, Foreman can tell right away that Cameron and Chase are no longer sleeping together. On a bright note, it means Chase the Kiss-Ass is back.
- House calls Cuddy's you-know-what a "squish mitten" when he's talking to Wilson. This tops the time he used the word "hoo-hoo" ("Need to Know").
- House is watching wrestling when he figures out the boy has a problem with aggression, which leads to the proper diagnosis. Fans have said the fight is an NWA World Heavyweight Title, Christian Cage versus Abyss, in an April 2006 Pay-Per-View Lockdown.
- When House asks Cuddy about the play she went to see with

Wilson, he references Abraham Lincoln's assassination, calling Cuddy "Mrs. Lincoln." Lincoln was shot during the third act of a comedy, *Our American Cousin*, at the Ford Theater on April 14, 1865.

- House also pays tribute to the movie *Casablanca* (1941) when he says "Round up the usual suspects." He last referenced *Casablanca* in "Lines in the Sand."

Booboos

We see again that the locker rooms are co-ed when Chase leaves the "Not Stolen" flowers on top of the locker.

3.20 House Training

First aired: April 24, 2007
Writer: Doris Egan
Director: Paul McCrane
Guest stars: Monique Gabriela Curnen (Lupe), Charles S. Dutton (Rodney Foreman), Beverly Todd (Alicia Foreman), Jane Adams (Bonnie)

Episode Differential

It's that time again. After a string of successes, the team will lose a patient in a turn of events that will lead directly to the team's own demise.

A young unemployed woman named Lupe observes a card-playing scheme in the street. She continually picks the con man's card correctly, until, on a third try, she becomes agitated and blurts that she can't make a decision. She passes out as cards tumble and both con man and audience dissipate. As the team will discover, Lupe suffers from a lack of blood to the brain, which temporarily paralyzed her ability to make decisions or exorcise free will.

As he did in "Histories" and "Deception," Foreman shows biases, calling Lupe a scam artist. In an unexpected twist, Chase accuses Foreman of racism. He immediately thinks that Lupe's condition stems from drug abuse, while Chase looks for other possibilities, such as toxins, in Lupe's apartment. The case becomes increasingly personal for Foreman as Lupe suspects he disagrees with her decisions in life. In terms of his own past, Foreman is made to go through many of the emotions that haunted him in his humble beginnings when his parents arrive in town. We meet Foreman's mom in the flesh for the very first time. She is increasingly showing signs of aging and progressed dementia, recognizing him at one point, but not another.

As Lupe's conditions worsens, the team suspects cancer and then autoimmune disease. Severe pain following a radiation treatment, however, changes the diagnosis to an infection. Her immune system has become so compromised by the treatment they gave her that she has no chance of recovery. Foreman eventually has to break the news, and she dies of what is later deemed a staph infection from a scratch made by her bra strap, which the staff failed to notice. As House and Foreman note within the show, this is the first time that the staff have directly contributed to a patient's death. As the title suggests, Foreman's lack of regard for the patient might mean he's learning too much from House, adopting his rude behavior and taking unnecessary risks.

Meanwhile, Cuddy and Wilson continue dating and House gets jealous, making investigations into Wilson's past habits with the ladies, even as he temporarily houses Wilson's dog. We meet Wilson's wife (most recent ex) for the first time. She tells House he didn't break up her marriage, but by accepting his friend on Christmas Eve (referencing "Damned If You Do"), and many other occasions when he knew Wilson ought to have been home with her, he didn't help.

Highlights

Wilson's ex-wife Bonnie, a new real estate agent, shows House a condo while he digs for information about Wilson's wooing tactics. She more or less compares Wilson to a tampon and House completes the comparison. She then goes on to show House the six-burner chef's oven while discussing how Wilson meets a woman's "needs."

Second in line for highlight of the episode is Wilson and Cuddy ending up at a bondage photography show.

Support Staff

- House uses it to move the blinds in the condo.
- He walks around the bed without it to perform the autopsy.

Lies

- The patient says she doesn't do drugs but later admits to having taken a few hits off the pipe in her time.
- Even though House always says that people thank Wilson after

he tells them they're dying, Wilson admits to Foreman that "It's not common." So this is a lie we've had throughout the series.
- House lies about his interest in a condo.
- Foreman confesses to Lupe that he did have a problem with her, and that he's also made bad decisions.
- When trying to convince Foreman of the people they'll save versus the people who will die in their care, House says that numbers don't lie.

Exam Room
- This episode, we hear House's formula for giving death news.
- Foreman's dad lets us know how long it's been since Foreman has been home — eight years.
- House is pleased that Cuddy thinks he's not a safe choice for a friend: "I'm not safe? Cool," he says.
- Chase gets tactical about Cameron. He lets her know that he's available, but also fine with her saying no — which she does, repeatedly.
- House meets the patient because he's interested in why she doesn't like Foreman. She says he's not as good as he thinks he is. Given the results of her treatment, she's right, and this is a heavy clue to the episode's outcome.
- House steals Wilson's coffee and comments on the sugar level. House himself uses sugar, but maybe not so much.
- House references James Bond films in general when he asks which is the better Bond, Sean Connery, or Daniel Craig. Craig plays in the recent *Casino Royale* (2006), Connery in films spanning 1962–1967 and again in 1971.
- Foreman loses his cool, punching the wall when he leaves Lupe's room after giving her the news of her impending death.
- Chase pulls his seminary background out of his pocket as he attempts to console Foreman. Even House, who doesn't believe in God, suggests Foreman go see a priest.
- "Guilt is irrelevant," House says about the whole matter, yet he has Wilson's marital dog waiting at home for him, so we know even he isn't above it.

Booboos
- House doesn't know Wilson's dog's name, which seems like House in terms of his inability to care about someone else's

life — though he's not usually so unobservant.

- Similarly, as we'll learn in the next episode, the dog is 17 but Bonnie and Wilson seem to have named him together. Was he adopted as a senior, perhaps from a rescue? If the references to Wilson's numerous ex-wives are to be believed, Bonnie and Wilson were together only a short while.

3.21 Family

First aired: May 1, 2007
Writer: Liz Friedman
Director: David Straiton
Guest stars: Dabier Snell (Matty), Jascha Washington (Nick), Adina Porter (Claudia), Thomas Mikal Ford (Scott)

Episode Differential

Following on last week's tragedy, this is another big episode for Foreman, and as in "Euphoria, Parts 1 and 2," Omar Epps handles the dramatic intensity well. This time, he's pushed not to his physical breaking point, but to his emotional one. It's also a big episode for House's cane, which can't keep it together. Is it symbolic that his cane should give out just as his staff is?

A 14-year-old leukemia patient, Nick, is presented with the option of a last resort bone marrow transplant from his younger brother, Matty. However, when young Matty sneezes, the medical team realizes they cannot proceed until they first determine his illness. They hope for something simple, but fate is not that kind, delivering again a zebra. All the while, Foreman is dealing with the emotional fall-out of the previous patient's death. Since Nick has only days left to live, the team decides to worsen Matty's condition in hopes of speeding up their ability to find its source, and ergo treatment. Matty becomes seriously ill, bleeding out of his ears.

A different marrow donor is found, but the transplant is unsuccessful. Nick is still dying. In a risky move, Foreman speeds up the process of transfer, extracting bone marrow without anesthesia to Nick, even as the boy protests, going back on the consent he had given Foreman verbally (before he knew what pain he would be in). In doing what needs to be done, Foreman saves the lives of both boys. As House applaudes Foreman's decision, Foreman comes to the conclusion that they are too alike, scarily so, and quits. The episode keeps within the themes of informed consent and doing wrong to do right that have been running all season.

House, meanwhile, has dog issues, including having his pet-on-loan, Hector, eat his pills and gnaw through his cane. House eventually resigns himself to the fact that he has found a canine version of himself.

Highlight

The scene in which Foreman defies the patient, attacking him to save his brother by painfully drawing enough of his bone marrow.

Support Staff

- The cane breaks due to the dog's chewing, and House falls.
- House says that the dog has had a long life, and holds the cane up as if he plans to whack with it.
- House tells Chase and Cameron that he tripped over Wilson's self-righteousness.
- He resorts to the granny cane that he used in "Whac-a-Mole."
- He and Wilson visit a tobacco shop and check out a variety of canes. A black one with no handle House calls "A little too Marilyn Manson in the retirement home." There's also one encased in a stretched bull penis, to which House replies, "Penis canes are murder," which is particularly funny considering the number of phallic references his cane usually draws in a given episode. In the end, he selects a black cane with orange flame detailing. Cameron is unimpressed by it.
- He walks without one when he goes into the clean room where Nick is.

Lies

- To House's dismay, Wilson refuses to tell the family the exact treatment they should follow or his confidence in it. The second time though, he does tell them what to do, which is a lie since he believes in patients making their own decisions.
- Foreman tells the family about the 4/6 donor — he's not supposed to yet.

- House is inadvertently trying to get rid of the dog. His "accidents" of leaving his pills open, and leaving the door open, are honest expressions of his resentment.
- The parents have made the decision for their son Nick, but House goes to the 14-year-old and coerces him to agree to what he wants.

Exam Room

- The cane Hector chews through is the collapsible one that House used in "Needle in a Haystack." Since it is largely metal, it's only the handle that Hector chews.
- While in the tobacco shop selecting his new cane, House also tries out an enormous curved Sherlock Holmes–style pipe — the writers and the actor having fun with their own creation.
- It's only been one week since their last patient died. Foreman is in the chapel. Although House recommended he speak to a priest at the end of the last episode, now House mocks him, calling God "Your imaginary friend."
- Chase continues to pursue Cameron with absolute reserve and dignity: "It's Tuesday. It's the day I remind you I like you and I want us to be together." Chase has always demonstrated an ability to allow himself to be humiliated (it's part and parcel of the kiss-ass role), but his choice to do so now reads more as tender than pathetic, and still completely in character.
- House references a condition known as The Yips, which is what happens when golfers or ball players lose their confidence. He's relating it to Foreman, but patient Matty is also into baseball.
- House isn't the only one into Vicodin this episode — he's got a pill-poppin' pup, whom he may or may not have inadvertently attempted to overdose.
- Foreman tosses House's death stats from the previous week back at him: "You'll save more, but I don't mind killing less." He gives his two-week notice. "I did what you would have done," Foreman says, driving home the parallel construction. In turn, the brothers each do what the other one would have.
- House tells Foreman that he's been like him since age eight. He's talking about Foreman's inquisitive mind and rule-breaking, but Foreman's not thrilled either way.

What's Up, Doc?

- Foreman does the bone marrow transplant, but it would be a specialist's job, and since bone marrow has nothing to do with neurology . . .
- If Matty was too sick for anesthesia, wouldn't having a needle driven down to the bone be as hard — or harder — on his system?

3.22 Resignation

First aired: May 8, 2007
Writer: Pamela Davis
Director: Martha Mitchell
Guest stars: Lyndsy Fonseca (Addie), Tony Spiridakis (Ben), Eve Gordon (Jody), Piper Perabo (Honey), Tracy Howe (Steve), Shonda Farr (Jamie)

Episode Differential

"Resignation" deals with Foreman's decision to leave, but the title also refers to the patient's attitude about her own failing health. Nineteen-year-old Addie is admitted to the hospital after coughing up blood during martial arts practice. As her condition deteriorates, House speculates that her body only "thinks" it has an infection, when in fact none can be found.

The side plot features House and Wilson having a drug-off when House suspects Wilson is taking anti-depressants. (Right now we ought to realize the clue to Addie's case will have something to do with depression.) To give Wilson a little pick-me-up, House puts amphetamines in his coffee, and Wilson takes House's Vicodin to counteract the effects once he realizes what has happened. In return, he drugs House's coffee with anti-depressants, though this is not revealed until later. They are showing unusual signs of caring for one another, though neither will admit it. This episode echoes their antics from "Safe."

Foreman, meanwhile, confirms his resignation, leaving the staff baffled as to why he would quit. The maniac in control? The Chase-Cameron trysts? Really, why would anyone quit? Both he and House refuse to talk about it, though everyone else at Princeton-Plainsboro wants to.

House treats a clinic patient with bowel issues whose girlfriend is a vegan and nutritionist. House informs both of them that the man's bowel problem is because he's cheating on her. She's not too upset until she realizes what House means: the man is cheating with hamburgers. The girlfriend is visibly outraged, and House jokingly propositions her. Eventually, House will ask her out under the guise of an interview at a bar, but she won't seem to mind when she finds out what he has done. House picks up a vegan? Even one played by Piper Perabo? It seems to go against his video-game-playing, wrestling-watching, potato-chip-eating, monster truck self, and yet when he does pick up, he does it well. (Why then all the call girls?)

Addie's condition, however, is rapidly deteriorating, and House and his team believe at this point that she is dying. House goes to her to break the news but before he can begin, she stops him, telling him she doesn't want to know why she's dying. This stumps the man obsessed with solving puzzles. He confronts her, speculating that she was trying to commit suicide. His theory is that the only reason she wouldn't want to know is that she already knew why and simply wasn't saying. She finally admits that she swallowed drain cleaner in capsules — making explicit the parallel in the plot, depression.

Of course, people and their silent — and not so silent — reasons will come to the fore in the season's final episode. Foreman tells Chase he doesn't like him and never has, and therefore he feels no reason to share his exit motives. Foreman is frequently abrupt in this manner — like the time he told Cameron he wasn't her friend — although strangely doesn't see that his detachment is one of the characteristics that makes him similar to House.

Highlight
Wilson saying the word "speed" while on it.

Support Staff
The cane got double-time in the last episode, so this one is virtually cane-free.

Lies
- House tells Chase that Foreman's leaving because he "wants to breed llamas."
- Foreman is honest about his dislike for Chase, but hides his

reasons for leaving.

- Foreman is honest with Cameron about why he's leaving.
- House doses Wilson's espresso.
- Wilson doses House's espresso.
- The clinic patient is "cheating" on his nutritionist girlfriend with cheeseburgers.
- Addie attempted suicide and keeps the information to herself, having gone about her ordinary activities and all their tests and treatments without revealing this.
- House lies to Addie, saying he won't tell her parents. He does.
- House lies to the nutritionist that it's a job interview when it's really a date.
- House does tell the truth when he admits all his character flaws to the nutritionist, including the fact that he doesn't always tell the truth.

Exam Room

- House is amused by the quote on his paper coffee cup. He keeps trying to interrupt his hard-working staff to share it with them. Since when is House amused by coffee quotes? Perhaps this is an indication that Wilson is dosing him as early as the first scene this episode, which would mean that Wilson actually got a leg up and dosed House *first*.
- "Personally, I can't believe I've had the same three employees for three years," House says, setting up the final episode.
- "The eager beaver combing his hair," House says when Chase continues working after the announcement of Foreman's leaving. The two have never been close, but with Chase having consoled Foreman recently about Lupe's death, and Foreman having offered advice about Cameron, it does seem like they've become closer.
- We finally get a needle-in-the-eye scene with no flinching!
- Just as he buys his cafeteria meals, we see that Wilson usually buys House's coffees, partly because House can't return the favor. It's hard to carry two coffee cups and a cane — although House did manage whenever Stacy was around.
- Unlike House, Wilson doesn't take pills dry.
- Once again, Cameron is the first to respond when the patient freaks out in the MRI machine.

- Again, House has a red sucker.
- House throws out his mail unopened. It seems characteristically House, and perhaps the reason Cameron started keeping his files in the first place.
- There's a protein theme deke-out. The clinic patient is eating the hamburgers for protein. House originally thinks Addie has a protein deficiency.

Booboos

- House says to the parents he's breaking the law by telling them Addie's suicidal, but legally he's obligated to report the suicide attempt.
- The one time the team would have found an easy clue to the patient's condition (the gell caps), they don't search her home.

3.23 The Jerk

First aired: May 15, 2007
Writer: Leonard Dick
Director: Daniel Sackheim
Guest stars: Nick Lane (Nathan), Colleen Flynn (Enid), Dustin Joiner (Mark), David Bowe (Doug)

Episode Differential

House takes on his rudest patient this episode. They go head-to-head and pawn-to-pawn. Sixteen-year-old prodigy Nathan collapses after losing control at a chess game he won. After being admitted to the hospital, he initially complains about head pain, but soon his organs begin to fail as well.

Many explanations are up for discussion, including chemical imbalance, which, the team thinks is the explanation for Nathan's rude personality, as he manages to upset each person on the medical team. His mom is surprisingly delighted since she's been subjected to his torments for years. In that, she shares a dream with the team members, who probably have wished that if only House dealt with his pain he himself might be less of a jerk. The team proposes that Nathan has a degenerative disease, Kelley-Seegmiller syndrome, which includes self mutilation and drastic behavior. But after concluding that this does not encompass all of Nathan's symptoms, House erases it from the board and starts again.

In an attempt to inspire another crash from which he can glean more (House's favorite method), House challenges Nathan at his own game. It's not until later, when Chase brings House one of the chess pieces and House watches Chase set it down that he realizes Nathan holds his pieces awkwardly. From this, House concludes that the patient's bones are not developed properly. Nathan is finally diagnosed with a rare, child form of hemochromatosis. Unfortunately, the treatment is not going to change his ascerbic personality — sorry, Mom.

All the while, there's a running mystery with the Princeton-Plainsboro staff. Foreman's interview at a New York hospital has been sabotaged, but he has no solid evidence as to who called and canceled on his behalf. He suspects House, who denies it and suggests Cuddy. The blame game continues around the medical team until House finally confesses to Chase that he canceled the interview, but would never tell Foreman, claiming that it wasn't the kind of place he would want to work. Is this House's way of showing he cares?

Chase coaxes the confession out of House by figuring out that he's the only one who would want to cause chaos — "Because as long as Foreman thought you were guilty, he'd been useless around here." House replies, "Sometimes I forget why I hired you." House is paying Chase a compliment here — that Chase is the one employee with deductive reasoning, who always knows the score.

Highlight
Chase hits on Cameron right after she implies that he's a petty, vindictive jerk. He reminds her, albeit through gritted teeth, that it's Tuesday and that he still likes her.

Support Staff
- House pretends to freak out, hiding behind his cane, saying, "Don't sneak up on me like that!" to Foreman who's not participating at all.
- House has it on the tray when he wheels the chessboard in.
- He also uses it to turn on the light over the board.
- "Arrogance has to be earned," House tells Nathan. Nathan's

oneupsmanship is very House as he says stonily, "I can walk."
"I don't bleed out of my penis," House fires back.

Lies

- The patient is absolutely honest to "stupid questions."
- "Are you accusing the symptoms of lying?" House asks Chase. "The symptoms never lie," he says, which is in itself a lie, since we've seen symptoms hide the true disease many times on the show.
- House called Manhattan General to cancel Foreman's interview but says that maybe Ashton Kutcher did it.
- Cuddy says she sabotaged the interview, then says she didn't. The first is the lie.
- The clinic patient's son doesn't at first admit to the $1.41 that is in his pocket.
- Wilson lies when he tells Cameron that Cuddy is going to fire him. He's baiting her to see if she's the one who canceled Foreman's interview.
- Chase suggests Nathan is lying or hiding something, simply because he's evil.
- House tells the truth to Chase when asked.
- House withholds information from Foreman — that he's figured out what's wrong with the patient — telling him to run the lab again.

Exam Room

- With the exception of the two tapeworms, this is the only time a disease has been trotted out again. In "Who's Your Daddy," the little girl, Leona, also had hemochromatosis.
- Following on that realization, however, this episode almost does a kind of verbal best-of as House and the team reference other episodes. Before House prescribes mushrooms, he references "Paternity" in which the patient hallucinated and almost jumped off the roof. Similarly, "hypogonadism" is mentioned again ("Sports Medicine"), and there's another Ashton Kutcher reference ("Poison" and "Heavy"). House remarks, "If he had tuberculosis, I still wouldn't let him cough on me," which references "TB or Not TB." At one point Foreman suggests an adrenal tumor, and House mocks him for it as if it is

Foreman's pet suggestion raised every time ("Acceptance").
There are likely many more, and now the torch is passed to
you. . . .

- The clue to the final diagnosis is planted early on: Cameron
  suggests hemochromatosis and House dismisses it as it doesn't
  fit with the personality disorder he wants to believe his patient
  has. This is one of the few times the title of the episode throws
  the audience a curve ball.

- Foreman breaks out all his best suits this episode as he prepares for other inteviews. Finally we see his character in
  something other than purple, the wardrobe's standby for
  Omar Epps. At least he does look good in purple though;
  can't say the same about Jesse Spencer and yellow. And then
  there's vest after vest on Jennifer Morrison. . . .

- In one scene, House searches under the desk for a dime, which
  the nurse hands to him. In either season one or two, where
  storylines were tighter in their parallels, the repetition of this
  small scene coupled with the coin boy in the clinic would have
  led us to believe the main case had something to do with
  metal toxicity. This episode doesn't fulfill on these hints
  though. They are only for our amusement.

- There's another Canadianism in the clinic. A sunburned (and
  obviously sun-stunned) father has quarter and nickel marks
  that are white, and a mischievous boy in tow. "Hey, one of
  these quarters is Canadian," House protests when the boy
  forks them over.

- Other than the Kutcher *Punk'd* reference, this episode includes
  a nod to the movie *Wayne's World* (1992), and the TV show
  about a wonder-boy doctor *Doogie Howser, MD*
  (1989–1993). Hmmm . . . Howser, MD, House, MD, no similarity in show titles there.

- "You do the nurse stuff, they'll do the doctor stuff," House
  tells a rushed Foreman, acknowledging the show's flaw where
  doctors draw blood and run all their own tests.

- Wilson also acknowledges the show's formula when he says,
  "Cameron's in love with him, Chase is afraid of him, and I
  enable him." In short, without Foreman, there'll be no
  dynamic to make House interesting.

What's Up, Doc?
- How does House get the mushrooms? He wouldn't have access to a Schedule 1 substance, and neither could Cuddy write the prescription.
- Basic blood tests would have shown hemochromatosis.

3.24 Human Error

First aired: May 29, 2007
Writers: Thomas L. Moran, Lawrence Kaplow
Director: Katie Jacobs
Guest cast: Mercedes Renard (Marina), Omar Avila (Esteban), Stephen Markle (Dr. Gooding)

Episode Differential

The third season ends with this abrupt episode, which surprised fans. It is hard to say what direction the show will take for season four. Some fans will be that much more eager to tune in; others may be walking away — just like House's underlings.

In a change of pace, and county of origin, the Coast Guard picks up a Cuban couple, Marina and Esteban, stranded in the water — a sick woman and her husband. When asked to leave his briefcase behind, Esteban refuses. As he eventually comes aboard the Coast Guard's helicopter, Esteban drops it; it spills into the water revealing (and destroying) his wife's medical documents. They then demand to see Dr. House for her treatment.

Between the drama and banter of the medical team, it is eventually theorized that Marina has MS. After a failed procedure accidentally breaking Marina's wrist, House concludes it might be cancer. Chase objects strongly to House's behavior and confronts him about his agreeing with Foreman. House promptly fires him, telling Chase that he has been at the hospital too long, has learned all he can from the job, and that it's time for a change. It is true that Chase is the longest-standing member of the team, as we saw back in the pilot episode. The staff, of course, is outraged and Cuddy demands that House take back what he said to Chase. House refuses, and dismisses other staff in a confrontation as well. Meanwhile, he still hasn't visited Esteban or Marina about their problem, and it is revealed that

Marina has a clot in her arm, suggesting that she has a heart defect.

After repeated attempts to get Marina's heart restarted in the operating room after they attempt surgery, Marina is put on temporary life support. Many, including Esteban, are confused by House's decision (and like the firing of Chase we also wonder if this is the "human error" of the episode title), but House refuses to answer any questions. At the end of the episode, Chase and Cameron finally sit down together and have dinner, during which Chase decides that House was correct in firing him.

Cuddy finally demands that House tell Esteban that his wife has died and the surgery was unsuccessful. They go to her bed, where she is still hooked up to machines, and shut them off. Esteban then notices her heart beating. Marina miraculously wakes up, declaring her pain to be gone. "Is it Heaven?" she asks as she comes to. "No, it's New Jersey," House answers, parodying the 1989 film *Field of Dreams* (a scene in which Shoeless Joe asks Ray Kinsella the same question and he replies, "No, this is Iowa"). Even though Marina claims her pain is gone, House double-checks with another angiogram, revealing the now-operable problem.

At the end of the episode, and after her talk with Chase, Cameron hands in her resignation letter as well. House also finally breaks down and asks Foreman to stay, but he declines, saying he wants to save lives, not solve mysteries. While the episode seems confusing with its international, dramatic set-up and its anti-climatic solution, the white board has been effectively wiped clean, with even Cameron leaving (and going back to Chase).

What will happen in season four? Interviews with Omar Epps indicate he'll still be involved, but as an old horror movie poster once asked, "Who'll survive and what will be left of them?" — an appropriate question about what it's like to work with House.

Highlight
House doing what's he's long threatened and once tried to do: fire Chase.

Support Staff
House plays his cane like an air guitar.

Lies
- As a season finale what would be lies are left as questions for the next season.

- Will Cameron really "miss" House?
- Is it true that Foreman doesn't want to leave?

Exam Room
- The U.S. Coast Guard is thanked in the end credits.
- The present that Cameron gives Foreman is a framed table of contents of the issue of *Midwest Journal of Experimental Medicine*. It's a tangible reminder of her forgiveness. His article is titled "Cerebral Magnetic Resonance Angiography enhanced by Rapid Auto-Transfusion During Hypothermic Circulatory Arrest."
- The God theme is explored again, with many pithy asides from House, such as whether Esteban traveled so far to put his wife's life in God's hands or in House's.

Booboos
During the rescue Esteban doesn't speak English, yet at the hospital his English becomes almost fluent.

What's Up, Doc?
- The hospital must be short staffed, as their head of oncology, Wilson, is performing surgery he's not certified to perform and the team, nary a cardiologist among them, are shown inserting catheters into Marina's heart.
- Bypass machines are only used for a few hours during surgeries, not as life support.

SOURCES

Abele, Robert. "The sour can be sweet," *The Los Angeles Times*, April 24, 2005.

Andreeva, Nellie. "Dr.'s orders: Salary boost for Laurie," *Hollywood Reporter*, http://www.hollywoodreporter.com/hr/search/article_display.jsp?vnu_content_id=1002838745

BBC News, "Laurie: reinvention as world star." http://news.bbc.co.uk/1/hi/entertainment/6216897.stm

Block, Marcelline. "An Interview with Robert Sean Leonard," *Play by Play*, March/April 1997.

Buckley, Christopher. "Bertie Wooster Meets James Bond," *New York Times*, June 8, 1997.

Byrne, Michelle. "A Bit of Laurie," *Time Out Dubai*, March 19–26, 2006.

Canadian Press, *"Is House the New West Wing?"* April 4, 2007. http://tv.yahoo.com/davidshore/contributor/943402/news/urn:newsml:cp.org:20070404:tv-25204020__ER:

Doyle, John. "The *House* that Shore built," *The Globe and Mail* (Toronto), May 6, 2006. http://www.theglobeandmail.com/servlet/story/RTGAM.20060506.wxshore06/BNstory/Entertainment/home

ET Online, "TV's Sexiest Women Revealed!" *ET Online*, March 20, 2007. http://www.etonline.com/celebrities/spotlight/47444/

Fernandez, Jay A. (Review of *The Gun Seller*) in *Washington Post Book World*, August 17, 1997.

Geary, Tim. "King of American prime time," *Telegraph.co.ok*, May 24, 2005. http://www.telegraph.co.uk/arts/main.jhtml?xml=/arts/2005/05/24/bvhugh24.xml

Harris, Will. "A Chat with Lisa Edelstein," Bullz-Eye Television Online, http://www.bullz-eye.com/television_reviews/interviews/2006/lisa_edelstein.htm

Holtz, Andrew. *The Medical Science of House, MD* (New York: Berkley Books, 2006).

House. TV Series. Exec. Prod. David Shore, Paul Attanasio, Katie Jacobs, Brian Singer. Fox. 2004–.

Jory, Amy. "I was miserable, self-absorbed and selfish until I finally faced up to the truth of my depression..." *The Evening Standard*, June 13, 2002.

Keveney, Bill. "Hugh Laurie gets into *House*," *USA TODAY*, November 15, 2004. http://www.usatoday.com/life/television/news/2004-11-15-hugh-laurie_x.htm

Kraft, Frances. "Emmy winner took a chance on television writing," *Canadian Jewish News*. http://www.cjnews.com/viewarticle.asp?id=7484

Kristine, Diane. "Inside *House*," Blogcritics magazine, June 26, 2006. http://blogcritics.org/archives/2006/06/26/213934.php

Lahr, John. "Petrified," *The New Yorker*, August 28, 2006, pp. 38–46.

Lane, Anthony. "Beyond a Joke: The Perils of Loving P.G. Wodehouse," *The New Yorker*, April 19 & 26, 2004, pp. 138–149.

Laurie, Hugh. "Talk today: *House* Star Hugh Laurie," (online chat transcript) February 11, 2007. http://cgi1.usatoday.com/mchat/20050211001/tscript.htm

————. "Books that made a difference to Hugh Laurie," O Magazine, February 2006. http://www.oprah.com/obc/omag/obc_omag_200602_books.jhtml

————. "Wodehouse Saved My Life," *The Daily Telegraph*, May 27, 1999. http://www.pgwodehousebooks.com/lauriesaved.htm

Lee, Luaine. "British actor doesn't know why he was hired to be 'Stuart's' dad," *Knight Ridder/Tribune News Service*, Juy 31, 2002.

————. "Laurie succeeds by doing a 'little' of everything," *Chicago Sun-Times*, July 26, 2002.

Lewisohn, Mark. "The BBC.co.uk guide to comedy: Alfresco," http://www.bbc.co.uk/comedy/guide/articles/a/alfresco_1299000062.shtml

McNamara, Mary. "Bedside manner: What will Hugh Laurie's grumpy super-doc do to lift season two?" *Los Angeles Times*. September 13, 2005.

Menon, Vinay. "The wry *House* that Shore built," *Toronto Star*, June 20, 2006.

Patterson, Troy. "Doc Hollywood," *Men's Vogue*, April 2007. http://www.mensvogue.com/arts/television/articles/2007/04/hugh_laurie

Reaney, James. "*House* episode references Canada," *Sun Media*, http://jam.canoe.ca/Television/TV_Shows/H/House/2007/04/05/3924772.html

Ryan, Maureen. "House-a-palooza part 2: Robert Sean Leonard," *Chicago Tribune Blog*, May 1, 2006. http://featuresblogs.chicagotribune.com/entertainment_tv/2006/05/houseapalooza_p.html

Sevetkey, Benjamin. "Monster House" *Entertainment Weekly*, August 25, 2006, pp. 30–36.

Spencer, Jesse. "Jesse Spencer's Official Web Site," www.jessespencer.com

Thompson, Emma. *The Sense and Sensibility Screenplay and Diaries*, New York, Newmarket Press, 1995.

USA Today, "TV stars jump off the screen and behind the mike," *USA TODAY*, August 28, 2006. http://www.usatoday.com/life/people/2006-08-28-celebbands-main_x.htm

Walton, Rob. "Jennifer Morrison: Woman on the Verge," *Playboy.com Arts & Entertainment*, http://www.playboy.com/arts-entertainment/wov/morrison/

Zap2It.com. "*House* Star Works the 'Night' Shift: Chris Evans will also join Reeves and Whitaker," http://www.zap2it.com/movies/news/zap-lauriee-vansnightwatchcasting,0,2409353.story

Other reference sources consulted

Fox Network official *House* site: www.fox.com/house

House M.D. Guide: www.housemd-guide.com

The Internet Movie Database: www.imdb.com

Polite Dissent: www.politedissent.com

Television Without Pity: www.televisionwithoutpity.com

Wikipedia: www.wikipedia.com